Socratic Dialogues

Meno, Euthyphro, Apology, Crito, and Phaedo

I0806039

Socratic Dialogues

Meno, Euthyphro, Apology, Crito, and Phaedo

Plato

Edited and Introduced by Andrew Bailey

Translated by Cathal Woods and Ryan Pack

broadview press

BROADVIEW PRESS
Peterborough, Ontario, Canada

Founded in 1985, Broadview Press is a fully independent academic publishing house owned by approximately twenty-five shareholders—almost all of whom are either Broadview employees or Broadview authors. Broadview is supported by a collaboration with Trent University, a liberal arts university located in Peterborough, Ontario—the city where Broadview was founded and continues to operate. Broadview is committed to environmentally responsible publishing and fair business practices.

Library and Archives Canada Cataloguing in Publication

Title: Socratic dialogues : Meno, Euthyphro, Apology, Crito, and Phaedo / Plato ;
edited and introduced by Andrew Bailey ; translated by Cathal Woods and Ryan Pack.
Other titles: Dialogues. Selections. English | Meno, Euthyphro, Apology, Crito, and Phaedo
Names: Plato, author | Bailey, Andrew, 1969- editor | Woods, Cathal, translator | Pack, Ryan, translator
Description: Includes bibliographical references and index.
Identifiers: Canadiana (print) 20240447638 | Canadiana (ebook) 20240447654 | ISBN 9781554815173 (softcover) | ISBN 9781460409190 (EPUB) | ISBN 9781037700064 (PDF)
Subjects: LCSH: Socrates. | LCSH: Philosophy, Ancient.
Classification: LCC B358 .B35 2024 | DDC 184—dc23

Broadview Press handles its own distribution in Canada and the United States:
PO Box 1243, Peterborough, Ontario K9J 7H5, Canada
555 Riverwalk Parkway, Tonawanda, NY 14150, USA
Tel: (705) 482-5915
email: customerservice@broadviewpress.com

Broadview Press acknowledges the financial support of the Government of Canada for our publishing activities.

Canada

Copy edited by Robert M. Martin
Typesetting and assembly by True to Type

PRINTED IN CANADA

Contents

Socrates statue at the Louvre.

Plato statue, a copy of Silanion's statue ca. 370 BC, at the Musei Capitolini.

Introduction

Who Were Plato and Socrates?

Plato

The historical details of Plato's life are somewhat obscure, though we know more about his life than about the lives of most ancient philosophers and he is the first whose entire body of philosophical work survives. He is traditionally thought to have been born in about 427 BCE and to have died in 347. His family, who lived in the Greek city-state of Athens, was aristocratic and probably wealthy. Legend has it that Plato's father, Ariston, was descended from Codrus, the last king of Athens. His mother, Perictione, was related to the great Solon, who around 570 BCE had completely reformed the notoriously harsh Athenian legal system laid out by Draco in the seventh century BCE, and replaced the hereditary aristocracy with a citizenship whose ranks were based on wealth. Solon's reforms were considered to have removed conditions that might otherwise have led to civil war and tyranny. When democracy was introduced in Athens in the fifth century BCE, Solon's constitution provided the basis from which the new constitution grew.

While Plato was still a boy, his father died and his mother married Pyrilampes, a friend of the revered Athenian statesman Pericles, who in the 450s had transformed Athens into one of the greatest cities in the Greek world. As a young man Plato fought in the Athenian army against Sparta during the Peloponnesian War (431–404)—which Athens lost—and he may have served again around 395 when Athens was involved in the Corinthian War (395–386).

Given his family connections, Plato seemed set to play a prominent role in Athenian political life, and, as it happened, when he was about 23, a political revolution occurred in Athens that could have catapulted him into public affairs. The coup swept the previous democratic rulers—who had just lost the war against Sparta—out of power and into exile and replaced them with the so-called Thirty Tyrants, several of whom were friends and relatives of Plato; two of these, Critias and Charmides, appear in his dialogues. It seems that Plato, then an idealistic young man, expected that this revolution would usher in a new era of justice and good government, but he was soon disillusioned: the new regime proved to be even more violent and corrupt than the old. He withdrew from public life in disgust.

The rule of the Thirty lasted only about nine months, and soon afterwards the exiled democrats were restored to power. Plato—impressed by the newly restored leaders' lenience toward the coup leaders—apparently thought again about entering politics. But then, in 399 BCE, the prosecution and conviction of his old friend and mentor Socrates caused him again to change his mind. Plato, along with some other philosophical followers of Socrates, fled Athens and went west to the city of Megara to stay with the philosopher Eucleides (a follower of the great Greek philosopher Parmenides of Elea). He may also have visited Egypt, though his travels at this time are shrouded in myth. It appears that Plato started writing in earnest at about this time; certainly, the earliest writings that have come down to us date from this period.

Almost all of Plato's writings are in the form of dialogues between two or more characters, and in most of them the character that takes the leading role in the discussion is Socrates. Writing in dialogue form was not unique to Plato; for example, a friend of Socrates, the general Xenophon, wrote a number of dialogues that provide another major source for Socrates' life. Plato, however, was by far the greatest practitioner of the dialogue form. Since Plato never wrote himself into any of his dialogues, it is often—though not uncontroversially—assumed that the views expressed by the character of Socrates more or less correspond with those that Plato is trying to put forward.

When Plato was about 40, he made another trip away from Athens, visiting Italy to talk with the Pythagorean philosophers who lived there, and traveling to Syracuse on the island of Sicily. There, during a long stay, he became close friends with Dion, the brother-in-law of the ruling tyrant Dionysius I. Dion became Plato's pupil and (according to legend) came to prefer a philosophical life of moral goodness to the pleasure, luxury, and power of his surroundings. Exactly what happened next is unclear, but there is some reason to believe that Plato was captured by a displeased Dionysius and sold into slavery, and that he was rescued from the slave market only by having his freedom purchased by a member of a different philosophical school influenced by Socrates (the Cyrenaics).

On his return to Athens, Plato bought some land in the precinct named for an Athenian hero called Academus, and there, in about 385

BCE, he founded the first European research center (or, at least, the first of which there is any real historical knowledge). Because of its location this school was called the Academy; it was to remain in existence for more than 900 years, until 529 CE. For most of the rest of his life, Plato stayed at the Academy, directing its studies. Very quickly, the school became a vital center for research in all kinds of subjects, both theoretical and practical: it was probably one of the first cradles for the study of metaphysics, epistemology, psychology, ethics, politics, aesthetics, and mathematical science, and members were invited by various Greek city-states to help draft new political constitutions. All known mathematicians of the fourth century had links to the Academy. Theaetetus of Athens and Eudoxus of Cnidus, together with Plato's Italian friend Archytas of Tarentum, helped to develop the mathematics that form the latter part of Euclid's *Elements*.

In 368, Dionysius I of Sicily died and Dion persuaded his successor, Dionysius II, to send for Plato so that the latter could advise him on how the state should be run. Plato, who was now about 60, agreed to go, albeit with some misgivings; possibly he hoped to make the younger Dionysius an example of a philosopher-king and to put his own political doctrines into practice. If so, the experiment was a disastrous failure, as Dion was soon sent into exile and Plato effectively held prisoner by Dionysius. After returning to Athens for a few years, Plato once again traveled to Sicily, at the urging of both Dion and Dionysius, and was again taken prisoner. In 360, he was finally able to escape and return to Athens for good. He died thirteen years later, at the ripe age of 80.

Socrates

Socrates was Plato's primary intellectual influence: though he left no writings, Socrates' personality and ideas were so powerful that he appears to have had a tremendous impact upon everyone he encountered, inspiring either intense devotion or powerful irritation. Born in about 470 BCE, Socrates would have been in his late 50s when a teenaged Plato fell under his influence, and he was about 70 when he was executed.

Socrates' father was a sculptor and his mother a midwife, and he initially earned his living as a stonemason. He married a much younger woman, Xanthippe, who bore him three sons. Little is known about the historical Xanthippe, but she has become a byword for spirited, argumentative women, and Socrates is depicted, in a dialogue written by another of his students, Xenophon, as saying that this fiery personality is why he married her.

Like Plato, Socrates served valiantly as a soldier—an infantryman—in the Athenian army during the ongoing wars with Sparta and its allies. Like all Athenian citizens he was also occasionally involved in civic politics, acting for a period as an overseer of the council of citizens appointed to run daily affairs of the city (the *boule*); however, in general Socrates steered clear of political life.

He lived very simply—some of his contemporaries thought, with ostentatious and unnecessary poverty—and was known for going barefoot even during bitterly cold weather. He was the butt of jokes, in which he often shared with apparent good humor, for his ugliness; he was short, with bandy legs—giving him a swaggering walk—a snub nose, bulging eyes, bristling eyebrows, and a paunch.

Socrates' main philosophical concern was the ethical question of how one's life should best be lived, and his method was to engage in systematic cross-examination (*elenchus*) of those he encountered, challenging them to state, and then to justify, their own beliefs about justice and virtue. Socrates frequently demonstrated to his interlocutors that their critically unconsidered beliefs about moral virtue were self-contradictory, and hence that those beliefs had no justification. The state of bewildered awareness of their own ignorance in which Socrates left his unfortunate victims is called *aporia*, and Socrates' technique of remorseless questioning is sometimes known as the "aporetic method."

Though Socrates was famous for insisting that he was wiser than his fellow Athenians only because he alone realized that he knew nothing, he did subscribe to a handful of substantive philosophical positions, two of which in particular he passed on to Plato. First, for Socrates, virtue (*arete*) is a kind of knowledge: that is, to be a virtuous person is, fundamentally, to *understand* what the good—the right thing to do—is, in much the same way as being an expert shoemaker consists in knowing everything there is to know about shoes. Socrates (and Plato after him) therefore held that it was vitally important to find correct definitions—or to understand the essence (*eidos*)—of ethical concepts; otherwise, we will not know how to live. In this way, ethical research would parallel mathematical research, in which the researcher tries to establish definitions for fundamental objects and then to prove results about those objects.

Wisdom is sufficient for virtue, Socrates thought, because no one does the wrong thing on purpose. We always desire to do what is best for us; it's just that sometimes we fail to understand what is in our own best interests. Every departure from moral virtue is a failure of wisdom—a failure, simply, to understand what is the right thing to do.

The second crucial Socratic doctrine is that the real essence of a person is not the body but the soul, and that this soul is immortal: the health of one's own soul is thus of paramount importance and is far more significant than the mere slings and arrows of physical life. Indeed, Socrates was convinced that, even while we are living in the physical world, the quality of our souls is a far more important determinant of our happiness than external circumstances like health, wealth, popularity, or power.

Socrates' goal, then, was the "care of the soul"—making one's soul as good and healthy as possible. And he thought that he had a mission, commanded by the god Apollo, to try to improve the souls of his fellow Athenians as well. This burnishing of the soul comes down to becoming as *wise* as possible—all virtue follows from wisdom, and it is wisdom that gives everything else, such as health and wealth, its value. What is the point of having money, for example, if you do not know what to do with it? The pursuit of wisdom requires questioning convention—refusing to do or believe things merely because they are expected or traditional—and committing oneself only to what is rationally justified. As Plato has Socrates famously put it in the *Apology*, the unexamined life is not worth living. Potentially, therefore, Socrates' philosophy is revolutionary. He was clear, too, that the point of examining one's presuppositions is not merely to come to possess more correct beliefs; it is to learn how one should *act* in life. The expression of a healthy soul is appropriate behavior.

Although wisdom is a kind of knowledge, it is not something that can be taught, in the standard sense of having things described or explained to you. Each individual must come to wisdom by grappling *themselves* with important ideas, such as justice, piety, courage, or balance. Here is one way to think of this. The nature of piety, for example, is to be understood by grasping the essence of *piety*—to put it a little anachronistically, it is a concept, and what it is to grasp a concept is to be able to define it. However, merely being able to rhyme off the definition is not adequate—it is not genuine understanding. A real grasp of the concept involves knowing *why* it is the way it is—why other ways of defining it are wrong, not just because some convention says so but because these *could not* be the way piety is. The aim of the Socratic method is to push people into thinking for themselves and performing the difficult mental activity that is the only way of coming to the genuine understanding of key concepts that constitutes knowledge of virtue.

As the Roman philosopher Cicero put it, more than 300 years after Socrates' death, "Socrates was the first to call philosophy down from the heavens and to place it in cities, and even to introduce it into homes and compel it to inquire about human life, ethical conduct, and goods and evils."[1] Though Socrates found many sympathetic students among the youth of Athens, his often-antagonistic rhetorical methods and his questioning of commonly held Athenian beliefs was not appreciated by all. In 399 BCE, three citizens brought trumped-up charges against Socrates, accusing him of impiety toward the city's gods and of corrupting the youth of Athens. It is not clear how far this prosecution was inspired by political opposition to Socrates, who had associated with members of the Thirty Tyrants, among others. Socrates was convicted by the majority of a jury of 500 citizens and—since he declared that he would rather die than give up philosophy (even though he would probably not have been killed had he chosen exile as a penalty)—he was executed by being given a poison, hemlock, to drink.

What Was Plato's Overall Philosophical Project?

Although the following dialogues, like nearly all of Plato's work, feature Socrates as their main protagonist, it is important to bear in mind that these dialogues were written by Plato, not Socrates—indeed, they were written after Socrates' death—and are expressions of *Plato's* philosophy, although undoubtedly Plato was heavily influenced by Socrates and held many very similar views, especially at the time these dialogues were written.

Plato is often regarded as the inventor of Western philosophy—and with some justification. His thought encompassed nearly all of the areas that are central to philosophy today—including metaphysics, epistemology, ethics, political theory, aesthetics, and the philosophy of science and mathematics—and for the first time in European history dealt with them in a unified way.[2] Plato thought of philosophy as a special discipline with its own intellectual method, and he was convinced that it had an absolutely foundational importance in human life. Only philosophy, Plato thought, could provide genuine understanding, since only philosophy scrutinized the assumptions that other disciplines left unquestioned. Furthermore, according to Plato, philosophy reveals a realm of comprehensive and unitary hidden truths—indeed, a whole level of reality that is undetectable by the senses—which goes far beyond everyday common sense and which, when properly understood, has the power to revolutionize how we live

1 *Tusculan Disputations* vol. 10, c. 45 BCE.

2 In fact, the mathematician and philosopher Alfred North Whitehead (1861–1947) famously was moved to say, "The safest general characterization of the European philosophical tradition is that it consists of a series of footnotes to Plato."

our lives and organize our societies. Philosophy, and only philosophy, holds the key to genuine human happiness and well-being.

This realm of objects that Plato claimed to have discovered is generally known as the Platonic Forms. The Forms, according to Plato, are changeless, eternal objects that lie outside of both the physical world and the minds of individuals, and they can be encountered only through pure thought (rather than by the senses). One of Plato's favorite examples of a Form is the mathematical property of Equality. In the *Phaedo* he argues that Equality itself cannot be identical with two equal sticks, or with any other group of physical objects of equal length, since we could always be mistaken about whether any two observed objects are really equal with one another, but we could not possibly be mistaken about Equality itself and somehow take *it* to be unequal. When two sticks are equal in length, therefore, they "participate in" Equality—it is their relation to Equality that makes them equal rather than unequal—but Equality itself is an abstract object that exists over and above all the instances of equal things. The Form of Equality is what one succeeds in understanding when one has a proper conception of what equality really is in itself: real knowledge, therefore, comes not from observation but from acquaintance with the Forms. Other central examples of Forms, for Plato, are Sameness, Number, Motion, Beauty, Justice, Piety, and (the most important Form of all) Goodness.

The relation of the ordinary world of perceivable, concrete objects to the realm of the Forms is described by Plato in Book VII of one of his major works, the *Republic*, using the allegory of a cave. Ordinary people, lacking the benefit of a philosophical education, are like prisoners trapped since birth in an underground cave and forced to look only at shadows cast on the wall in front of them by puppets behind their backs, dancing in front of a fire. With the proper philosophical encouragement, they can—if they have the courage to do so—break their bonds and turn around to see that what they believed was reality itself was really only an illusory puppet show. The philosophers among them can even leave the cave and once outside will encounter the true reality—of which even the puppets are only copies—illuminated by the light of the sun, which, for Plato, represents the Form of the Good. The perceptible world is thus merely an imperfect image of—and is sustained by—the quasi-divine, eternal realm of the unchanging and unobservable Forms.

What Is the Structure of These Dialogues?

Three of the dialogues collected here are among the first works Plato wrote: the *Apology*, *Crito*, and *Euthyphro* were probably written sometime between 399 and 387 BCE—that is, in the years immediately following the death of Socrates, when Plato was in his late 20s and 30s. The *Meno* and *Phaedo* were likely written sometime later and are part of a sequence of dialogues in which the mature Plato moves away from the views of Socrates and develops ideas that depart from what Socrates taught (even though Plato still uses Socrates as the main protagonist in these dialogues). The *Meno* shows Socrates in typical philosophical discussion; but the other dialogues take place at times closely preceding and including his trial and execution. In the *Euthyphro*, Socrates is waiting to attend a preliminary hearing before the city's magistrates when he strikes up a conversation with another legal petitioner, Euthyphro. In the *Apology*[1] we hear Socrates' unsuccessful defense in response to the indictment against him. The *Crito* takes place in Socrates' prison cell, where he is waiting to be executed, and deals with Socrates' reasons for refusing to accept the help of his wealthy friend Crito and escape from Athens. Finally, the *Phaedo* takes place during Socrates' last moments, in which he talks about why he does not fear his own death.

These dialogues are instances of a fourth-century BCE literary genre called "Socratic conversations" (*Sokratikoi logoi*) in which people who knew Socrates wrote imagined reconstructions of his conversations. Dialogues by Plato and the historian Xenophon (c. 430–354 BCE) are the only examples of this genre that survive, but others were written by many of his contemporaries.

Plato attended Socrates' trial and, although the *Apology* is certainly not a verbatim account of what Socrates actually said, it is likely that it does not depart too far from the flavor and spirit of Socrates' words (since Plato's dialogue would have been read by many people who were actually there). Plato was not personally present at Socrates' death, but he knew people who were. The *Meno*, *Euthyphro*, and *Crito*, by contrast, although they involve real people, were not literal records of actual conversations or events—and would not have been expected to be so by Plato's readers—but rather exemplify the thoughts, manners, and personality of Socrates, and in so doing they use Socrates to explore Plato's own ideas.

Some Useful Background Information

The Political Context

In ancient Greece, the city (*polis*) was the primary political unit—approximately equivalent to states today. Although the Greeks at the time

---

1 *Apology* is the traditional name for this dialogue, but it might be better named *Socrates' Defense*; the standard name comes from the Greek *apologia*, which means defense.

did think of themselves as members of a common people, their main allegiance was to their home *polis*, and cities differed widely in their culture and forms of government. Socrates and Plato lived during a period of major transition for their home state of Athens. Athens was the most powerful and culturally influential Greek city-state in the Athenian "Golden Age" of the 440s and 430s BCE, but 431 saw the beginning of brutal wars for dominance between Athens and the competing city-state of Sparta, ending with the humiliating defeat of Athens in 404. (This was followed by yet another turn of fortune: the decline of Sparta and partial re-establishment of Athenian fortunes in the 370s.)

The crucial political event that forms the background for Socrates' trial and execution was the final defeat of Athens in the long Peloponnesian War against Sparta, which took place in 404 BCE, five years before Socrates' trial. This, obviously, was a crushing blow for Athenian self-confidence and brought about a crescendo in the already ongoing search for someone to blame for the city's misfortunes. The democratic government and its generals naturally shouldered a large part of this guilt, and so this government was toppled and replaced by a puppet junta of Athenian aristocrats supported and controlled by the Spartan army: these were known as the Thirty Tyrants. The Tyrants sought to secure their political position with a bloody campaign of repression, but this had the effect of sparking a civil war in Athens in which, the following year, the forces of the democrats were victorious. This new government tried to bring order back to the Athenian state by forming an alliance with moderate members of the anti-democratic, oligarchical faction and proclaiming a blanket amnesty for crimes committed during the previous few years, including under the rule of the Thirty.

Socrates was overtly apolitical throughout his life, refusing to take sides with the various factions that fought over control of Athens, but he was also adamant in refusing to participate in anything that he considered to be unjust or illegal, even when such refusals endangered his own safety. (He describes some of these episodes in his speech in the *Apology*.) In both these ways he was unusual for his time, and—perhaps ironically—both were causes for public suspicion of him.

Furthermore, despite his intention to steer clear of politics, he nevertheless was associated with several figures who were perceived to be enemies of democracy in Athens, three powerful men in particular. Alcibiades—a close friend of Socrates who often boasted of his association with him—was a rich, charming, arrogant man who had led Athens to crushing military disaster, blasphemed against one of the most important Athenian religious cults, the Eleusinian Mysteries, and then turned traitor and fled to the Spartans and helped them attack his former home city. Critias, Socrates' student and a first cousin of his mother, was the aristocratic leader of the Thirty Tyrants who controlled Athens after its defeat by Sparta and the suspension of democracy. Another one of the tyrants, Charmides, was Socrates' pupil (and Plato's uncle).

Socrates publicly denounced the illegal actions of the Thirty Tyrants (not because they were undemocratic, but because they were unconstitutional and unjust) and refused Critias' demand that he stop associating with and influencing the young men of the city. Instead of executing him, however, Critias sought to implicate him in the short-lived oligarchy by commanding him to arrest a wealthy enemy of the regime, Leon of Salamis, seize his property, and execute him; as recounted in the *Apology*, Socrates refused to participate, but Leon was nevertheless killed.

During the rule of the Thirty Tyrants, some 1,500 Athenians were murdered by the regime. None of the main culprits were available to be officially tried for their crimes, because of the general amnesty or because they had already died or escaped the city—though in one way or another almost all of them met untimely ends—and so it is quite possible that one of the undercurrents in Socrates' trial was that he was being made a scapegoat for the recent horrors.

The Religious Context

Ancient Greek religious beliefs form an important background to the Platonic dialogues collected here. Greek religion was polytheistic,[1] and different cities and regions worshipped somewhat different collections of deities. The gods mentioned in these dialogues include Zeus, god of the sky and leader of the gods; Hera, goddess of women and Zeus's wife (and sister); Athena, goddess of wisdom and craft; Hephaistos (sometimes spelled Hephaestus), god of blacksmiths and fire; and Asclepius, the god of healing. The city of Athens bears the same name in Greek as Athena, who was considered the divine patroness of the city, and the Parthenon—named for Athena Parthenos, or the virgin Athena—was a major temple and center of worship for her. Hephaistos was also a particularly important god for Athens, because the city was a center of manufacturing and craftsmanship. Lastly, a principal god who is mentioned obliquely is Apollo, god of poetry and prophecy, among other things; it is Apollo to whom the or-

1 Although Socrates and Plato were both attracted to, and perhaps persuaded by, the idea of monotheism.

acle at Delphi is sacred, and thus he is the god who gave Socrates his divine mission (and may be the god who speaks to him through his "divine sign").

In addition to the gods, the Greeks believed in a number of demigods: half-god, half-mortal children of liaisons between gods and mortals. Of these, Heracles and Tantalos are both mentioned in the dialogues. Heracles (known to the Romans as Hercules) was a son of Zeus and the ideal hero to the Greeks, a semi-divine figure who used both his strength and his intelligence to fight against various monsters on behalf of humanity. Tantalos (or Tantalus) was another son of Zeus, but instead of being a hero he murdered his son and tried to feed him to the gods as an offering. For this he was punished by being placed in the deepest part of the Underworld, where he was constantly offered food and drink, which then receded just beyond his grasp when he tried to take them.[1] The text mentions "the money of Tantalos"; as he was a king who derived great wealth from mines he controlled, his association with the Underworld in Greek myth would have had overtones for Plato's contemporaries, who saw the realms below ground as a source of mineral riches.

The ancient Greeks believed in beings even older than the gods of Olympus, two of whom are mentioned in these dialogues: the giant Titans including Cronos, father of Zeus, and Cronos' own father Ouranos (sometimes spelled Uranus), who was the elemental Greek god personifying the sky.

Life in Plato's Athens, and in classical Greece generally, was thoroughly permeated by religion. The year was shaped by a succession of regular religious festivals, and everything—from politics to warfare to crafts to agriculture to the arts—had a religious character. Of particular importance was the role of religion in contributing to the solidarity of the community, and religious observance was a public act often enforced by civic laws. Ritual sacrifice of animals such as oxen, sheep, and pigs was a central, and frequent, feature of Greek religious life and served to reinforce the proper relationship not only between humans and gods but also between members of the community. Social groups—families, demes (local regions), clubs, cities, and even the wider Greek nation—were defined as those who worshipped the same gods.[2]

---

1 This is the origin of the verb *to tantalize*.

2 The period of upheaval in Athens caused by the disruptions of the Peloponnesian War and the defeat at the hands of Sparta and its allies led to a flowering of new cults and religious rites in Athens. For example, the worship of Asclepius—mentioned in the *Phaedo*—was a new import to Athens during the war.

Since religious ritual was what kept the gods' good will and support of one's community alive, impiety was a serious crime: piety was a form of patriotism, which, it was believed, had serious real-world consequences if it was neglected. There was no separation between the modern concepts of "church" and "state" in ancient Greece, and so religious authority was inseparable from secular power. Major sacred rites were performed by magistrates or prominent citizens on behalf of the city. Individual gods had their priests, but these were typically part-time holy men with secular "day jobs," and there were no institutions to train and certify priests or to ensure any kind of doctrinal orthodoxy.

The closest things to religious professionals in classical Greece were seers and oracles. A seer was someone who interpreted dreams or various patterns in nature, such as the flight of birds or the entrails of a sacrificed animal, in order to answer questions put to the gods. Seers—such as Euthyphro—were consulted often, including before public activities such as military campaigns or political decisions; they were frequently influential members of the social elite and were taken extremely seriously, although decision-making power remained with the generals or citizen assembly.

Oracles were specific sacred locations at which, at particular times, the gods spoke directly to people, together with the priestesses and priests who interpreted these pronouncements. In the *Apology* Socrates mentions the oracle at Delphi (about 100 km northwest of Athens), which was the most important oracle in ancient Greece, and thought to stand at the center of the world; the oracle there was generally considered to be infallible, so Socrates' allusion to it has great weight. When Socrates asserts that he has a mission from god to examine and improve the people of Athens, he is being perfectly sincere and literal.

An example of the tight integration of religion into civic life, and of its life-and-death importance, is the episode of the mutilations of the herms (*hermai*), statues of the face and phallus of the god Hermes that served as sacred boundary markers surrounding the city. In 415, at the height of the Peloponnesian War, Athens was mounting an invasion of Sicily. On the eve of the departure of the fleet, the shocking discovery was made that almost all of the herms had been vandalized overnight. The city was appalled by this act of sacrilege and also feared a conspiracy against the democracy, and a commission was swiftly established to investigate not only who had defaced the herms, but also any crimes of irreverence toward the city's gods. Rewards were offered for those who informed on their neighbors, and the ensuing few months saw a spreading moral panic in which hundreds of people were tortured, imprisoned, exiled, and executed for the crime of impiety. Among the accused were many of Socrates' close friends and students, such as Alcibiades, Phaedrus, Charmides, and Critias. In the end, it turned out that the actual culprits in the mutilations of the herms were members of a young men's drinking club, one of whom confessed, and that many of the accusations of impiety had been trumped up by lying informants. But by then, of course, the damage had been done.

One final point regarding the religious context of these dialogues: the notion of the soul, as Plato understands it, is not precisely the same as the modern notion (although Platonic doctrines of the soul were important precursors to the Christian concept). According to Plato, the soul, or *psyche*, is the thing that brings life to the body; it is the "shade" that persists after the death of the body; and it is essentially rational. However, it is not a kind of non-physical substance; instead, it is more analogous to a really existing but abstract object such as the Form of the Good. The Greeks had no clear theory of an afterlife and paid no special attention to life after death; their religious hopes were generally focused on success in this life.

The Legal Context

Athenian law, unlike modern legal systems, made no distinction between private and public interests: private individuals were entitled to prosecute people, not because they had been personally wronged, but on behalf of the public interest. It was not unusual for citizens to consider it their moral duty to prosecute other individuals for harming the city, and this is what happened to Socrates.

In the Athenian legal system there was no equivalent of an attorney general—no one to either permit or to disallow a legal process. And during the trial there was no presiding judge able to make decisions about the adequacy or relevance of the evidence being presented. There was also no judge to decide on a penalty for plaintiffs found guilty: in cases like Socrates', the prosecutor would argue for a penalty, the accused would make a counter-argument for a different penalty, and the jury would vote to decide between the two.

The charge of impiety—of not showing proper respect to the city's gods—was not an unusual one. Some of the most famous citizens of Athens had to respond to similar legal accusations, including the sculptor and architect Phidias, the playwrights and poets Sophocles and Euripides, and the philosophers Anaxagoras, Aristotle, and Theophrastus. (On the other hand, the charge of corrupting the youth does seem to be unusual, and it may have been formulated specifically for Socrates.)

To us, this process may seem flawed and unsatisfactory. But to Socrates (and Plato) his trial was a perfectly normal and acceptable instance of Athenian law and democracy in action.

The trial took place in a large building—basically just an open space with walls and seating—in the marketplace at the corner of the Acropolis. It lasted no more than a single day. Present were the 500 (or possibly 501) jury members, chosen by lottery, plus a crowd of curious onlookers, as even at the time the trial was attracting a great deal of attention. A substantial proportion of the jury and audience would have known Socrates personally and many more would have heard of him—Athens at the time had a population of about 150,000 people, about the size of Alexandria, Virginia, or Guelph, Ontario, or Oxford, England; of these, perhaps 20,000 would have been eligible for jury duty.

Imprisonment was not a normal punishment in ancient Greece—standard punishments were fines, loss of citizenship, exile, or death—and so it was unusual to keep prisoners more than a day or two before their execution or while they arranged payment of their fine. Socrates' imprisonment was extended to some thirty days, since no execution was permitted during the sacred festival of Apollo, and the end of the festival, marked by the return of a special boat from the holy island of Delos, was delayed by contrary winds that kept the boat at sea. Socrates, then, had ample opportunity to escape from his prison, which he could have done by simply digging through its earthen wall or through bribery. It appears that his friends had arranged the possibility of his escape, and that this escape was widely anticipated. But Socrates chose to remain.

Sophism

Another factor in the trial of Socrates was the (false) popular association of Socrates with the school of Sophism. Sophists were traveling teachers who, for payment, would teach young male citizens the art of rhetoric, or persuasive public speaking. This was a skill of great practical importance since legal and political decisions were made by assemblies of citizens and were based on the persuasiveness of the parties involved. Because their teaching was in great demand, Sophists were often popular, courted by the powerful, and became very wealthy from the fees their students paid.

On the other hand, they were not to be trusted and their teachings were often thought to have a corrosive effect on democracy and good governance because they explicitly taught the art of making the weaker of two arguments appear to be the stronger. That is, they were not concerned with rationality or good judgment but simply with persuasion, and they prided themselves on their ability to make true claims seem false. In this way, they were a clear and present danger to conventional or traditional belief. Gorgias, for example, a prominent Sophist, advertised himself as being able to make even paradoxical, absurd positions appear reasonable; and he taught a particular, theatrical style of speaking that was intended, literally, to cast a kind of spell on the audience, one that acted like a drug to make them more suggestible.

How Important and Influential Are These Dialogues?

It is difficult to overestimate the influence of Plato's thought on the history of philosophy. The dialogues collected here contain seminal early explorations of several big ideas: the relationship between religion and morality (and whether it is coherent to suppose that morality is grounded in religious belief); the nature of death, and whether or not it is a harm; the health of the immortal soul; the nature of goodness and of the good life; and the question of what we owe to the state and its laws, including a view, influentially expressed by Plato, that there is some sort of implicit contract between the state and its citizens that is the grounding for our obligation to obey the law.

Furthermore, these short dialogues provide a powerful introduction to what philosophy *is*: the examination of every preconception, no matter how conventional or comfortable, and following the arguments wherever they may lead, in service of the overriding goal of uncovering the truth.

A second way in which these dialogues are important is as the main source for the inspirational example of Socrates. Over the centuries his "martyrdom" at the hands of his fellow citizens has been held up as an iconic moral example, perhaps second in the Western tradition only to Jesus, with whom he is often compared, for Socrates' unwavering commitment to his own moral principles and his steadfastness in the face of death.

Timeline

478 BCE	Defeat of the Persian invasion of Greece by a coalition led by Athens (the Delian League), and the start of the Athenian "Golden Age."
c. 470	Birth of Socrates.
454	The Delian League becomes, in effect, the Athenian empire, as Athens takes control of the league's finances and military.
445	Pericles is elected main democratic leader and general of the army, a position he holds until his death by being repeatedly re-elected.

c. 437	Anaxagoras is banished from Athens after being tried for impiety.
431	Start of the Peloponnesian War between the Athenian empire (a mainly naval power) and Sparta and its (mostly land-based) allies.
430	Outbreak of plague (typhoid fever) in Athens.
429	Death of Pericles from plague.
c. 427	Birth of Plato.
423	Public performance of Aristophanes' play *Clouds*, mocking Socrates and probably making him notorious in the city.
c. 416	Socrates marries Xanthippe.
415	There is a rash of trials and executions for impiety, including of many of Socrates' associates, following the mutilations of the *hermai*, the symbolic Athenian border markers.
413	Another play by Aristophanes, *Birds*, is performed, which also includes an attack on Socrates.
412	Athenian morale is at a low point, following revolts by several of its subject-allies.
411	An Athenian coup briefly overthrows democracy and replaces it with oligarchy: the rule of the Four Hundred.
406	Athens wins a sea battle (the battle of Arginusae), but at such a major cost that the city's military power is effectively destroyed. Socrates is an overseer of the Athenian citizens' council (the *boule*) at this time and refuses to allow the responsible generals to be illegally prosecuted. After his term ends, the generals are prosecuted anyway and executed.
404	Athens is finally defeated; this is followed by a reaction against its democratic leaders, who were blamed for the defeat, and the rule of the Thirty Tyrants (backed by the Spartan army).
403	Restoration of Athenian democracy after a brief civil war.
399	Trial and execution of Socrates.
399–387	Plato writes *Euthyphro*, *Apology*, *Crito*.
395	Start of the Corinthian War, sparked by Spartan imperialism.
387	Plato's first visit to Sicily.
387–367	Plato writes *Meno* and *Phaedo*.
c. 385	Plato founds the Academy.
384	Birth of Aristotle.
371	Defeat of Sparta and establishment of the second Athenian League.

c. 367	Aristotle joins the Academy. Plato's second visit to Sicily.
360	Plato escapes Sicily.
c. 347	Death of Plato.
338	Athens is defeated by Macedonia, and soon after ceases to be an independent power.

Suggestions for Further Reading

Part of the fun of grappling with these dialogues is learning about the very different, and fascinating, way of life of ancient Athens. A couple of interesting and accessible resources for this include Robert Parker, "Greek Religion," in *The Oxford History of the Classical World*, ed. John Boardman, Jasper Griffin, and Oswyn Murray (Oxford University Press, 1986), and K.J. Dover's *Greek Popular Morality in the Time of Plato and Aristotle* (Basil Blackwell, 1974, reprinted by Hackett in 1994). The British Joint Association of Classical Teachers has produced a reliable, readable (illustrated) book called *The World of Athens: An Introduction to Classical Athenian Culture* (Cambridge University Press, 2008). Another interesting read is *The Mutilation of the Herms: Unpacking an Ancient Mystery*, self-published by Debra Hamel in 2012 (http://www.dhamel.com/the-mutilation-of-the-herms).

Further context comes from *Xenophon, Conversations of Socrates*, translated by Hugh Tredennick and revised by Robin Waterfield (Penguin, 1990), and an enjoyable modern translation of Aristophanes' *Clouds* is by Peter Meineck (Hackett, 1998).

Probably the best short introduction to the philosophical context in which Plato was writing is still Terence Irwin's superb *Classical Thought* (Oxford University Press, 1989). Paul Johnson, *Socrates: A Man for Our Times* (Penguin, 2011) vividly describes the "celebrity culture" of ancient Athens, while Robin Waterfield, *Why Socrates Died: Dispelling the Myths* (Faber and Faber, 2009) is, as well as being an outstanding account of the context of Socrates' trial, particularly interesting as a defense of Socrates' accusers, or at least an attempt to explain their actions as being rational and understandable. (As Waterfield puts it, "Socrates would have been the last to want to leave a cultural icon unexamined.") Also well worth consulting are C.C.W. Taylor, *Socrates: A Very Short Introduction* (Oxford University Press, 1998); *A Companion to Socrates*, edited by Sara Ahbel-Rappe and Rachana Kamtekar (Blackwell, 2006); T.C. Brickhouse and N.D. Smith, *The Routledge Philosophy Guidebook to Plato and the Trial of Socrates* (Routledge, 2004); and James A. Colaiaco, *Socrates Against Athens* (Routledge, 2001).

There is a *Cambridge Companion to Socrates*, ed. Donald R. Morrison (Cambridge University Press, 2010); *The Cambridge Companion to Plato*, ed. Richard Kraut (Cambridge University Press, 1992), is also of interest, especially the chapters by Terry Penner on "Socrates and the Early Dialogues" and by Michael L. Morgan on "Plato and Greek Religion." Lastly, two more scholarly works of very high quality are Gregory Vlastos, *Socrates: Ironist and Moral Philosopher* (Cambridge University Press, 1991), and T.C. Brickhouse and N.D. Smith, *Socrates on Trial* (Oxford University Press, 1989).

Translators' Note

The translations of *Euthyphro*, *Apology*, and *Crito* were made from the 1995 Oxford Classical Text of Duke et al. (However, we prefer ἐρῶντα τῷ ἐρωμένῳ at *Euthyphro* 14b4, retain οὐ at *Apology* 27e7, and give ἀληθῆ λέγεις to Crito at *Crito* 48b1.) The commentaries of Adam (*Euthyphro*, *Apology*, *Crito*) and Burnet (in *Plato: Euthyphro, Apology of Socrates*, *Crito*) proved invaluable throughout. In addition, for *Euthyphro*, some useful suggestions were found in the editions by Graves, Heidel, and Wells; for *Apology*, Flagg, and Helm's *Plato: Apology*; for *Crito*, Cron/Dyer, Flagg, Tyler, and Wagner.

The translation of *Meno* was made from the Oxford Classical Text of Burnet, 1903 (Platonis Opera Vol. III). The commentaries of Thompson (*The Meno of Plato*, MacMillan, 1901), Bluck (*Plato's Meno*, Cambridge, 2010 [1961]), McKirahan (*Plato's Meno*, Bryn Mawr, 1986) and Sharples (*Plato: Meno*, Aris & Phillips, 1985) were all useful.

The translation of *Phaedo* was made from the Oxford Classical Text of Burnet, 1903, with a few small emendations. The textual commentaries of Archer-Hind (*The Phaedo of Plato*, MacMillan, 1883), Geddes (*The Phædo of Plato*, Williams & Norgate, 1863), Stanford (*Plato's Apology of Socrates, Crito, and Phædo*, Curry and Co, 1834), and Steadman (*Plato's* Phaedo, 2015) were consulted.

We express our gratitude to Virginia Wesleyan College for supporting both translators during the preparation of the translations of *Euthyphro*, *Apology*, and *Crito* in 2007, from the Faculty Summer Development Fund (Woods) and from the Undergraduate Research Fund (Pack). The translations of *Meno* and *Phaedo* were undertaken solely by Woods.

We would also like to thank Dustin Platter and Seosamh Mac Coille, and Laura Buzzard, Stephen Latta, Robert M. Martin, and Michel Pharand at Broadview Press, for commenting on drafts of the translations.

Readers are encouraged to send corrections to the translations. This is best done by email to cathalwoods@gmail.com.

Cathal Woods
Ryan Pack

Meno

Introduction

The *Meno* begins with the question whether virtue can be taught. 'Virtue' here is the usual translation for Plato's Greek term *arete*. Another possible translation is 'excellence'. It's a general term, encompassing all the more particular virtues such as strength, bravery, and so on. It might be understood as the state of actualizing full human potential, or as achieving full human function.

Socrates asserts that Meno's questions couldn't be answered until there's understanding of exactly what virtue is, and (as usual) confesses, perhaps with false modesty, ignorance. Meno confidently replies with a list of the different virtues for a man, a woman, a child, or a slave; but Socrates says that this is inadequate: what's wanted is a definition of "virtue" that covers all these particulars: what they all have in common—their essence. Meno replies that virtue in general is the ability to rule men. This may seem to readers to be very far off the mark; but perhaps what Meno is thinking is that "ruling" one's self or others is the only way to produce the excellence that all virtue involves. In any case, Socrates quickly shows the inadequacy of this definition, pointing out that a slave might possess virtues, though he rules nobody, and the ruling is virtuous only if it is just. He illustrates the generality he's looking for in a definition by comparing it to other general terms like 'shape', whose definition must apply to all particular shapes (circle, rectangle, etc.).

Meno tries again: virtue, he suggests, is desiring and owning beautiful things. Socrates again points out that these are virtuous only if done in a good way. Meno then admits to being confused and at a loss, perplexed and at an impasse. He wonders how anyone can discover what he does not already know: how could he recognize it if he came across it? (This has become known as Meno's Paradox.) Socrates dismisses this as a debaters' trick, but nevertheless responds to it with his doctrine of knowledge as *recollection*. As a demonstration of this doctrine, he gets Meno's uneducated slave boy to come up with truths of geometry, not by teaching him these truths, but by (it's claimed) getting the boy to "recollect" them—discovering what in some sense he already potentially knew. Readers may be skeptical about Socrates' account of the mind's remembering these truths learned during its previous pre-birth existence; however, accounting for this sort of knowledge (called *a priori*, meaning prior to, independent of, teaching or other experience) is a perennial question faced by philosophy.

The two return to the original question. Socrates argues that virtue is always a good thing, but that the only way something can be good for anyone is if it's exercised with the person's knowledge; so virtue is knowledge. But all knowledge is teachable, so virtue can be taught.

Surprisingly, however, Socrates then proceeds to argue for the reverse conclusion: that if a subject can be taught, there must be teachers who could be paid to teach it; but such teachers of virtue do not exist. Anytus, who has joined the discussion, agrees with Socrates that the Sophists cannot teach virtue, but claims that any good and capable person—any Athenian "gentleman"—can teach it. Socrates responds with several examples of wealthy, competent men, known to be good and to produce good results, but whose sons turned out to be far from virtuous. Anytus, at this point, warns Socrates about the dangers of speaking ill of people; this is an ominous foreshadowing: Anytus will later be one of Socrates' prosecutors at his trial.

Anytus stops participating in the dialogue, but Socrates pursues the question, attempting to resolve the contradiction he arrived at earlier, by distinguishing real knowledge from mere true belief (true opinion). The latter, despite being capable of "running away," can bring one results as good as the former can. Socrates claims that nobody has the genuine theoretical knowledge required for genuine virtue; those who are respected as good people, and who do good deeds, lack this knowledge. They are good only because of a "gift from the gods," like the inspiration of poets.

Cast of Characters

Anytus: One of Socrates' prosecutors. A wealthy democrat, he had been a not-very-successful general during the wars with Sparta and had escaped punishment for his failures by bribing the courts. He hated the Sophists and, probably influenced by Aristophanes' play *Clouds* (originally produced in 423 BCE), associated Socrates with them. He is probably Meno's host in Athens.

Gorgias: Nicknamed "the nihilist," Gorgias was a prominent Sophist from Sicily who settled in Athens as an old man and became extremely popular and in great demand as a teacher of wealthy young men, including Meno. When he died he was rich enough to commission a gold statue of himself for a public temple.

Meno: Meno in real life was rich and privileged, a political/military leader involved in a notorious wartime treachery against the Greeks. But this dialogue represents him before these events, as a youth deeply interested in philosophical questions but not terribly skilled in Socrates' methods of approaching them. Meno was not from Athens but from a region of central Greece called Thessaly. This dialogue, though not historically accurate, is probably meant to take place in early 402 BCE, when Meno was around 19 years old and on his way to join the mercenary army of Cyrus the Younger in Asia Minor.

Meno's slave: Uneducated, as would be expected, but intelligently cooperative with Socrates' demonstration.

Meno

Meno: Can you tell me, Socrates, is virtue acquired by teaching? Or 70a
not by teaching but by training? Or neither by training or learning, but
it comes to men naturally or in some other way?

Socrates: Before now, Meno, Thessalians were famous among the
Greeks, admired for their horsemanship and their wealth, but now, it b
seems, for their wisdom too, especially the Larisaians,[1] the townsfolk
of your friend Aristippus.[2] Gorgias brought this about among you.
When he arrived in the city he made the leading men of the Aleuadai,[3]
including your lover Aristippus, lovers of his wisdom, along with the
other Thessalians. And in particular, he has gotten you into this habit
of answering fearlessly and grandly if anyone asks a question, as befits
someone with knowledge, as indeed he himself does, when he puts c
himself forward for any Greek who wishes to ask whatever he wants,
and refuses no one an answer.

---

1 *Larisaians* Larisa was (and still is) the major city in the region of Thessaly.

2 *Aristippus* Aristippus was a powerful aristocrat involved in power struggles in Thessaly, who—a year or two after the time this dialogue is set—placed Meno in charge of thousands of mercenary troops hired by the Persian prince Cyrus the Younger.

3 *Aleuadai* The Aleuadai were an old and prominent family in Thessaly.

But around here, my friend Meno, the opposite is the norm, as
71a though some shortage of wisdom had occurred, and wisdom might have migrated from our territory to yours. If you put a question like that to anyone here, there's no one who won't laugh and say, "My friend, you must think me to be one of the fortunate few, to know whether virtue is acquired by teaching or in what way it comes to be. I am so far from knowing whether or not it is teachable that I don't at all know just what virtue itself is."

b And indeed I myself, Meno, am in the same state. I am impoverished along with my townsfolk in this matter and I scold myself for not knowing the first thing about virtue. And when I don't know what some thing is, how can I know what sort of thing it is? Or do you think it is possible, if someone doesn't know who Meno is at all, to know whether he is handsome or wealthy or, further, noble, or the opposites of these? Does it seem possible to you?

c Meno: Not to me. But do you truly not know, Socrates, what virtue is? Is this the report we will carry home about you?

Socrates: Not only that, my friend, but further, that I had not met anyone else who knew, as it seemed to me.

Meno: What?! Didn't you meet Gorgias when he was here?

Socrates: I did.

Meno: And you didn't think he knew?

Socrates: I don't really remember, Meno, and so I can't say at the moment how he seemed to me then. Maybe he did know and you know
d what he said. So, remind me how he put it, or you yourself speak, if you like, since you presumably have the same view.

Meno: I do.

Socrates: Well then let's not talk about him, since in fact he's not here. But you yourself, divine Meno, what do you say virtue is? Speak and don't deny me, so that I spoke a most fortunate untruth, and you and Gorgias prove knowledgeable, even though I had said I had never met anyone who knew.

e Meno: But it's not hard to say, Socrates. To begin with, if you want the virtue of a man, it's easy. A man's virtue is this: to attend to the

affairs of the city effectively and, in the process, to benefit his friends and harm his enemies and make sure that he suffers nothing similar himself. If you're looking for the virtue of a woman, it's not hard to express: it's to manage her home well, preserving her possessions and being obedient to her husband. And there's a different virtue for children, both male and female, and for an old man, and, if you want, for a free man and, if you like, for a slave. And there are so many 72a
other virtues that there's no problem saying what virtue is, since there's a virtue for each occupation and stage of life with respect to each function of each person. And I take the same to apply to vice, Socrates.

Socrates: It seems I've had some great good fortune, Meno, if, when looking for a single virtue, I have discovered you possess a kind of swarm of virtues. And in keeping with that image of swarms, if I asked b
what the essence of a bee was and you were to say that there are many different kinds, how would you answer me if I asked, "Do you mean that with respect to *this*, their being bees, that there are many different kinds, different from one another? Or do they differ not at all in this respect, but in some other, such as beauty or size or something else of this sort?" Tell me, how would you answer when asked this?

Meno: To this I would say that they do not differ at all insofar as they are bees, one from another.

Socrates: And if after this I said, "Now tell me this, Meno. *By what* do c
they not differ but are all alike, what do you say this is?" Presumably you would have something to say to me?

Meno: I would.

Socrates: The same applies to the virtues, too. Even if there are many different kinds, they all have some one, same form, on account of which they are virtues, and which, I suppose, a person who is answering another who asked for what virtue actually is to be made clear would rightly have paid attention to. Or don't you understand what I d
mean?

Meno: I think I understand, though I don't yet quite grasp the point of your question as I would like.

Socrates: Does it seem this way to you only concerning virtue, Meno, that there is one for a man, another for a woman, and so on, or is it the same

for health and size and strength, too? Do you think there is one health for a man and another for a woman? Or is it the same form in every case,
e wherever health might be, whether in a man or anywhere else at all?

Meno: I think that with health, at least, it's the same in both a man and a woman.

Socrates: And what about size and strength? If a woman really is strong, won't she be strong because of the same form and because of the same strength? By the words "the same" I mean this: there's no difference, with respect to being strength, whether strength is in a man or in a woman. Or do you think there's any difference?

Meno: I don't.

73a Socrates: Will virtue be any different, with respect to being virtue, whether it's in a child or an old man, or in a woman or a man?

Meno: Somehow, to me, Socrates, this case no longer seems to be similar to those other cases.

Socrates: What? Didn't you say that a man's virtue is to organize a city well, and a woman's virtue to organize a house?

Meno: I did.

Socrates: But is it possible to manage a city or a house or anything at all well unless they do so moderately and justly?

b Meno: Of course not.

Socrates: And if they manage justly and moderately, they will manage by means of justice and moderation?

Meno: Necessarily.

Socrates: So, both of them, if they are going to be good, the woman and the man, need justice and moderation?

Meno: Apparently.

Socrates: What about a child and an old man? Could they be good if they were immoderate and unjust?

Meno: Of course not.

Socrates: But moderate and just instead?

Meno: Yes.

Socrates: Then all people are good in the same way, since they are c
good by possessing the same things.

Meno: It seems so.

Socrates: And surely they wouldn't be good in the same way unless they possessed the same virtue.

Meno: Of course not.

Socrates: Now since they all have the same virtue, try to say and remember what Gorgias says it is, and with which you agree.

Meno: What else than the ability to govern men, if you're looking for d
a single thing in all cases?

Socrates: That is indeed what I'm looking for. But is this also the same virtue of a child, Meno, or of a slave, for these to be able to rule the master, and do you think the person who rules would still be a slave?

Meno: I hardly think so, Socrates.

Socrates: It's not likely, best of men. And further, take a look at this, too: you say it's to be able to rule. Won't we add to that "justly, and not unjustly"?

Meno: I think so, since justice, Socrates, is a virtue.

Socrates: Virtue, Meno, or *a* virtue? e

Meno: What do you mean by that?

Socrates: The same as about anything else. For example, if you like, roundedness, about which I would say that it is a kind of shape, not simply that it is shape. I wouldn't speak that way about it for this reason, that there are other shapes too.

Meno: You are speaking correctly, since I too say that not only justice but others, as well, are virtues.

74a Socrates: What are they? Tell me, just as I could tell you other shapes, if you asked me to, tell me other virtues too.

Meno: I think bravery is certainly a virtue, and moderation and wisdom and benevolence and a whole lot of others.

Socrates: Again, Meno, the same thing has happened to us: we have discovered many virtues when looking for one, though in a different way than just now. The one thing which runs through all of these, we are unable to find.

b Meno: Somehow I'm not able, Socrates, in the way you're looking for, to get hold of one virtue over all, as in the other cases.

Socrates: That's not surprising. But I'm eager, if I can, to keep going, since you understand, I presume, that this point applies to everything. If someone asked you what I did just now, "What is shape, Meno?" and you said that it is roundedness, and he said to you what I did, "Is roundedness shape or *a* shape?," you would certainly say that it is a shape.

Meno: Certainly.

c Socrates: And, based on this, that there are other shapes in addition?

Meno: Yes.

Socrates: And if he went to ask you what kinds, you would tell him?

Meno: I would.

Socrates: And again, if he asked in the same way what color is, and you told him that it is whiteness, and the questioner followed this up with "Is whiteness color or *a* color?," you would say that it is *a* color, because there happen to be others too?

Meno: I would.

Socrates: And if he requested that you state other colors, you would tell
d him others that are colors just as much as white is?

Meno: Yes.

Socrates: And then if, in the same way as I pursued the argument, he
said, "We always arrive at many things. But don't speak to me like
that. Instead, since you call all of these by a single name, and you say
that none of them is not a shape even though they are opposites of
one another, say what it is that applies just as much to roundedness
as to straightness, and which you call 'shape' when you say that e
roundedness is no more a shape than straightness?" Or don't you say
this?

Meno: I do.

Socrates: Well then, when you say this, do you maintain that roundedness is no more rounded than straight, nor straightness more straight than rounded?

Meno: Of course not, Socrates.

Socrates: Rather, you say roundedness is no more a shape than straightness, and the latter no more than the former.

Meno: That is true.

Socrates: What is it then that this names? Try to say. If you say to the 75a
one questioning you in this way, either about shape or color, "But I
don't understand what you want, sir, or even know what you are saying," he would probably be amazed and say "Don't you understand
that I am looking for what is the same in all these cases?" Or would
you have nothing to say, Meno, if someone asked you, "What is it in
roundedness and straightness and the others that you call 'shape', the
same in all of them?" Try to say, so that you can also get some practice for the answer about virtue.

Meno: No, Socrates. You tell me instead. b

Socrates: You want me to indulge you?

Meno: Very much.

Socrates: Will you then be willing to tell me about virtue, too?

Meno: I will.

Socrates: Then I must be strong; it's worth it.

Meno: It certainly is.

Socrates: Come, then, let us try to tell you what shape is. See if you will accept that it is the following: to us, shape is the only thing among existing things that always follows color. Is that satisfactory to you, or
c are looking for something else? I would be happy if you defined virtue for me in this way.

Meno: But this is silly, Socrates!

Socrates: What do you mean?

Meno: That shape, according to your account, is supposed to be what always follows color. Well, then, what if someone were to say that he did not know what color is, but was having difficulties, just as with shape? What do you think your response would have been?

Socrates: The truth, I think. And if the questioner were one of the clever people, fond of arguing and contentious, I would say to him,
d "What was said is my response, but if I speak incorrectly, it is your job to examine the definition and refute it." If they are friends, as you and I are, and want to interrogate one another, they should answer more gently and dialectically.[1] It is more dialectical, perhaps, not only to answer with the truth but also in terms that the questioner acknowledges are familiar. And so, I will try to speak in this way to you.

Tell me, then, is there something you call an "extremity"? I mean
e this in the sense of "limit" and "terminal"; all of these I take to mean the same thing. Perhaps Prodicus[2] would disagree, but you, at least, no doubt say that something has "reached a limit" and is "at an extremity." I want to say something like this, nothing fancy.

Meno: I do. And I think I understand what you mean.

76a Socrates: What about this: is there something you call "a surface," and something else "a solid," the ones from geometry?

---

1 "Dialectical" speaking is a conversation between two people with different points of view, with each trying to find out the truth through reasoned argument.

2 *Prodicus* In Plato's dialogue *Protagoras*, Prodicus—a Sophist philosopher—pays a lot of attention to fine distinctions among terms that most people would regard as synonymous.

Meno: Yes, I do.

Socrates: Then from this you might now understand me and how I define shape. For, of every shape I say this: that in which the solid ends, this is shape. To put it briefly, I would say that shape is the limit of a solid.

Meno: But what do you say about color, Socrates?

Socrates: You are outrageous, Meno! You impose the trouble of an-
swering on an old man[1] and aren't willing to recollect and tell me what b
Gorgias says virtue is.

Meno: Just tell me this, Socrates, and I will tell you.

Socrates: Even someone blindfolded would know, Meno, from your conversation, that you are beautiful and still have lovers.

Meno: What?

Socrates: Because you do nothing but give orders, like spoiled children
do, behaving like tyrants for as long as they are young. You have prob-
ably detected in me the fault of being susceptible to the beautiful, so I c
will please you by answering.

Meno: By all means, do me the favor.

Socrates: Do you want me to answer in the style of Gorgias, the way that you would be most likely to follow?

Meno: I do, of course.

Socrates: Don't both of you talk about things having certain effluences, as Empedocles[2] does?

Meno: Absolutely.

---

1 *an old man* If this dialogue is set around 402 BCE, Socrates would have been in his late 60s at the time.

2 *effluences ... Empedocles* Empedocles was an earlier Greek philosopher/scientist. His theory of vision involved "effluences": tiny particles that flow out of things continually and into the eye of the observer.

Socrates: And channels into which and out of which the effluences travel?

Meno: Certainly.

Socrates: And some of the effluences fit some of the channels, while
d others are smaller or larger?

Meno: That's right.

Socrates: Don't you also call something "sight"?

Meno: I do.

Socrates: From this, then, "please take my meaning," said Pindar.[1] Color is an effluence from shapes, which fits sight and is perceived.

Meno: I think you have stated your reply brilliantly, Socrates.

Socrates: Perhaps because it was given in a way familiar to you. And I think you can work out from this statement what sound is, and smell,
e and others of this sort.

Meno: Certainly.

Socrates: It's a grandiose response, Meno, and so it's more pleasing to you than the one about shape.

Meno: It is to me, anyway.

Socrates: And yet it isn't, son of Alexidemus, as I am persuaded that the other is better. And I think it wouldn't seem so to you if you didn't have to leave before the mysteries,[2] as you mentioned yesterday, but could stick around and be initiated.

77a Meno: But I would stay, Socrates, if you were to tell me lots of things like this.

---

1 *Pindar* the greatest lyric poet of ancient Greece. This was a popular quotation—roughly, "pay attention to what I'm about to say"—but the poem from which it comes has been lost.

2 *mysteries* The Eleusinian Mysteries were mystical initiations, held near Athens, into the religious cult of Demeter and Persephone. Plato is drawing a parallel between initiation into a religious cult and 'initiation' into philosophy.

Socrates: I will spare no effort, both for your sake and mine, to say such things, but I might not be able to tell you many of them. But you come on and try to keep your promise to me, to say of virtue in general what it is. And quit making many out of one, as those who make jokes say whenever someone shatters something, but keeping it whole b
and healthy, tell me what virtue is. I've given you some models, at least.

Meno: Well then, it seems to me, Socrates, that virtue is, as the poet says, "to delight in fine things and be capable of them." I too say that this is virtue, desiring fine things and being able to bring them about.

Socrates: Do you mean that the person who desires fine things desires good things?

Meno: Most of all.

Socrates: This is assuming that among people, some desire bad things and some good things? Best of men, you don't think that everyone de- c
sires good things?

Meno: No, I don't.

Socrates: Then some desire bad things?

Meno: Yes.

Socrates: Thinking the bad things to be good, you mean? Or also knowing that they are bad and nonetheless desiring them?

Meno: I think there are both.

Socrates: Do you really think someone, knowing that the bad things are bad, desires them?

Meno: Absolutely.

Socrates: Desires what, do you think? To get them for himself?

Meno: Yes, to get them. What else? d

Socrates: Thinking that the bad things will help the person who gets them, or knowing that the bad things harm the person who has them?

Meno: There are some who think they are beneficial and there are others who know that they harm.

Socrates: Do you really think that they know that the bad things are bad, those who think bad things are beneficial?

Meno: I don't believe that at all.

Socrates: So, it is clear that these people do not desire bad things, those who are ignorant of them, but desire things they believe to be good,
e even though they are in fact bad. These ignorant people, then, who think they are good, it's clear that they desire good things. Or not?

Meno: They probably do.

Socrates: What then? Those who desire bad things, according to you, thinking that bad things harm the person who suffers them, do they know that they will be harmed by them?

Meno: Necessarily.

78a Socrates: But they think anyone who is harmed is miserable, to the extent that they are harmed?

Meno: This is also necessary.

Socrates: Aren't miserable people unhappy?

Meno: I, for one, think so.

Socrates: Is there anyone who wishes to be miserable and unhappy?

Meno: I don't think so, Socrates.

Socrates: Then no one, Meno, wants bad things, if they don't want to be miserable and unhappy. What else is there to being miserable than desiring and possessing bad things?

b Meno: It's likely what you say is true, Socrates, and no one wants bad things for himself.

Socrates: So, just now you were saying that virtue is desiring and being capable of good things?

Meno: I did say that.

Socrates: And with respect to what was said, the desiring occurs in everyone, and no one is better than anyone else in this respect?

Meno: Apparently.

Socrates: Then it's clear that if one person is better than another, it would be in connection with superior capability.

Meno: Certainly.

Socrates: This, then, it seems, is your account of virtue: the power to
bring about good things. c

Meno: To me, Socrates, it seems to be exactly as you now express it.

Socrates: Let us examine this too, then, to see if you are right. Perhaps you spoke well. To be able to bring about good things, you say, is virtue?

Meno: I do.

Socrates: And by "good things" don't you mean things such as health and property?

Meno: And I mean possessing gold and silver coins, too, and political honor and power.

Socrates: Do you think there are other good things besides these kinds?

Meno: No, but I mean everything of these kinds.

Socrates: Well, then, virtue is the acquisition of gold and silver coins. d
So says Meno, the hereditary guest-friend of the Great King.[1] Do you add "justly" or "piously" to this acquisition, Meno, or does it make no difference to you? If someone acquires these things unjustly, do you similarly call this "virtue"?

Meno: Certainly not, Socrates.

---

1 *hereditary guest-friend of the Great King* The king of Persia, ruler of the Achaemenid Empire.

Socrates: But "vice," instead?

Meno: Absolutely.

Socrates: Then we must, it seems, add justice or moderation or piety
e to this acquisition, or some other part of virtue. If we don't, it won't be virtue, even if it is the acquisition of good things.

Meno: How could there be virtue without these?

Socrates: So, not acquiring gold and silver, whenever it wouldn't be just, whether for oneself or someone else, isn't this lack of acquisition virtue also?

Meno: It seems so.

Socrates: Then virtue would be the provision of good things no more than the non-provision, but, as seems likely, virtue will be whatever is
79a done with justice, and anything without all of these kinds of thing is vice.

Meno: I think it must be as you state.

Socrates: And each of these we said a little while ago is a part of virtue: justice and moderation and everything like this?

Meno: Yes.

Socrates: Well then, are you toying with me, Meno?

Meno: What?

Socrates: Just now I begged you not to shatter or cut up virtue, and gave you models of how you should answer, but you take no heed and
b tell me that virtue is to be able to bring about good things with justice; but this, you say, is a part of justice?

Meno: I do.

Socrates: It follows from what you agree to that doing what one does with some part of virtue is virtue, since justice, you say, is a part of virtue, as are each of those parts. Then why do I say this? Because I begged you to state what virtue is as a whole but you are a long way from saying what it is. You say that every action is virtue, so long as it is done with a part of virtue, as though you had told me the whole of virtue and I recognize it now, even as you break it up into parts. c

I think, my dear Meno, that we need you to answer the same question over again from the start, "What is virtue?," if every action done with a part of virtue is virtue. For this is what a person who says this means, that every action done with justice is virtue. Don't you think the same question needs answering, or do you think that someone knows what a part of virtue is without knowing virtue itself?

Meno: I don't think so, anyway.

Socrates: And furthermore, if you remember, when I answered you just d
now about shape, we threw out the kind of answer which attempts to answer in terms of what is still being sought and not yet agreed upon.

Meno: And we were right to throw it out, Socrates.

Socrates: So, don't think, you best of men, that, when still looking for what virtue as a whole is, by answering in terms of its parts you will clarify what it is, or anything else by talking in this way, but rather that there's a need to ask the same question again: What is virtue about e
which you say what you say? Or do you think I'm talking nonsense?

Meno: I think what you say is right.

Socrates: Then answer again from the beginning. What do you say virtue to be, both you and your friend?

Meno: Socrates, I heard before I even met you that you are always
perplexed and making others perplexed. And now, as it seems to me, 80a
you are bewitching and flattering me and being totally enchanting, so that I have become completely perplexed. You seem to me, if it is possible to joke a little, to be, in appearance and in every way, exactly like the broad electric ray[1] of the sea, for it too numbs anyone who ap-

1 *broad electric ray* A type of electric ray fish; the species referenced here is likely either the marbled electric ray (*torpedo marmorata*) or the common torpedo (*torpedo torpedo*). Sometimes translators of this dialogue give the alternate name 'torpedo fish'. This name antedates the reference to the undersea weapon; its source in Latin means *numbness* or *paralysis*, as produced by the fish's electric sting. The suggested comparison occurs in Plato's Greek: he calls the fish *narkē* and making-numb is *narkan.* Socrates also notoriously had flat, snub-nosed features, perhaps like a fish.

proaches and comes in contact with it, and now you seem to have put
b me in something like the same state. For truly I am numb, both my
spirit and my tongue, and I do not know what response I could give
you.

And even though I have on countless occasions said many things to many people about virtue, and spoke well, as it seemed to me, anyway, now I cannot say at all what it is. I think you are wise not to sail away from here or go abroad, because if you acted in this way as a foreigner in another city,[1] you would probably be arrested for sorcery.

Socrates: You're a rascal, Meno, and you nearly deceived me.

Meno: Why, precisely?

c Socrates: I know why you drew an image of me.

Meno: Why, do you think?

Socrates: So that I will draw one of you in return. I know this about all handsome men, that they enjoy images being made of them, because it benefits them, I think because the images of handsome men are also handsome. But I won't draw an image of you in return.

If the electric ray makes others numb by being itself numb, I am
like it; if not, I am not. I do not make others perplexed by being with-
d out doubts myself; rather, I am utterly perplexed and in this way I
make others perplexed. And now, concerning virtue, I don't know
what it is, and you probably knew previously, until I got hold of you
and now you're certainly like someone who doesn't know. Nonethe-
less, I want to investigate it with you and seek out what on earth it
is.

Meno: How will you seek it, Socrates, when you have no idea what it is? What kind of thing, from among those you are ignorant of, will you set before yourself to look for? And even if you happened exactly upon it, how would you recognize that this is what you didn't know?

e Socrates: I understand what you want to say, Meno. Do you see how
sophistical this argument is that you're dragging up, that a person can-
not search either for what he knows or what he doesn't know? For he
cannot search for what he knows—he knows it, and there is no need

---

1 *as a foreigner in another city* That is, in a place where Socrates would not have the legal protection of being a citizen.

to search for such a thing—nor for what he doesn't know—since he doesn't know what he's searching for.[1]

Meno: Well, doesn't this argument seem to be finely stated, Socrates? 81a

Socrates: Not to me.

Meno: Can you say how?

Socrates: I can, since I have heard wise men and women, about divine affairs …

Meno: Saying what?

Socrates: Something true and beautiful, it seems to me.

Meno: What is it, and who is saying it?

Socrates: Those saying it are some of the priests and priestesses whose business it is to be able to give an account of their practices. And Pindar says it too and many other poets, those who are divinely inspired. b
And what they say is the following—see if you think they speak the truth:

They say that the soul of man is immortal. At one time it comes to an end—which people call "dying"—and at another it is reborn, but it is never destroyed, and so one must live life as piously as possible, since to those from whom …

> … Persephone[2] accepts compensation for her ancient grief,
> To the sunlight above, in the ninth year, their
> Souls she again returns.
> From them come noble kings, c
> Increasing in strength and wisdom, men both swift and great,
> And for the rest of time called "hallowed heroes" by men.[3]

When the soul is immortal and has been born many times, and has seen the things here and the things in that land of Hades—every-

---

1 The puzzle presented in this paragraph has become known as Meno's paradox.

2 *Persephone* Persephone was queen of Hades, where all souls go post mortem; here it's supposed she reincarnates souls to our world once they have paid for their sins. Her "ancient grief" is the murder of her son by the ancient Titans, and humans have to pay the price for this as the descendents of the Titans.

3 Pindar, Fragment 133.

thing, in fact—there is nothing that it has not learned, and so it's no surprise that it can recollect about virtue and other things that it knew before. And because all of nature is of the same kind and the
d soul has learned everything, nothing prevents a soul that has recollected just one thing—which people call "learning"—from rediscovering everything for itself, so long as it is brave and doesn't give up the search. For searching and learning are, as a whole, recollection.

Therefore, we must not be persuaded by this sophistical account, since that one would make us lazy and is pleasant for faint-hearted
e men to hear, whereas this one makes them energetic and eager to search. Believing this one to be true, I want to search with you for what virtue is.

Meno: Yes, Socrates. But what do you mean by this, that we do not learn and what is called "learning" is recollection? Can you teach me that this is so?

Socrates: As I was saying a moment ago, Meno, you are a rascal, and
82a now you are asking if I can *teach* you what I say is *not teaching* but recollection, so that I will immediately be seen to contradict myself!

Meno: By Zeus, no, Socrates. I didn't say it for that reason, but out of habit. But if you can somehow show me that what you say is true, show me.

Socrates: Although it's not easy, nonetheless I want to exert myself for your sake. Summon one of these many attendants of yours for me,
b whichever you like, so that I can prove it to you in his case.

Meno: Certainly. [To the slave:] Step forward here.

Socrates: Now, is he Greek and does he speak Greek?

Meno: Absolutely, yes. He was born in the house.

Socrates: Then pay close attention to see which you think is happening, whether he is recollecting or is learning from me.

Meno: I certainly will.

Socrates: Tell me, boy, do you know that a square is like this?

Slave: I do.

Socrates: And so, a square has these lines, four of them, all equal? c

Slave: Of course.

Socrates: And these ones going through the center are also equal?

Slave: Yes.

Socrates: Okay. And there could be larger and smaller versions of this area?

Slave: Certainly.

Socrates: Now, if this side were two feet and this side two feet also, how many feet would the whole be? Look at it like this: if this one[1] were two feet but this one[2] only one foot, wouldn't the area have to be two feet taken once?

Slave: Yes.

Socrates: When this one is also two feet, there would be twice two? d

Slave: There would.

Socrates: An area of twice two feet?

1 The top edge.
2 The side edge.

Slave: Yes.

Socrates: How much is twice two feet? Calculate and tell me.

Slave: Four, Socrates.

Socrates: Now, couldn't there be one different from this, doubled, but of the same kind, with all the lines equal, as in that one?

Slave: Yes.

Socrates: And how many feet in area?

Slave: Eight.

Socrates: Come then, try to tell me how long each line of that one will
e be. In this one, it's two, but what about in that doubled one?[1]

Slave: It's clearly double, Socrates.

Socrates: You see, Meno, that I am not teaching anything, but put everything as a question. He now believes he knows what sort of line the eight-foot area comes from. Or don't you think so?

Meno: I do.

Socrates: And does he know?

Meno: Not at all.

Socrates: He believes it comes from the double?

Meno: Yes.

Socrates: Observe him recollecting in sequence, as one ought to rec-
83a ollect. Tell me, you say the double area comes to be from the double

---

1 *In this one ... that doubled one* This is the math problem Socrates sets out to have the slave boy solve: if you double the area of a square, how much must you have increased the length of its sides (its 'lines')? Initially the slave boy asserts, incorrectly, that you will have doubled the length of its sides. In the subsequent parts of the dialogue Socrates helps the boy to realize that this is incorrect, and then to come to the right answer. However, (according to Socrates) he does so entirely by helping the boy recall and put together things he already knows—by asking him questions—rather than by teaching him anything new.

line? I mean this kind, not one with this one long and this one short, but equal all around like this one, but double its size, that is, eight feet. See if you still think it comes from the double.

Slave: I do.

Socrates: Wouldn't this [line] itself become double if we add another of the same length here?

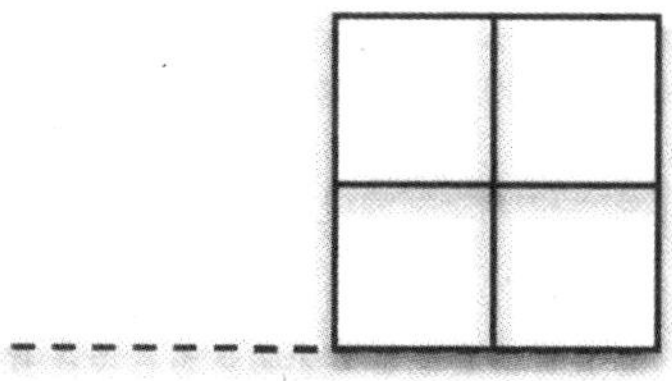

Slave: Of course.

Socrates: From this, you say, there will be an eight-foot area, if there are four of the same length? b

Slave: Yes.

Socrates: Let us use it to draw four equal lines. Isn't this exactly what you say the eight-foot area is?

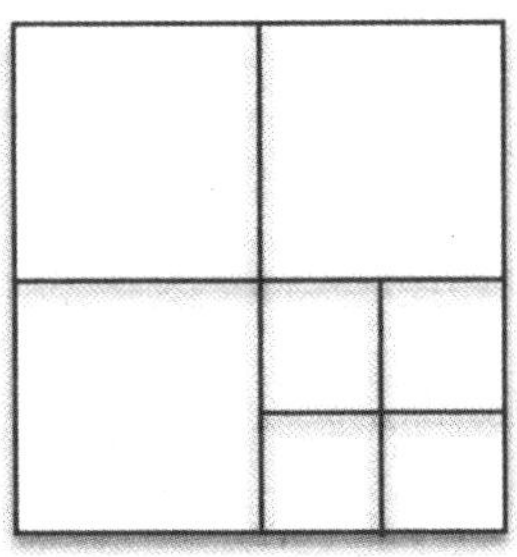

Slave: Absolutely.

Socrates: Within this there are these four, each of which is equal to this four-foot area?

Slave: Yes.

Socrates: What area is this? Isn't it four times as large?

Slave: Yes, by Zeus.

Socrates: It is double, the one four times as large?

Slave: No, by Zeus.

Socrates: But how many times larger is it?

Slave: Four times.

c Socrates: Then the area that comes from the double line, boy, is not double but four times the area.

Slave: You are right.

Socrates: Since four times four is sixteen, is it not?

Slave: Yes.

Socrates: The eight-foot area comes from what line? Based on this line, isn't it four times the size?

Slave: So I say.

Socrates: But the quarter area is based on this one here, half its size?

Slave: Yes.

d Socrates: Well then. The eight-foot area is double this one, and half that one?

Slave: Yes.

Socrates: Won't it come from a line longer than this, but shorter than that? Or not?

Slave: It seems so to me.

Socrates: Well said; answer as it seems to you. Now tell me, was this line not two feet long, and that one four?

Slave: Yes.

Socrates: So, the eight-foot area must come from a line longer than two feet but less than four?

Slave: It must.

Socrates: Then try to say how long you say it is. e

Slave: Three feet.

Socrates: If it really were three feet, we will take half as much again of this one and it will be three feet? For this is two and this is one. And from here, this is two and this is one. And the area you mentioned comes into being.

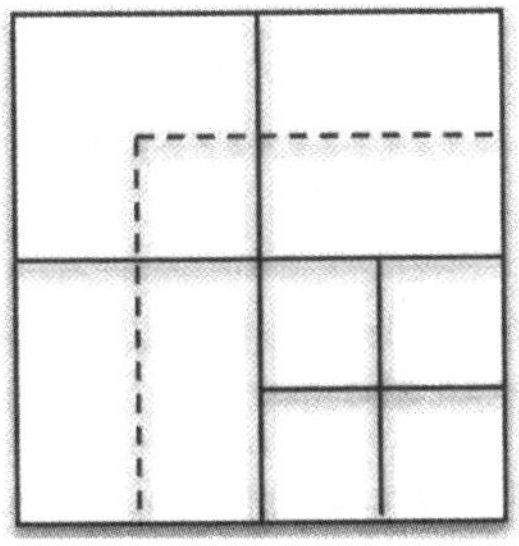

Slave: Yes.

Socrates: So, if this side is three and this one also three, the whole area is three times three?

Slave: It seems so.

Socrates: Three times three are how many feet?

Slave: Nine.

Socrates: But we need the double area to be how many feet?

Slave: Eight.

Socrates: Then the eight-foot area certainly doesn't come from the three-foot line.

Slave: Not at all.

Socrates: But from what length? Try to tell us clearly. And if you do not want to calculate it, point out the length instead. 84a

Slave: By Zeus, Socrates, I have no idea.

Socrates: Consider again, Meno, as he proceeds in the recollection, what point is he now at? The first time, he did not know what the line

of the eight-foot area is, just as he still doesn't know now. But whereas
he thought then that he did know it, and answered confidently like
someone who knows, and did not think himself in any difficulty, now
he actually thinks he is in trouble; he doesn't know and likewise does
b not think he knows.

Meno: That's true.

Socrates: Is he now in a better position concerning the thing he does not know?

Meno: I think that's also true.

Socrates: Putting him in difficulties and numbing him, like the electric ray, is there any harm in it?

Meno: I don't think so.

Socrates: In fact, it's likely we have done him a good deed, with regard
to finding out how things are. For now, he doesn't know and would be
glad to know, whereas before, he thought it would be easy to speak
c well in front of many people and on many occasions about the doubled
area, how it must have a line double in length.

Meno: Probably.

Socrates: Do you think that before he would try to search for or understand what he thinks he knows but doesn't know, until he fell into difficulty and realized he doesn't know, and yearned to know?

Meno: I don't think so, Socrates.

Socrates: He has benefited from becoming numb?

Meno: I think so.

Socrates: Observe, then, how, from this perplexity, he will discover it
after all, searching along with me, and I doing nothing except posing
d questions and not teaching. Be on the lookout for me teaching and
spelling it out for him, and not asking for his opinions.

Tell me: we have here our four-foot area? Do you understand?

Slave: I do.

Socrates: And we can add another one to it, this one, equal?

Slave: Yes.

Socrates: And this third one, equal to each of these?

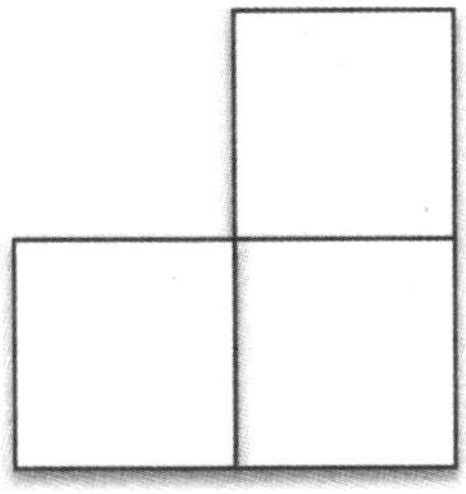

Slave: Yes.

Socrates: And we can fill in this space here in the corner?

Slave: Of course.

Socrates: So that there are precisely these four equal areas?

Slave: Yes. e

Socrates: Well then, this whole thing would be how many times this one?

Slave: Four times.

Socrates: But we need to produce double. Or don't you remember?

Slave: Of course.

Socrates: Now isn't there this same line, going from corner to corner, cutting each of these areas in two? 85a

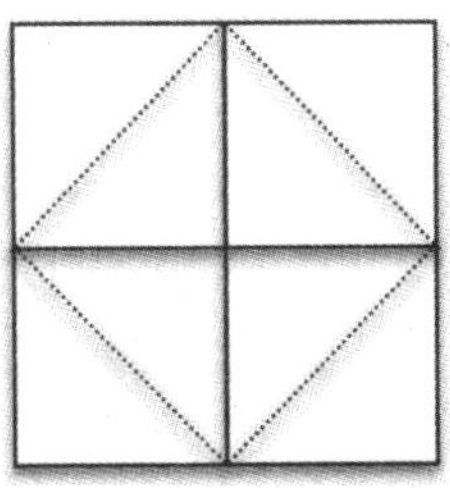

Slave: Yes.

Socrates: So, there will be these four equal lines, enclosing this area?

Slave: There will.

Socrates: Look, then. How large is this area?

Slave: I don't understand.

Socrates: There are four areas, and each line has divided each of them in half internally? Or not?

Slave: Yes.

Socrates: And how many feet are in this area?

Slave: Four.

Socrates: And how many in this one?

Slave: Two.

Socrates: And four is how many times two?

Slave: Double.

b Socrates: So, this, then, would be how many feet?

Slave: Eight.

Socrates: Coming from what line?

Slave: From this one.

Socrates: From the one stretching from corner to corner of the four-foot area?

Slave: Yes.

Socrates: The experts call this the "diagonal." And so, if we name this the diagonal, it would be from the diagonal, according to you, slave of Meno, that the double area comes into being.

Slave: Exactly so, Socrates.

Socrates: What do you think, Meno? Is there any answer that he gave that was not his own belief?

Meno: No, they were his own. c

Socrates: Even though he did not know, as we were saying a little earlier.

Meno: You are right.

Socrates: These beliefs, then, were within him. Or not?

Meno: Yes.

Socrates: The man who does not know, then, concerning what he does not know, has within himself true beliefs about what he doesn't know?

Meno: Apparently.

Socrates: At present, these beliefs are like a dream to him, having just now been stirred up. But if someone will put these questions to him on many occasions and in many ways, you know that his knowledge of these matters will eventually be as accurate as anyone's. d

Meno: It's likely.

Socrates: Won't he know it not by anyone teaching but through questioning and him regaining the knowledge from within himself?

Meno: Yes.

Socrates: And isn't him regaining the knowledge from within himself recollection?

Meno: Absolutely.

Socrates: The knowledge he now has, he either gained at some time or always had it?

Meno: Yes.

Socrates: If he always had it, he was always knowing, and if he gained it at some point, he would not have acquired it in his present life, at any e rate. Or has someone taught him geometry? Because he will do the same thing for all geometry, and all other learning. Is there someone who has taught him all these? I suppose you would be one to know, especially since he was born and raised in your household.

Meno: And I know that no one ever gave him instruction.

Socrates: But does he have these beliefs, or not?

Meno: It seems necessary, Socrates.

Socrates: If he didn't acquire them in this life, then, the following be-
86a comes immediately obvious, that he possessed them and learned them at some other time.

Meno: Apparently.

Socrates: And this is the time when he was not a human?

Meno: Yes.

Socrates: If there are true beliefs within him during the time when he both is and is not a human being, which become knowledge when stirred up by questioning, then won't his soul be in a state of having learned throughout all time? Since it's clear that throughout all time he was or was not a human?

Meno: Apparently.

b Socrates: Then, if we always possess the truth about things in the soul, the soul would be immortal, so that the person who doesn't happen to have knowledge now, that is, who hasn't recollected, should be brave and try to search for it and recollect?

Meno: Your words seem good to me, Socrates, somehow or other.

Socrates: And to me too, Meno. I wouldn't strongly insist on the other aspects of the argument, but that we would become better men and braver and less lazy if we believe it is necessary to search for what one doesn't know, rather than if we think that we can't discover what
c we don't know and should not look for it; for this I will fight strongly, if I am able, in both word and deed.

Meno: There again, your words seem good to me, Socrates.

Socrates: Since we agree that one must inquire into what one doesn't know, do you want us to try to look together for what virtue is?

Meno: Certainly. Although, of course, I would be most pleased to look
into and hear about what I asked at the start, whether we should pur-
sue virtue as something teachable, or natural, or occurring in men in d
some other way.

Socrates: If I were in charge, Meno, not only of myself but of you too,
we wouldn't examine whether virtue is teachable or not teachable until
we had discovered the main point, *what it is*. But since you aren't even
trying to control yourself, so that you would in fact be free, but instead
you attempt to rule me and take charge, I will agree with you: what else
can I do? So, it seems we must investigate what kind of thing it is when
we don't yet know what it is. e

But if nothing else, at least loosen your control a little bit for me and
agree to examine whether it is acquired by teaching or however it is ac-
quired on the basis of a hypothesis. By "on the basis of a hypothesis"
I mean in the way geometers often examine things, whenever some-
one asks them something, such as whether a certain area can be in- 87a
scribed within a circle in the shape of a triangle, and one of them might
say, "I don't yet know if it can be, but I think I have a sort of hypoth-
esis that's useful for such a problem: if this area, when applied to the
given line, is the kind that leaves behind an area like this one which
was stretched out, I think one thing follows, or another, if this is im-
possible. So, by hypothesizing, I am willing to tell you what follows
concerning its inscription within the circle, whether it is possible or b
not."[1]

It's the same way with virtue; since we don't know what it is or
what it's like, let's examine whether it is teachable or not teachable on
the basis of a hypothesis, and say the following: If virtue were what
kind of thing, of the things related to the soul, would it then be teach-
able or not teachable? First of all, if it is different from, or some sort
of, knowledge, is it acquired by teaching or not—or, as we put it just
now, by recollection; it makes no difference to us what name we use.
Is it teachable? Or is it clear to everyone that a man can be taught noth- c
ing except knowledge?

---

1 What the geometrical reasoning is here is not clear; scholars have made varying guesses.

Meno: I think so.

Socrates: Then, if virtue is a type of knowledge, it would clearly be acquired by teaching.

Meno: Of course.

Socrates: We finished that quickly, that if it is of one kind, it's teachable, but not, if it's of another.

Meno: Certainly.

Socrates: After this, we should probably investigate whether virtue is knowledge, or of a different kind than what knowledge is.

d Meno: That does seem to be what should be examined next.

Socrates: What then? Don't we say that this thing—virtue—is good? Does that hypothesis still hold for us, that it is good?

Meno: Absolutely.

Socrates: If there is also something else that is good and distinct from knowledge, perhaps virtue wouldn't be a kind of knowledge. But if nothing is good that knowledge does not embrace, we would be right to suspect that it is some kind of knowledge.

Meno: That's right.

Socrates: And next, by virtue we are good?

Meno: Yes.

e Socrates: And if we are good, we are beneficial? Since anything good is beneficial. Or not?

Meno: Yes.

Socrates: Virtue also is beneficial, then?

Meno: Necessarily, based on what has been agreed.

Socrates: Let's examine then, taking each one in turn, what kinds of things benefit us: health, we say, and strength, and beauty and property, of course. We say that these and things like them are beneficial. Or not?

Meno: Yes.

Socrates: But we say that these same things sometimes also are harmful. Or would you say something different from this? 88a

Meno: No, exactly that.

Socrates: Do you see, then, what it is that guides each of these when it benefits us, and what when it harms us? Isn't it true that when correctly used, it benefits, but when not, it harms?

Meno: Certainly.

Socrates: In addition, then, let us examine the things related to the soul. You call something "moderation" and "justice" and "bravery" and "intelligence" and "memory" and "magnanimity" and everything of this sort?

Meno: I do. b

Socrates: Of these, examine, then, the ones that seem to you not to be knowledge but different from knowledge, whether they don't sometimes harm and sometimes benefit? Bravery, for example, when bravery is without prudence and is a kind of daring. Isn't it that whenever a man is daring without understanding, he is harmed, but with understanding he is benefited?

Meno: Yes.

Socrates: And similarly for moderation and intelligence: when acquired by learning and discipline they are beneficial, but without understanding, harmful?

Meno: Very much so. c

Socrates: In sum, all of the soul's endeavors and acts of endurance result in happiness when guided by prudence, but in the opposite when they lack prudence?

Meno: It's likely.

Socrates: If virtue is one of the things in the soul and is necessarily beneficial to it, it must be prudence, since all of these things of the soul
d are in themselves neither beneficial nor harmful, but become beneficial or harmful when accompanied by prudence or foolishness. According to this account, since virtue is beneficial, it must be a kind of prudence.

Meno: I think so.

Socrates: And the other things too that we were just now talking about, wealth and such like, that are sometimes good and sometimes harmful; in the way that prudence made the goods of the soul beneficial by guiding the
e rest of the soul, in the same way doesn't the soul make them beneficial by using and guiding them correctly, but, if incorrectly, harmful?

Meno: Certainly.

Socrates: The soul with intelligence guides correctly, while the one without misses the mark?

Meno: That's correct.

Socrates: And don't we say the same in every case, all the other goods a person has depend upon the soul, and the goods of the soul itself de-
89a pend upon prudence, if they are going to be good? By this reasoning, the beneficial would be prudence. And do we say virtue is beneficial?

Meno: Certainly.

Socrates: Do we say virtue is prudence, either the whole or some part of it?

Meno: What you've said seems well said to me, Socrates.

Socrates: Then if this is how things are, good men would not be good by nature?

Meno: I think not.

b Socrates: If they were, I suppose the following would be true: if good men were good by nature, there would no doubt be some people who knew which of the young people had good natures, and we would have taken the ones so designated and guarded them in the treasury, sealing them up more carefully than gold, so that no one would corrupt them and they would be useful to the city when they come of age.

Meno: That's quite likely, Socrates.

Socrates: But since the good things are not good by nature, are they so
by learning? c

Meno: I think it must be, now. And clearly, Socrates, according to the hypothesis that virtue is knowledge, it's acquired by teaching.

Socrates: Perhaps, by Zeus. But maybe we did not properly agree to this.

Meno: A moment ago it seemed fine to me.

Socrates: But it needs to seem finely stated not just a moment ago but in the present and in the future, if any of it is going to be sound.

Meno: But why? What do you see that makes you dissatisfied with it d
and skeptical that virtue is not knowledge?

Socrates: I will tell you, Meno. That it is teachable *if* it is knowledge, I don't take that back or think it wasn't well said, but rather, that it is knowledge. See if my doubt seems reasonable to you. Tell me this: if something is teachable, not just virtue, wouldn't there have to be teachers and learners of it?

Meno: I think so. e

Socrates: And again, conversely, if there are neither teachers of it nor learners, would we be right to infer that it is not acquired by teaching?

Meno: That's true. But don't you think there are teachers of virtue?

Socrates: I often investigated whether anyone is a teacher of it, doing everything I can but not able to find anyone. Indeed, I search with the cooperation of many people, and especially with those I think are most experienced in the matter. And now, perfectly for us, Anytus[1] here has sat
down, with whom we can share the search. It would be fitting for us to 90a
make him a partner, because, first, Anytus here had a father, Anthemion, both wealthy and wise, who became wealthy not by accident or because of a gift, like Ismenias the Theban who recently acquired Polycrates'

1 *Anytus* Anytus was one of Socrates' accusers, in *Socrates' Apology*. See in particular 94e below, where Anytus warns Socrates to be careful.

fortune.[1] Rather, he acquired it by his own wisdom and dedication, and
b besides, he did not seem to be an arrogant citizen or puffed up and offensive, but a decent and orderly man, and further, the majority of the Athenians believe he reared and educated this man here well, since they are electing him to the highest offices. It is proper to investigate with someone like this whether there are or are not teachers of virtue, and who they are. So, join the search with us, Anytus, myself and your guest-friend[2] Meno here, related to who might be teachers in this matter.

Look at it this way: if we want Meno to become a good doctor, to
c what teachers would we send him? Would it not be to the doctors?

Anytus: Certainly.

Socrates: And what if we want him to become a good shoemaker, to the shoemakers?

Anytus: Yes.

Socrates: And others similarly?

Anytus: Certainly.

Socrates: Repeat that again for me. Sending him to the doctors, we say, would be a good place to send him, if we wanted him to become
d a doctor. When we say this, are we saying that we would be sensible to send him to these people, those who lay claim to the craft rather than those who don't, and who charge fees for this very thing, declaring themselves to be teachers of anyone who wants to come and learn? Thinking along these lines, would we assign him properly?

Anytus: Yes.

Socrates: And also with flute-playing and the others of the same kind? If we wanted to make someone a flute-player it would be very stupid to
e be unwilling to send him to those who promise to teach him the craft and who charge a fee, and to instead cause problems for others by wanting

---

1 *Polycrates' fortune* Polycrates was a democratic Athenian politician, and the 'gift' in this case was probably an attempted bribe from Polycrates to Ismenias to induce him to intervene and restore democracy to Athens during the rule of the Thirty Tyrants.

2 *guest-friend* There was a special relationship of hospitality between these two families, perhaps established by Anthemion and Meno's grandfather. Meno is about 19 years old. Anytus is of the previous generation (and Socrates is about 67). See also 78d.

him to learn from those who neither put themselves forward as teachers nor have any students in the subject which we wanted him, the one we would send, to learn. Doesn't that seem very irrational to you?

Anytus: Yes, by Zeus, it does, and what's more, ignorant.

Socrates: Well said. And now you can deliberate along with me about 91a
your guest-friend Meno here. For he has been telling me for a long time, Anytus, that he desires the wisdom and virtue by which men manage households and cities, and take care of their parents, and know how to receive and send off citizens and foreigners in the manner wor-
thy of a good man. Think about to whom we would be right to send b
him, with respect to this virtue. Or is it clear, according to our recent principle, that it is to those who promise to be teachers of virtue and declare themselves available to any Greek who wants to learn, and who set a fee and collect it?

Anytus: And who do you say these are, Socrates?

Socrates: You know very well that these are the men people call "sophists."

Anytus: By Heracles! Quiet, Socrates! Let none of my household or c
friends, whether Athenian or foreigner, be seized by the kind of madness that would send them to be ruined by these people, since they are obviously the ruin and corruption of those they associate with.

Socrates: How do you mean, Anytus? Are they, alone of those who claim to know how to do some benefit, so different from the others that they like the others, do not benefit whatever one might entrust to
them but also, on the contrary, corrupt it? And think they are worthy d
of openly collecting money for this? I don't know if I can believe you.

I know of a certain man—Protagoras[1]—who made more money from this wisdom than did Phidias[2] (who produced such noticeably fine works) and ten other sculptors besides. Surely what you say is outrageous, if, on the one hand, those who repair old sandals and mend
cloaks would be found out within a month if they returned the sandals e
and cloaks in a worse state than they received them, and if they did

1 *Protagoras* An influential sophist philosopher, who died in c. 420 BCE, and the protagonist of another Platonic dialogue of the same name.

2 *Phidias* An Athenian sculptor, painter, and architect, who died in about 430 BCE. He created the giant statue of Zeus at Olympia, which was one of the Seven Wonders of the Ancient World, and the two major statues of Athena on the Acropolis.

this, would quickly die of hunger, while Protagoras, on the other hand, avoids detection by the whole of Greece as he corrupts his associates and sends them away worse than when he received them, and for forty years—since I believe he died at nearly seventy and was forty years at his work—for all that time, even today has lost none of his reputation, and not just Protagoras but a whole lot of others too, some born before
92a him and some still alive now.

Should we really say, then, according to what you said, that they swindle and ruin the young knowingly? Or do they deceive even themselves and in this way we will judge them to be mad, whom some people say to be the wisest of men?

Anytus: They are far from being mad, Socrates. Much more so are the young men who give them money, and still more those who entrust
b their young men to them, their relatives, and most especially of all, the cities, who allow them to enter and don't drive them away, whether it's a foreigner who tries to do something like this or a citizen.

Socrates: Did one of the sophists wrong you, Anytus, or why are you so harsh towards them?

Anytus: By Zeus, I have never associated with any one of them, nor would I allow anyone I know to do so!

Socrates: You have no experience whatsoever with these men?

Meno: May it always be so!

c Socrates: But how, then, you strange fellow, would you know about the matter, whether there's anything good or bad in it, if you've had no experience of it at all?

Anytus: Easily! I know who they are anyway, whether I have experience of them or not.

Socrates: Perhaps you are a seer, Anytus, since, from what you yourself say, I would be puzzled how else you would know about them.
d But, in fact, we won't look into who these people are, who Meno would go to and become worse—they are, if you wish, the sophists—but tell us, the people, and do your family friend here a good deed by telling him to whom should he go, in a city so large as this, to gain, worthy of the title, the virtue I was just now describing.

Anytus: Why don't *you* tell him?

Socrates: But I said whom I thought were teachers of it, though it turns
out I was saying nothing, according to you. And perhaps you are say-
ing something. But you take your turn and tell him which of the Athe- e
nians he might go to. Give the name of anyone you like.

Anytus: Why should he hear the name of any one person? No matter what Athenian gentleman he meets, there is not one of them who wouldn't improve him more than the sophists would, if he is willing to be persuaded.

Socrates: Did these gentlemen become the way they are sponta-
neously, learning from no one and yet are nonetheless able to teach
others these things they didn't learn? 93a

Anytus: I should think that they too learned from their predecessors, who were also gentlemen. Or don't you think there are many good men in this city?

Socrates: I think, Anytus, that there are people here who are good at
public affairs, and what is more, just as many as there were in the past.
But they were not good *teachers* of their virtue, were they? This happens
to be the focus of our argument, not whether there *are* good men here
or not, and not whether there were in the past. Instead, we've been ex-
amining for a while whether virtue is teachable. This is what we're look- b
ing for when we're investigating whether the good men, both now and
in the past, also knew how to pass on the virtue that made them good,
or whether this can't be passed on to a man or accepted by one man
from another. This is what Meno and I were investigating all along.

Look at it this way: given what you yourself say, would you not
say that Themistocles[1] was a good man? c

Anytus: I would; the best of all.

Socrates: And so, a good teacher, too. If anyone else was a teacher of his own virtue, you would say he was?

---

1 *Themistocles* An Athenian populist politician and general (c. 524 – c. 459 BCE), thought of as a hero of the Greek struggle against the Persian empire. Cleophantus is the first in a sequence of apparently disappointing offspring of prominent Greek figures that Socrates is about to list off.

Anytus: I believe so, if he wanted to, anyway.

Socrates: But do you believe that he did not want various others to be-
come gentlemen, especially his own son? Or do you think he refused
d him this and purposefully did not pass on the virtue which made him
good? Or have you not heard that Themistocles taught his son Cleo-
phantus to be a good horseman? Cleophantus could stand upright on
horses while throwing a javelin and perform many other amazing feats
that his father had him taught and made skilled at, any that were pos-
sessed by good teachers. Or haven't you heard this from your elders?

Anytus: I have.

Socrates: So, no one could allege that his son's nature was bad.

e Anytus: Presumably not.

Socrates: But then what? That Cleophantus, son of Themistocles, became a good and wise man, with respect to the things that his father was—have you ever heard anyone, young or old, say that?

Anytus: Certainly not.

Socrates: But are we then to believe that he *did* want to teach his son these things, but to make him no better than his neighbors with respect to the wisdom in which he himself was skilled, if virtue were indeed teachable?

Anytus: Presumably not, by Zeus.

Socrates: Well, there you have the kind of teacher of virtue he was, the
man you affirm was one of the best in the past. But let's look at another
94a one, Aristides, son of Lysimachus. Or don't you agree that he was good?

Anytus: I do, absolutely.

Socrates: This man too gave his son Lysimachus[1] the finest education in Athens, with respect to all the things that are the province of good

1 *Lysimachus* Aristides' father and son were both named Lysimachus. Aristides (c. 530–c. 468 BCE) was another revered politician and general from Athens' golden age. He was nicknamed "the Just," and the contemporary historian Herodotus, in his *Histories* (c. 430 BCE), called him "the best and most honorable man in Athens."

teachers, but do you think he was made a better man than anyone else? You associate with him, in fact, and you see what kind of man he is.

Or take Pericles,[1] if you like, a man of such magnificent wisdom. b
You know that he raised two sons, Paralus and Xanthippus?

Anytus: I do.

Socrates: And they, as I'm sure you know, he taught to be horsemen second to none in Athens, and in music and athletics and anything else that there's an art of, he brought them up to be second to none. And did he not want to make them good men? I think he wanted to, but maybe it's not teachable.

And so that you don't think that it was only a few and the least able
Athenians who were unable to succeed in this endeavor, remember c
that Thucydides[2] also raised two sons, Melesias and Stephanos, and taught them well in various things, and in particular to be the best wrestlers in Athens. He placed one with Xanthias and the other with Eudoros.[3] These had a reputation as the best wrestlers of the time. Or don't you remember?

Anytus: So I've heard.

Socrates: Clearly, he would never have taught his sons those things that
require spending money to teach, but fail to teach them what would d
make them good men, without paying anything, *if* it was teachable? Perhaps Thucydides was an inferior man, without many friends in Athens or among the allies? But he came from an important family and had great power in the city and among the Greeks, such that if this were teachable, he could find someone who would make his sons good, some-
one at home or abroad, if he himself lacked the time on account of at- e
tending to the city. But in fact, Anytus my friend, virtue is not teachable.

Anytus: I think, Socrates, that you readily speak ill of men. I would advise you, if you are willing to listen to me, to be discreet. As is prob-

1 *Pericles* A very prominent figure in Athens' rise to cultural and political dominance in the 460s BCE, and Archon (ruler) of the city from about 461 to 429 BCE.

2 *Thucydides* Yet another Athenian politician, general, and historian, who wrote a *History of the Peloponnesian War*. He died in about 400 BCE.

3 *Xanthias ... Eudoros* Wrestling was the most popular organized sport in Ancient Greece, and for hundreds of years at this time had been a competition at the Olympic games.

ably the case in other cities, it is easier to do men harm than good, and
95a certainly in this one. But I think you already know that.

Socrates: Meno, Anytus seems angry, and it's no wonder, since he thinks, first, that I am slandering these men, and second, includes himself among them. But if he ever learns what slander is, he will stop being angry, though at the moment he doesn't know. Tell me, don't you think there are fine and noble men where you come from, too?

Meno: Very much so.

b Socrates: Well, then, are they willing to offer themselves as teachers of the young, and do they agree that there are teachers and that virtue is teachable?

Meno: By Zeus, no, Socrates. Sometimes you might hear that it's teachable, and sometimes that it's not.

Socrates: Shall we say that people who can't even agree on this are teachers of this subject?

Meno: I don't think so, Socrates.

Socrates: What, then? These sophists, who are the only people to declare themselves able, do you think they are teachers of virtue?

c Meno: Now, this is something that strikes me about Gorgias in particular, that you'll never hear him promising this, and he mocks others when he hears them promising it. Though he does think people must be made clever speakers.

Socrates: Then you don't think that the sophists are teachers either?

Meno: I'm unable to say, Socrates. I feel the same way as many others: sometimes I think they are, sometimes not.

Socrates: Do you realize that it's not only you and the other men in public life who sometimes think that it's teachable and sometimes not,
d but that the poet Theognis,[1] too, you know, says the same thing?

---

1 *Theognis* Theognis of Megara was a lyric poet from the previous century (sixth century BCE), whose poems offer advice about life from the perspective of an aristocrat confronting the social and political upheaval of the time.

Meno: In which verses?

Socrates: In the elegies, where he says …

> Eat and drink with them and among them
> Sit, and please them, whose power is great.
> For you will teach yourself goodness from the good. If with the bad
> You spend time, you will lose what intelligence you already have. e

You see that in these words he speaks as though virtue is teachable?

Meno: Apparently.

Socrates: But elsewhere he makes a small change …

> "If good sense could be formed," he says, "and implanted in man,"
> he says, roughly, that,
> "Fees many and large would they receive"
> —those who are able to do this. And
> "Never from a good father comes bad,
> Obeying wise commands. But by teaching 96a
> Never will you make the bad man good."[1]

Doesn't it strike you that he is contradicting himself on these matters?

Meno: It seems so.

Socrates: Can you name any other subject of which the people who claim to be teachers are not agreed to be teachers of others, and even thought not to know it, and to be bad teachers of the very thing b
they profess to teach, while those who are agreed to be gentlemen sometimes say it is teachable, and sometimes not? Would you say that people who are so confused about anything are properly teachers?

Meno: By Zeus, not I.

Socrates: Then if neither the sophists nor those who are gentlemen are teachers of this subject, clearly there are no others?

Meno: I don't think so.

---

1 Theognis, *Elegiac Poems* 33–36 and 434–38.

c Socrates: But if there are no teachers, there are no learners?

Meno: I think what you say is right.

Socrates: We are agreed, then, that a subject which has neither teachers nor learners is also not teachable?

Meno: We are agreed.

Socrates: And so, there don't seem to be any teachers of virtue?

Meno: That's right.

Socrates: And if no teachers, no learners?

Meno: It seems so.

Socrates: Then virtue would not be teachable?

d Meno: It's not likely, if we have been examining things correctly. As a result, I am wondering, Socrates, whether there are any good men at all, or what method there is by which good men come into being.

Socrates: There's a chance, Meno, that you and I are inferior men, and that Gorgias didn't educate you sufficiently, nor Prodicus me.[1] More than anything, then, we should turn our attention to ourselves and
e search for someone who will improve us at least in some way. I say this looking back over our recent investigation, how we embarrassingly failed to notice that men do things well and properly not only when they are guided by knowledge, and that is, perhaps, also why detecting whatever way men become good escapes us.

Meno: How do you mean, Socrates?

Socrates: This: we rightly agreed that good men must be beneficial,
97a and that this can't be any other way. Right?

Meno: Yes.

Socrates: And that they will be beneficial if they guide us properly in our affairs, this too we correctly agreed to, I suppose?

1 *nor Prodicus me* Socrates is being ironic here.

Meno: Yes.

Socrates: But that someone cannot guide correctly if he is not a wise man, we are alike in having agreed to this incorrectly.

Meno: How do you mean?

Socrates: I will tell you. If someone knew the road to Larisa,[1] or anywhere you like, and could walk there and guide others, surely he would guide them correctly and well?

Meno: Certainly.

Socrates: And what if someone correctly believed which was the cor- b
rect road, though he had not taken it, and lacked knowledge, wouldn't he also guide them correctly?

Meno: Certainly.

Socrates: And as long as he holds onto the correct belief, I suppose, of which another had knowledge, he won't be any worse a guide than the one who has knowledge, believing the truth but lacking knowledge of it.

Meno: No worse at all.

Socrates: Then true beliefs are no worse a guide to correct actions than prudence. And this is what we left out in our previous investigation
into what virtue is, when we said that prudence alone guides correct ac- c
tion. As a matter of fact, there was also true belief.

Meno: Very likely.

Socrates: True belief is thus just as beneficial as knowledge.

Meno: Less, Socrates, to the extent that the person who has knowledge would always be successful, while the person with the true belief would sometimes be, and sometimes not be, successful.

Socrates: How do you mean? Won't the person who always has true belief always succeed, for as long as he believes correctly?

---

1 *Larisa* The major town and region in Thessaly, Meno's home.

Meno: It seems necessary, to me. And so, I wonder, Socrates, if this
d is so, why knowledge is valued so much more than true belief, and what makes one of them different from the other.

Socrates: Do you know what makes you wonder, or shall I tell you?

Meno: Please, tell me.

Socrates: Because you haven't paid attention to Daedalus's[1] statues. Perhaps there are none where you live.[2]

Meno: What are you thinking about when you say this?

Socrates: Because if one of them is not tied down, it sneaks off and runs away, but if it is tied down, it remains by you.

e Meno: So what?

Socrates: Acquiring one of his unbound statues is not worthy of any great honor, like a runaway slave, since it won't stay with you. But a bound one is worth much, since Daedalus' works are very beautiful.

What am I thinking about when I say this? About the true beliefs. Since the true beliefs, too, for as much time as they stay with you, are fine possessions and bring about entirely good results. But they are
98a unwilling to stick around for long, and they run away out of the soul of a man and so are not worth much, until someone binds them by working out the reason.

And this, Meno my companion, is recollection, as we agreed previously. Whenever they are bound, first, they become knowledge, and second, steadfast. For these reasons knowledge is more honored than true belief, and knowledge differs from true belief in being bound.

Meno: Yes, by Zeus, Socrates, it's something like that.

b Socrates: Of course, I'm speaking as someone who doesn't know but is guessing. That true belief and knowledge are different from one another, I certainly don't think I'm guessing about that, and if I claim to

1 *Daedalus* Mythological sculptor, to whom were attributed archaic sculptures that were so lifelike that they appeared ready to run off.

2 *Perhaps there are none where you live* A little dig at Thessaly as being less cultured than Athens.

know anything at all—and there are few things I would say that about—I would put this down as one of the things I know.

Meno: And what you say is right, Socrates.

Socrates: Well, then, isn't this right, that being guided by a true belief makes the outcome of each of our actions no less beneficial than when guided by knowledge?

Meno: This too seems right to me.

Socrates: And a true belief is no worse and no less beneficial in our actions than knowledge, nor the man who has true beliefs than the man who has knowledge. c

Meno: It is.

Socrates: And we agree that the good man is beneficial?

Meno: Yes.

Socrates: Since, therefore, men are good and useful to their cities not only because they have knowledge, if there are any such men, but also because of their correct belief, and neither of these two arises naturally in men, neither knowledge nor true belief … or do you think either of them comes naturally? d

Meno: I don't.

Socrates: Then, since they're not by nature, neither would good men come to be by nature.

Meno: Certainly not.

Socrates: And since they are not by nature, we began examining the next thing, whether it is teachable.

Meno: Yes.

Socrates: And it seemed that it was teachable, if virtue is prudence?

Meno: Yes.

Socrates: And if it was teachable, it would be prudence?

Meno: Certainly.

e Socrates: And if there were teachers of it, it would be teachable, but if none, not teachable?

Meno: That's right.

Socrates: But we have agreed that in fact there are no teachers of it?

Meno: We have.

Socrates: And then we agreed that it was neither teachable nor prudence?

Meno: Certainly.

Socrates: But we do agree that it is good, at least?

Meno: Yes.

Socrates: And what guides correctly is beneficial and good?

Meno: Certainly.

99a Socrates: And that these are the only two things that guide correctly, true belief and knowledge, and any man who guides correctly has these. For things that happen correctly by chance do not occur by human guidance; but whenever a man guides towards what is correct, these two things guide: true belief and knowledge.

Meno: It seems so to me.

Socrates: But since it is not teachable, virtue can no longer be knowledge?

Meno: Apparently not.

b Socrates: Since there are two good and beneficial things and one has been "acquitted," knowledge would not be a guide of political activity.

Meno: I think not.

Socrates: So, it's not by some kind of wisdom, or by being wise, that such men as Themistocles and the like, and those whom Anytus here was talking about just now, guide their cities. And this is why they are unable to make others the same kind of person as they are, because they are not like this through knowledge.

Meno: It's likely to be as you say, Socrates.

Socrates: If it is not knowledge, then right belief is what remains. And by using this the political men organize the cities, and are no different, c
as far as knowledge goes, from those who deliver oracles and prophesy, since these say true things when they are inspired, lots of true things, but know nothing about what they're saying.

Meno: This is probably how it is.

Socrates: So, Meno, are these men worthy of being called "divine," those who bring about many great things by what they do and say without any intelligence?

Meno: Certainly.

Socrates: Then we could properly call "divine" those soothsayers and seers we were just talking about and all of the poets; and no less than d
these we could call the politicians "divine" and "inspired," filled with the breath and possessed by the god, whenever they successfully speak on many great matters without knowing what they're talking about.

Meno: Certainly.

Socrates: And women, too, of course, Meno, call good men "divine," and the Spartans, whenever they praise someone as a good man, say, "A divine man, he."

Meno: And apparently, Socrates, they speak correctly. Though Any- e
tus here is annoyed at what you say.

Socrates: It matters nothing to me; we will talk with him again. But for now, if we have investigated and spoken well in the course of all this talk, virtue would be neither by nature nor by teaching, but, to those in whom it is present, by a share of the divine, without intelligence, un-

100a less there was someone among the political men who could make others political too. If there were, he would be pretty much the only one among the living of the sort Homer said Tiresias was among the dead, saying of him, "Of those in the land of Hades, he alone is wise; the others flit around as shadows."[1] In the same way, in this world also, with respect to virtue, such a man would be a real thing compared to shadows, as it were.

b Meno: I think you put it superbly, Socrates.

Socrates: Based on this reasoning, then, Meno, it seems to us that virtue is present to those who have it by a share of the divine. We will have clear knowledge of it when, before we ask in what way virtue comes to be in man, we first try to discover what exactly virtue is in its own right.

But now it is time for me to go somewhere. As for you, on the other hand, persuade your guest-friend here, Anytus, of the very things you
c have been convinced of, so that he might become gentler. If you persuade him, you will also benefit the Athenians.

Suggestions for Critical Reflection

1. Socrates is dissatisfied with Meno's attempt to provide a definition of anything by listing various items that count as instances of such a thing. What does he think is wrong with this sort of definition? What sort of definition does he prefer? Why? Do you think that a Socratic definition is always possible? Look up the dictionary definitions of various nouns. Do they satisfy Socrates' requirements? If not, would a Socratic definition be possible?
2. Meno presents Socrates with a paradox that has come to be known as "The Paradox of Inquiry" or "Meno's Paradox" (80e), which apparently shows that inquiry of a certain sort is impossible. What is this paradox? Socrates provides what he thinks is a response, explaining how inquiry is possible after all. What is Socrates' response? Is this response adequate?
3. Do you think that Socrates' dialogue with the slave boy shows that some knowledge is recollection? What are alternative ways to explain the slave boy's apparent knowledge?

1 Homer, *Odyssey* 10.494–95.

4. If the soul knows everything, when did it learn it? If all 'learning' is recollection how can a soul learn anything in the first place?
5. Socrates says, "if we always possess the truth about things in the soul, the soul would be immortal" (86b). What do you think of this argument?
6. Why does Socrates give all those examples of virtuous parents with less-than-virtuous sons? What does he presuppose, such that these examples would prove his point? Is he correct in that presupposition?
7. "We are agreed, then, that a subject which has neither teachers nor learners is also not teachable" (96c). Is this too hasty? If it is, how does this affect Socrates' argument?
8. Do you agree with Socrates that real knowledge differs from mere true opinion (or belief that just happens to be true)? What do you think Socrates supposes that difference to be? The story of the statues that walk away (97d) is clearly just a picturesque metaphor: what really is this difference, if anything? Why do you think it's often supposed that real knowledge is superior?
9. Socrates apparently concludes that virtue is neither learned nor inborn, but is instead a gift from the gods. Do you think he means this, literally, and that this is his real point? If not, what is the real point?

Euthyphro

Introduction

In this dialogue, which takes place a few weeks before Socrates' trial, Socrates is on his way to "the porch of the king"—that is, the open building or walkway in the Agora that was the meeting place for the King Archon, who despite his archaic title was of one of nine elected officials in Athens with mostly formal functions. Socrates had to attend on the "king" in order to hear the charges being brought against him by Meletus and to have the date set for his trial.

On his way, he bumps into a professional religious prophet, or soothsayer, named Euthyphro, who is also there to meet with the King Archon—though in Euthyphro's case it is to bring an indictment rather than to receive one. As is Socrates' habit, he falls into conversation with Euthyphro and is soon quizzing him about whether he has really thought through the justification for his actions.

The main subject of the *Euthyphro* is a particular moral virtue—that of piety or holiness, which is to say showing proper respect for religion and the gods (literally, knowledge of how to properly perform ritual prayers and sacrifices). However, the notion is somewhat broader than it might initially seem: insofar as the gods approve generally of morally good behavior, to show proper respect for the gods will involve behaving well more generally.

Socrates fairly quickly turns the discussion to an attempt to find the essence or definition of piety—the fundamental thing that all pious actions have in common. (The particular murder that Euthyphro is prosecuting is merely an example of something that might be an impious action, and not the central topic of the dialogue.) Euthyphro's first attempt to answer this question is to say that "what is beloved by the gods is pious, and what is not beloved by them is impious," but Socrates shows him that this is inadequate as a definition. He argues against it in two ways, but it is the second that really counts; this more fundamental objection to the definition emerges when Socrates asks, "Is the pious loved by the gods because it's pious, or it is pious because it is loved?"

The final stage of the dialogue deals with piety as a particular type of right action ("the pious is a part of the just")—pious actions are those that constitute appropriate interaction with the gods. Euthyphro is confident that he is on solid ground here, as an expert on dealing with the gods, but Socrates once again ties him into logical knots and shows that merely identifying what the gods like is not yet to show what about it *makes* it worth liking. (Analogously, your favorite music is not *made into* good music by the mere fact that you like it: there must be something about it that is already good, and it is for this reason that you like it.)

At this point Euthyphro suddenly remembers that he has urgent business elsewhere, and to Socrates' disappointment the conversation comes to an abrupt end.

Cast of Characters

Euthyphro: A seer or prophet; that is, someone who was a professional interpreter of the wishes of the gods. Little is known about him beyond what is revealed in Plato's dialogues.

Meletus: The main presenter of the case against Socrates. He was a fairly young man and a religious zealot who had previously been involved in bringing legal charges of impiety.

Euthyphro

2a Euthyphro: What new thing has happened, Socrates, that you have abandoned your stomping grounds in the Lyceum[1] and are now spending your time here, around the porch of the king[2]? For surely you too are not involved in some suit before the king,[3] as I am.

Socrates: No, Euthyphro, the Athenians don't just call it a suit, but a public indictment.[4]

1 *Lyceum* A gymnasium outside the walls of Athens.

2 *the porch of the king* The "porch" is a covered walkway in the Athenian *agora* (marketplace or forum).

3 *before the king* The "king" was one of nine *archons* or magistrates. At this stage of the proceedings, accusations would be lodged and testimony recorded from those involved and from witnesses. The King Archon was in charge of religious matters. Socrates is there because he has been charged with a religious crime (not acknowledging the gods of the city); Euthyphro is there because he believes that his father, as a murderer, is polluting the religious spaces of the city, which therefore need to be purified. (See section 57 of Aristotle's *Athenian Constitution*.)

4 *a public indictment* It was up to individuals (in Socrates' case, Meletus, along with Anytus and Lycon) to bring cases on behalf of the city.

Euthyphro: What do you mean? Someone has indicted you, I suppose, b
since I certainly wouldn't accuse you of the opposite, you indicting someone else.

Socrates: Certainly not.

Euthyphro: So someone else is indicting you?

Socrates: Absolutely.

Euthyphro: Who is this person?

Socrates: I don't know the man very well myself, Euthyphro; I think he is a young and unknown person. Anyway, I believe they call him Meletus. He is from the Pitthean deme,[1] if you know of a Meletus from Pitthos with straight hair, not much of a beard, and with a slightly hooked nose.

Euthyphro: I don't know him, Socrates. But what charge has he in- c
dicted you on?

Socrates: On what charge? A not undistinguished one, I think, as it's no small thing for a young man to be knowledgeable about so important an issue. For he, he says, knows how the young are corrupted and who their corruptors are. He's probably somebody wise, and having seen how I in my ignorance corrupt the people of his generation, he is coming to tattle on me to the city, as though it were his mother. And he alone seems
to me to be starting out in politics correctly, because the correct way is d
to first give one's attention to how our young people will be the best possible, just as a good farmer probably cares first for his young plants, and after this for the others as well. And so Meletus too is presumably
first weeding out those of us who corrupt the sprouting young people, 3a
as he puts it. Then after this it's clear that, having turned his attention to the older people, he will become a source of many great goods for the city—this is likely to happen to him, having started off in this way.

Euthyphro: I wish it were so, Socrates, but I'm terrified that the opposite might happen. Because it seems to me that by trying to wrong you he is starting out by recklessly harming the hearth of the city. Do tell me, just what does he say you're doing to corrupt the young?

---

1 *deme* An administrative division of Attica, the broader region in which Athens is located.

b Socrates: Extraordinary things, you remarkable man, at least to hear him describe them. For he says I am a maker of gods, and because I make novel gods and do not acknowledge the old ones, he indicts me for their sake, he says.

Euthyphro: I understand, Socrates. It's because of the divine sign[1] that you say comes to you occasionally. And so he has lodged this indictment on the grounds that you are an innovator concerning religious ideas and he is surely coming to the court intending to slander you, knowing that such things are easily misrepresented to the many. In-
c deed in my case too, whenever I say something in the assembly about religious matters, foretelling the future for them, they ridicule me as a madman, even though nothing in my foretelling was untrue. Even so, they envy all of us who are like this. We should think nothing of them but fight them on their own ground.

Socrates: But my dear Euthyphro, being ridiculed is probably no big deal; indeed it seems to me that it doesn't matter much to the Athenians if they think someone is clever, provided that he is not capable of teaching his wisdom. They become outraged, though, with anyone
d they suspect of also trying to shape others in some way, whether because they are envious, as you claim, or for some other reason.

Euthyphro: Which is why I have no great desire to have it put to the test, how they feel about me.

Socrates: It's perhaps because you seem to rarely make yourself available and appear unwilling to teach your wisdom, whereas I fear that, because of my love of people, I strike them as someone who is bursting to talk to everybody, and not just without demanding payment, but would even be glad to compensate anyone who was willing to listen to me. So as I was saying, if they intend to laugh at me, as you said hap-
e pens to you, there would be nothing unpleasant about spending time in court playing around and laughing. But if they are going to be serious, in that case it's unclear how things will turn out, except to you prophets.

Euthyphro: Well, it will probably be nothing, Socrates, and you will fight your case satisfactorily, as I think I will fight mine, too.

Socrates: Yes, what exactly is your suit, Euthyphro? Are you defending or prosecuting it?

---

1 *divine sign* See *Apology* 31b–d and 41a–c.

Euthyphro: I am prosecuting.

Socrates: Whom?

Euthyphro: A man whom by pursuing I will again appear mad. 4a

Socrates: But why? You're pursuing someone who flies?

Euthyphro: He is a long way from flying; indeed he happens to be well advanced in years.

Socrates: Who is he?

Euthyphro: My own father.

Socrates: Your father, you fantastic fellow?!

Euthyphro: Absolutely.

Socrates: But what is the charge, and what are the circumstances?

Euthyphro: Murder, Socrates.

Socrates: Heracles! Surely most people don't know what is correct in such a situation, since I don't think that just anyone could take care of this correctly, but only someone, I suspect, who has progressed a long b
way in wisdom.

Euthyphro: By Zeus, a long way indeed, Socrates.

Socrates: Surely the person killed by your father is one of your relatives? It must be, since you would not prosecute him for murder on behalf of a stranger?

Euthyphro: It's ridiculous, Socrates, that you think it makes a difference whether the man killed is a stranger or a relative, rather than that it is necessary to attend only to this: whether the killer killed legally or not—and if it was legal, to let him go, and if not, to prosecute him, even if the killer shares your hearth and eats at the same table. Be- c
cause the pollution is the same, if you knowingly associate with such a man and do not purify both yourself and him by prosecuting him in law.

The victim, as a matter of fact, was one of my hired men, and when we were farming in Naxos[1] he was working for us there. Well, he got drunk, became angry with another one of our household slaves, and slit the man's throat. So my father bound his feet and hands, threw him into some ditch, and sent a man here to inquire of the interpreter of re-
d ligious law about what should be done. But during that time he paid no attention to the bound man and neglected him, thinking him a murderer and that it would be no big thing if he died as well, which then in fact happened, as he died of hunger and cold and of his bonds before the messenger returned from the interpreter.

That's why both my father and my other relatives are angry, because I am prosecuting my father on behalf of a murderer, when he didn't kill him, they say, or if he did in fact kill him, well, since the man he killed was a murderer, one should not be concerned about such
e people—because it's unholy for a son to prosecute his father for murder, they say, not really knowing, Socrates, how the religious law stands with respect to holiness and unholiness.

Socrates: But before Zeus, Euthyphro, do you think you have such accurate knowledge about how the religious laws stand, about both piety and impiety, that, with these things having taken place in the way you describe, you are not afraid that by prosecuting your father you in turn might be committing an impiety?

5a Euthyphro: I would be of no use, Socrates, and neither would Euthyphro be better than the majority of men, if I did not have accurate knowledge of all such matters.

Socrates: In that case it would be excellent for me to become a student of yours, marvelous Euthyphro, and prior to this dispute with Meletus I will challenge him exactly as follows, saying that while even in the past I used to make knowing the religious law my top priority, now, because he says I err by judging rashly and innovating with respect to the religious laws, I have even become your student. And I could say,
b "If you agree, Meletus, that Euthyphro is wise in such matters, then believe that I worship properly, too, and do not charge me. If not, see about bringing a charge against him, my teacher, rather than me, since he corrupts the elderly—me and his father—by teaching me and by rebuking and chastising him." And if I don't convince him and he doesn't withdraw the charge or indict *you* in my place, shouldn't I say in court the exact same thing as I said when challenging him?

---

1 *Naxos* A Greek island that was an Athenian colony.

Euthyphro: Yes, by Zeus, Socrates. If he tried to indict me I think I c
would uncover in what way he is unsound and we would find that the
discussion in court would be about him, long before it was about me.

Socrates: And indeed, my dear Euthyphro, I recognize this and want
to become a student of yours, seeing how practically everyone else
and Meletus himself pretends not to notice you, but he sees through me
so clearly and easily that he indicts me for impiety. So now, by Zeus,
explain to me what you were just now claiming to know clearly: what
sort of thing do you say holiness is, and unholiness, with respect to d
murder and everything else as well? Or isn't the pious the same as it-
self in every action,[1] and the impious in turn is the complete opposite
of the pious but the same as itself, and everything that in fact turns out
to be impious has a single form with respect to its impiousness?

Euthyphro: It certainly is, Socrates.

Socrates: So tell me, what do you say the pious is, and what is the impious?

Euthyphro: Well then, I claim that the pious is what I am doing now,
prosecuting someone who is guilty of wrongdoing—either of murder
or temple robbery or anything else of the sort, whether it happens to
be one's father or mother or whoever else—and the impious is failing e
to prosecute. For observe, Socrates, how great a proof I will give you
that this is how the law stands, one I have already given to others as
well, which shows such actions to be correct—not yielding to impious
people, that is, no matter who they happen to be. Because these very
people also happen to worship Zeus as the best and most just of the 6a
gods, and agree that he put his own father in bonds because he un-
justly swallowed his sons, and the father too castrated his own father
for other similar reasons.[2] Yet they are sore at me because I am pros-
ecuting my father for his injustice. And so they say contradictory
things about the gods and about me.

Socrates: Maybe this, Euthyphro, is why I am being prosecuted for this crime, that whenever someone says such things about the gods, for some reason I find them hard to accept? For this reason, I suppose,

1 *the same as itself in every action* That is, there is just one kind of piety—all pious actions have something in common (and ditto for impiety).

2 *Zeus ... other similar reasons* For the stories of Zeus, Cronos, and Ouranos, see Hesiod, *Theogony*, 154–82 and 453–506.

someone will claim I misbehave. But now if you, with your expertise in such matters, also hold these beliefs, it's surely necessary, I suppose,
b that we too must accept them—for indeed what *can* we say, we who admit openly that we know nothing about these matters? But before the god of friendship[1] tell me, do you truly believe these things happened like this?

Euthyphro: These and still more amazing things, Socrates, that most people are unaware of.

Socrates: And do you believe there is really a war among the gods, with terrible feuds, even, and battles and many other such things, such as are recounted by the poets and the holy artists, and that have been
c elaborately adorned for us on sacred objects, too, and especially the robe covered with such designs which is brought up to the acropolis at the great Panathenaea?[2] Are we to say that these things are true, Euthyphro?

Euthyphro: Not only these, Socrates, but as I said just now, I could also describe many other things about the gods to you, if you want, which I am sure you will be astounded to hear.

Socrates: I wouldn't be surprised. But you can describe these to me at leisure some other time. For the time being, however, try to state more
d clearly what I asked you just now, since previously, my friend, you did not teach me well enough when I asked what the pious was but you told me that what you're doing is something pious, prosecuting your father for murder.

Euthyphro: And I spoke the truth, too, Socrates.

Socrates: Perhaps. But in fact, Euthyphro, you say there are many other pious things.

Euthyphro: Indeed there are.

---

1 *the god of friendship* Zeus Philios, or Zeus in his aspect of the champion of friendship.

2 *robe ... great Panathenaea?* The Panathenaea was a celebration of Athena's birthday, held annually, with a larger ("great") celebration every four years. A new robe would be presented to the statue of the goddess Athena.

Socrates: So do you remember that I did not request this from you, to teach me one or two of the many pious things, but to teach me the form itself by which everything pious is pious? For you said that it's by one form that impious things are somehow impious and pious things pious. e
Or don't you remember?

Euthyphro: I certainly do.

Socrates: So then tell me whatever this form itself is, so that, by looking at it and using it as a paradigm, if you or anyone else do anything of that kind I can say that it is pious, and if it is not of that kind, that it is not.

Euthyphro: Well if that's what you want, Socrates, that's what I'll tell you.

Socrates: That's exactly what I want.

Euthyphro: Well, what is beloved by the gods is pious, and what is 7a
not beloved by them is impious.

Socrates: Excellent, Euthyphro! And you have answered in the way I was looking for you to answer. Whether you have done so truly or not, that I don't quite know—but you will obviously spell out how what you say is true.

Euthyphro: Absolutely.

Socrates: Come then, let's look at what we said. An action or a person that is beloved by the gods is pious, while an action or person that is despised by the gods is impious. It is not the same, but the complete opposite, the pious to the impious. Isn't that so?

Euthyphro: Indeed it is.

Socrates: And this seems right?

Euthyphro: I think so, Socrates. b

Socrates: But wasn't it also said that the gods are at odds with each other and disagree with one another and that there are feuds among them?

Euthyphro: Yes, it was.

Socrates: What is the disagreement about, my good man, that causes hatred and anger? Let's look at it this way. If we disagree, you and I, about quantity, over which of two groups is greater, would our disagreement over this make us enemies and angry with
c each other, or wouldn't we quickly resolve the issue by resorting to counting?

Euthyphro: Of course.

Socrates: And again, if we disagreed about bigger and smaller, we would quickly put an end to the disagreement by resorting to measurement?

Euthyphro: That's right.

Socrates: And we would weigh with scales, I presume, to reach a decision about heavier and lighter?

Euthyphro: How else?

Socrates: Then what topic, exactly, would divide us and what difference would we be unable to settle such that we would be enemies and angry with one another? Perhaps you don't have an answer at hand, so
d as I'm talking, see if it's the just and the unjust, the noble and the shameful, and the good and the bad. Isn't it these things that make us enemies of one another, any time that happens, whether to me and you or to any other men, when we quarrel about them and are unable to come to a satisfactory judgment about them?

Euthyphro: It is indeed this disagreement, Socrates, and over these things.

Socrates: And what about the gods, Euthyphro? If they indeed disagree over something, don't they disagree over these very things?

Euthyphro: It's undoubtedly necessary.

e Socrates: Then some of the gods think different things are just—according to you, worthy Euthyphro—and noble and shameful, and good and bad, since they surely wouldn't be at odds with one another unless they were disagreeing about these things. Right?

Euthyphro: You're right.

Socrates: And so whatever each group thinks is noble and good and just, they also love these things, and they hate the things that are the opposites of these?

Euthyphro: Certainly.

Socrates: Then according to you the things some of them think are just, others think are unjust, and by disagreeing about these things they 8a
are at odds and at war with each other. Isn't this so?

Euthyphro: It is.

Socrates: The same things, it seems, are both hated by the gods and loved, and so would be both despised and beloved by them?

Euthyphro: It seems so.

Socrates: And the same things would be both pious and impious, Euthyphro, according to this argument?

Euthyphro: I'm afraid so.

Socrates: So you haven't answered what I was asking, you remarkable man! I didn't ask you for what is both pious and impious at once: what is beloved by the gods is also hated by the gods, as it appears. As a result, Euthyphro, it wouldn't be surprising if in doing what you're doing b
now—punishing your father—you were doing something beloved by Zeus but despised by Cronos and Uranus, and while it is dear to Hephaestus, it is despised by Hera,[1] and if any other god disagrees with another on the subject, your action will also appear to them similarly.

Euthyphro: But I believe, Socrates, that none of the gods will disagree with any other on this matter at least: that any man who has killed another person unjustly need not pay the penalty.

Socrates: What's that? Have you never heard any *man* arguing that someone who killed unjustly or did something else unjustly should not c
pay the penalty?

Euthyphro: There's no end to these arguments, both outside and inside the courts, since people commit so many injustices and do and say anything to escape the punishment.

---

1 See the Introduction, on the religious context for these dialogues.

Socrates: Do they actually agree that they are guilty, Euthyphro, and despite agreeing they nonetheless say that they shouldn't pay the penalty?

Euthyphro: They don't agree on that at all.

Socrates: So they don't do or say *everything*, since, I think, they don't
d dare to claim or argue for this: that if they are in fact guilty they should *not* pay the penalty. Rather, I think they claim that they're not guilty. Right?

Euthyphro: That's true.

Socrates: So they don't argue, at least, that the guilty person shouldn't pay the penalty, but perhaps they argue about who the guilty party is and what he did and when.

Euthyphro: That's true.

Socrates: Doesn't the very same thing happen to the gods, too, if indeed, as you said, they are at odds about just and unjust things, some saying that a god commits an injustice against another one, while others deny it? But absolutely no one at all, you remarkable man, either
e god or human, dares to say that the guilty person need not pay the penalty.

Euthyphro: Yes. What you say is true, Socrates, for the most part.

Socrates: But I think that those who quarrel, Euthyphro, both men and gods, if the gods actually quarrel, argue over the particulars of what was done. Differing over a certain action, some say that it was done justly, others that it was done unjustly. Isn't that so?

Euthyphro: Certainly.

9a Socrates: Come now, my dear Euthyphro. So that I can become wiser, teach me too what evidence you have that all gods think the man was killed unjustly—the one who committed murder while he was working for you, and was bound by the master of the man he killed, and died from his bonds before the servant could learn from the interpreters what ought to be done in his case, and is the sort of person on whose behalf it is proper for a son to prosecute his father and make an allegation of murder. Come, try to give me a clear indication of how in this

case all the gods believe beyond doubt that this action is proper. If you b
could show me this satisfactorily I would never stop praising you for
your wisdom.

Euthyphro: But this is probably quite a task, Socrates, though I could explain it to you very clearly, even so.

Socrates: I understand. It's because you think I'm a slower learner than the judges, since you could make it clear to *them* in what way these actions are unjust and how the gods all hate such things.

Euthyphro: Very clear indeed, Socrates, if only they would listen to me when I talk.

Socrates: Of course they'll listen, so long as they think you speak
well. But while you were speaking the following occurred to me: c
I'm thinking to myself, "Even if Euthyphro convincingly shows me
that every god thinks this kind of death is unjust, what more will I
have learned from Euthyphro about what the pious and the impious
are? Because while this particular deed might be despised by the
gods, as is likely, it was already apparent, just a moment ago, that the
pious and impious aren't defined this way, since we saw that what is
despised by the gods is also beloved by them." So I acquit you of
this, Euthyphro. If you want, let us allow that all gods think this is d
unjust and that all of them despise it. But this current correction to
the definition—that what all the gods despise is impious while what
they love is pious, and what some love and some hate is neither or
both—do you want us to now define the pious and the impious in
this way?

Euthyphro: Well, what is stopping us, Socrates?

Socrates: For my part nothing, Euthyphro, but think about whether adopting this definition will make it easiest for you to teach me what you promised.

Euthyphro: I do indeed say that the pious is what all the gods love, e
and the opposite, what all gods hate, is impious.

Socrates: Then let's look again, Euthyphro, to see whether it's well stated. Or will we be content to simply accept our own definition or someone else's, agreeing that it is right just because somebody says it is? Or must we examine what the speaker is saying?

Euthyphro: We must examine it. But I'm quite confident that what we have now is well put.

10a Socrates: We'll soon know better, my good man. Think about this: Is the pious loved by the gods because it's pious, or it is pious because it is loved?

Euthyphro: I don't know what you mean, Socrates.

Socrates: I'll try to express myself more clearly. We speak of something being carried and of carrying, and being led and leading, and being seen and seeing, and so you understand that all of these are different from one another and how they are different?

Euthyphro: I think I understand.

Socrates: So there's a thing loved and different from this there's the thing that loves?

Euthyphro: How could there not be?

b Socrates: Then tell me whether what is carried is a carried thing because it is carried, or because of something else?

Euthyphro: No, it's because of this.

Socrates: And also what is led because it is led, and what is seen because it is seen?

Euthyphro: Absolutely.

Socrates: So it is not that because it is something seen, it is seen, but the opposite, that because it is seen it is something seen.[1] And it is not because it is something led that it is led, but because it is led it is something led. And it is not because it is something carried that it is carried, but because it is carried, it is something carried. Is it becoming clear
c what I'm trying to say, Euthyphro? I mean this: that if something becomes or is affected by something, it's not because it is a thing coming to be that it comes to be; but because it comes to be it is a thing coming into being. Nor is it affected by something because it is a thing

---

1 *So it is not ... is something seen* That is, someone seeing something gives it the property of being seen, rather than the other way round (something being seen makes it the case that someone sees it).

that is affected; but because it is affected, it is a thing that is being affected. Or don't you agree?

Euthyphro: I do.

Socrates: And is a loved thing either a thing coming to be or a thing affected by something?

Euthyphro: Certainly.

Socrates: And does the same apply to this as to the previous cases: it is not because it is a loved thing that it is loved by those who love it, but it is a loved thing because it is loved?

Euthyphro: Necessarily.

Socrates: So what do we say about the pious, Euthyphro? Precisely d
that is it loved by all the gods, according to your statement?

Euthyphro: Yes.

Socrates: Is it because of this: that it is pious? Or because of something else?

Euthyphro: No, it's because of that.

Socrates: Because it is pious, then, it is loved, rather than being pious because it is loved?

Euthyphro: It seems so.

Socrates: Then because it is loved by the gods it is a loved thing and beloved by the gods?

Euthyphro: How could it not? e

Socrates: So the beloved is not pious, Euthyphro, nor is the pious beloved by the gods, as you claim, but the one is different from the other.

Euthyphro: How so, Socrates?

Socrates: Because we agree that the pious is loved because of this—that is, because it is pious—and not that it is pious because it is loved. Right?

Euthyphro: Yes.

Socrates: The beloved, on the other hand, because it is loved by gods, is beloved due to this very act of being loved, rather than being loved because it is beloved?

Euthyphro: That's true.

Socrates: But if the beloved and the pious were in fact the same, my
11a dear Euthyphro, then, if the pious were loved because of being the pious, the beloved would be loved because of being the beloved; and again, if the beloved was beloved because of being loved by gods, the pious would also be pious by being loved. But as it is, you see that the two are opposites and are completely different from one another, since the one, because it is loved, is the kind of thing that is loved, while the other is loved because it is the kind of thing that is loved.

So I'm afraid, Euthyphro, that when you were asked what in the world the pious is, you did not want to reveal its nature to me, but wanted to tell me some one of its qualities—that the pious has the qual-
b ity of being loved by all the gods—but as for what it *is*, you did not say at all. So if I am dear to you, don't keep me in the dark but tell me again from the beginning what in the world the pious is. And we won't differ over whether it is loved by the gods or whatever else happens to it, but tell me without delay, what is the pious, and the impious?

Euthyphro: But Socrates, I have no way of telling you what I'm thinking, because somehow whatever we put forward always wanders off on us and doesn't want to stay where we put it.

Socrates: Your statements, Euthyphro, seem to belong to my ancestor
c Daedalus.[1] And if I were saying them and putting them forward, perhaps you would be joking about how, on account of my relationship to him, my works made of words run away even on me and don't want to stay wherever a person might put them. But at present these propositions are yours, and so we have to find some other joke, since they don't want to stay put for you, as even you yourself admit.

---

1 *Daedalus* The statues made by the mythical Daedalus were said to be so lifelike that they appeared to move (see *Meno* 97d). Daedalus is most famous for making wings for himself and his son Icarus to use to escape from Crete. Socrates calls him his 'ancestor' because Socrates' father was a stonemason.

Euthyphro: It seems to me that pretty much the same joke applies to
the statements, Socrates, since I am not the inspiration for their wan- d
dering off and their refusal to stay in the same place. Rather, it seems to me that you are the Daedalus, since they would stay in place just fine for me, at least.

Socrates: Then I'm afraid, my friend, that I've become more skilled in the craft than the man himself, to the extent that while he could only make his own works move, I can do so to others' works as well as my own. And to my mind this is the most exquisite thing about my skill, that I am unintentionally clever, since I wanted the words to stay put
for me and to be fixed motionless more than to have the money of e
Tantalos[1] and the skill of Daedalus combined. But enough of this. Since I think you are soft,[2] I myself will help you educate me about the pious. So don't give up the task. See whether you believe that everything pious is necessarily just.

Euthyphro: I do.

Socrates: And is everything just pious? Or is every part of piety just
but the just is not the whole of piety, but some part of it is pious, and 12a
some other part is different?

Euthyphro: I can't keep up with what you're saying, Socrates.

Socrates: And yet you are younger than me by at least as much as you are wiser than me! But, as I say, you are spoiled by your abundance of wisdom. Pull yourself together, you blessed man, since what I'm saying is not difficult to get your head around. I mean, of course, the opposite of what the poet meant when he wrote:

> Zeus who created it and who produced all of these
> You do not want to revile; for where there is fear there is also b
> respect.[3]

I disagree with this statement from the poet. Shall I tell you how?

Euthyphro: Yes indeed.

---

1 *Tantalos* A mythical son of Zeus who derived great wealth from mines.

2 *soft* Slacking (in the task of defining the pious).

3 *there is also respect* The quotation is from Stanisos' *Cypria*, a collection of tales describing the events prior to the beginning of Homer's *Iliad*.

Socrates: I don't think that "where there is fear there is also respect" since I think many people who fear sickness, poverty and many other things feel fear, but they feel no respect at these things they fear. Don't you think so, too?

Euthyphro: Certainly.

Socrates: Where there is respect, though, there is also fear, for is there
anyone who feels respect and is ashamed at some act who doesn't also
c feel fear and dread a reputation for cowardice?

Euthyphro: He does indeed dread it.

Socrates: So it's not right to claim that "where there is fear there is also respect," for respect is not in fact everywhere fear is, but instead where there is respect there is also fear. Because I think fear covers more than respect since respect is a part of fear, just as oddness is a part of number, so that it's not the case that where there is number there is also oddness, but where there is oddness, there is also number. Do you follow now, at least?

Euthyphro: I certainly do.

Socrates: This is the kind of thing I was talking about earlier when I
was questioning you: where there is justice, is there also piety? Or is
d it that where there is piety, there is also justice, but piety is not every-
where justice is, since piety is a part of justice? Do you think we should
speak in this way or in some other?

Euthyphro: No, in this way. I think you're speaking properly.

Socrates: Then see what follows this: if the pious is a part of the just, we must, it seems, discover what part of the just the pious might be. If, to go back to what we were just discussing, you now asked me something such as what part of number the even is, and what kind of number it happens to be, I would say that it would be the number that can be divided into two equal and not unequal parts.[1] Doesn't it seem so to you?

Euthyphro: It does.

---

1 *divided into two equal and not unequal parts* Literally (in the Greek) "isosceles and not scalene," presumably because isosceles triangles have two equal legs.

Socrates: So try to teach me in this way, Euthyphro, what sort of e
part of the just piety is, so that we can also tell Meletus not to do us wrong and charge me with impiety, since I have already learned enough from you about what is holy and what is pious and what is not.

Euthyphro: It seems to me now, Socrates, that holiness and piety is the part of justice concerned with attending to the gods, while the remaining part of justice is concerned with attending to human beings.

Socrates: I think you put that well, Euthyphro. But I still need just one 13a
small thing: I don't know quite what you mean by "attending." Surely you don't mean that attending to the gods is like the other kinds of attending, even though we do say so. We say, for example, that not everybody knows how to attend to a horse, just the horse-trainer. Right?

Euthyphro: Certainly.

Socrates: Since horse-training is attending to horses?

Euthyphro: Yes.

Socrates: And no one but the dog-trainer knows how to attend to dogs?

Euthyphro: Right.

Socrates: And dog-training is attending to dogs?

Euthyphro: Yes. b

Socrates: And cattle-herding is attending to cattle?

Euthyphro: Absolutely.

Socrates: Naturally, then, piety and holiness are to the gods, Euthyphro? That's what you say?

Euthyphro: I do.

Socrates: Then does all attending bring about the same effect? Something of the following sort: the good and benefit of what is attended to, in just the way you see that horses, when attended to by horse-trainers, are benefited and become better? Or don't you think they are?

Euthyphro: They are.

c Socrates: And dogs by the dog-trainer somehow, and cattle by the cattle-herder, and all the others similarly? Or do you think the attending is aimed at harming what is attended to?

Euthyphro: By Zeus, I do not.

Socrates: But at benefiting them?

Euthyphro: How could it not be?

Socrates: And since piousness is attending to the gods, does it benefit the gods and make the gods better? Do you agree to this, that whenever one does something pious it results in some improvement of the gods?

Euthyphro: By Zeus, no, I don't.

Socrates: Nor did I think that that's what you meant, Euthyphro—far
from it, in fact—and that's why I was asking what you really meant by
d "attending to the gods," because I didn't think you mean this kind of
thing.

Euthyphro: And you're right, Socrates. Because I mean no such thing.

Socrates: Alright then. But what kind of attending to the gods would piousness be, then?

Euthyphro: The kind, Socrates, when slaves attend to their masters.

Socrates: I understand. It would be a kind of service to gods, it seems.

Euthyphro: Certainly.

Socrates: Can you tell me about service to doctors, what end result is such service aimed at? Don't you think it's at health?

Euthyphro: I do.

Socrates: And what about service to shipbuilders? What end result is e
that service aimed at?

Euthyphro: Clearly it's aimed at a ship, Socrates.

Socrates: And service to house-builders, I suppose, is aimed at houses?

Euthyphro: Yes.

Socrates: Tell me then, best of men, what end result is service to the gods aimed at? It's obvious that you know, since you claim to have the finest religious knowledge—of any human, at least.

Euthyphro: And as a matter of fact, Socrates, I speak the truth.

Socrates: So tell me, by Zeus, what in the world is that magnificent task which the gods accomplish by using us as servants?

Euthyphro: Many fine tasks, Socrates.

Socrates: Well, and so do the generals, my friend. But nevertheless 14a
one could easily say what their key purpose is: that they achieve victory in war. Is that not so?

Euthyphro: How else could it be?

Socrates: And I think the farmers accomplish many fine tasks. And yet their key purpose is nourishment from the soil.

Euthyphro: Very much so.

Socrates: So what, then, about the many fine things that the gods accomplish? What is the key purpose of their labor?

Euthyphro: As I said a little earlier, Socrates, it is a great task to learn ex- b
actly how all these things are. But I will put it for you generally: if a man knows how to speak and act pleasingly to the gods in his prayers and sacrifices, those are pious, and such things preserve both his own home and the common good of the city. But the opposites of these pleasing things are unholy, and they obviously overturn and destroy everything.

Socrates: If you were willing, Euthyphro, you could have told me the heart of what I was asking much more briefly. But in fact you are not
c eager to teach me, that much is clear—since now when you were just about to do so, you turned away. If you had given your answer, I would already have a satisfactory understanding of piousness from you. But for the present, the lover must follow his beloved wherever he might lead. So what do you say the pious and piousness are, again? Aren't you saying it's a certain kind of knowledge, of how to sacrifice and pray?

Euthyphro: I am.

Socrates: And sacrificing is giving to the gods, while praying is making a request of the gods?

Euthyphro: Very much so, Socrates.

d Socrates: Based on this, piousness would be knowledge of making requests and giving things to the gods?

Euthyphro: You have understood my meaning very well, Socrates.

Socrates: It's because I am eager for your wisdom, my friend, and pay close attention to it, so that nothing you might say falls to the ground. But tell me, what is this service to the gods? You say it is making requests of them and giving to them?

Euthyphro: I do.

Socrates: And proper requests would be requests for what we need from them, asking them for these things?

Euthyphro: What else?

e Socrates: And again, giving properly would be giving what they happen to want from us, to give these things to them in return? Since to give a gift by giving someone what he has no need of would not be too skillful, I suppose.

Euthyphro: That's true, Socrates.

Socrates: So piousness for gods and humans, Euthyphro, would be some skill of trading with one another?

Euthyphro: If naming it that way is sweeter for you, call it "trading."

Socrates: As far as I'm concerned, nothing is sweeter unless it is true. Tell me, how do the gods benefit from the gifts they receive
from us? What they give us is clear to everyone, since every good 15a
we have was given by them. But what they receive from us, what good is it? Or do we fare so much better than them in the trade that we get everything that's good from them, while they get nothing from us?

Euthyphro: But do you think, Socrates, that the gods are benefited by what they receive from us?

Socrates: Well then what in the world would they be, Euthyphro, these gifts from us to the gods?

Euthyphro: What else, do you think, but honor and admiration and, as I said just now, gratitude?

Socrates: So being shown gratitude is what's pious, Euthyphro, but it b
is neither beneficial to the gods nor dear to them?

Euthyphro: I think it is dear to them above everything else.

Socrates: So the pious is once again, it seems, what is dear to gods.

Euthyphro: Very much so.

Socrates: Are you at all surprised, when you say such things, that your words seem not to stand still but to move around? And you accuse me of making them move around like a Daedalus when you yourself are much more skilled than Daedalus, even making things go around in circles? Or don't you see that our discussion has gone
around and arrived back at the same place? You remember, no doubt, c
that previously the pious and the beloved by the gods seemed to us not to be the same but different from one another. Or don't you remember?

Euthyphro: I certainly do.

Socrates: Well, don't you realize now that you're saying that what is dear to the gods is pious? But this is nothing other than what is beloved by the gods, isn't it?

Euthyphro: It certainly is.

Socrates: So either what we decided then was wrong, or, if we were right then, we are wrong now.

Euthyphro: So it seems.

Socrates: Then we must examine again from the beginning what
the pious is, as I am determined not to give up until I understand
d it. Do not scorn me, but by applying your mind in every way, tell
me the truth now more than ever. Because you know it if anybody
does and, like Proteus,[1] you cannot be released until you tell me.
Because unless you knew clearly about the pious and impious
there is no way you would ever have, on behalf of a hired laborer,
tried to pursue your aging father for murder. Instead you would
have been afraid before the gods, and ashamed before men, to run
the risk of conducting this matter improperly. But as it is, I am
e sure that you think you have clear knowledge of the pious and the
impious. So tell me, great Euthyphro, and do not conceal what you
think it is.

Euthyphro: Well, some other time, Socrates, because I'm in a hurry to get somewhere and it's time for me to go.

Socrates: What a thing to do, my friend! By leaving, you have cast me
down from a great hope I had: that I would learn from you what is
pious and what is not, and moreover would free myself from Mele-
16a tus' charge by showing him that, thanks to Euthyphro, I had already
become wise in religious matters and that I would no longer speak
carelessly and innovate about these things due to ignorance, and most
of all that I would live better for the rest of my life.

Suggestions for Critical Reflection

1. Socrates often speaks ironically. For example, at the start of the *Euthyphro* he begins by praising Meletus for his wisdom in bringing the indictment against him, and he reacts similarly to Euthy-

1 *Proteus* A mythical sea god who could change shape. The Spartan hero Menelaus had to hold on to Proteus as he changed shape in order to get him to prophesy. (See Homer, *Odyssey* 4.398–463.)

phro when he learns that he is bringing charges against his own father. What do you think is the purpose of this ironical tone?

2. In the *Euthyphro* Socrates famously asks whether right actions are loved by the gods *because they are right*, or if instead an action is right simply *because it is approved of by the gods* (10a). What is the difference between the two options? Socrates does not seem to take the second option seriously, instead focusing on the first; why do you think this might be?

3. Socrates claims that "the beloved is not pious, Euthyphro, nor is the pious beloved by the gods, as you claim, but the one is different from the other" (10e). How does he reach this conclusion?

4. Socrates argues that piety can't be what's approved of by the gods because the gods quarrel. That reply doesn't appeal to today's adherents of religions that believe in just one God, who is consistent in his approval. Explain why Socrates' reply might have relevance to these people, today.

5. This dialogue centers around the idea of *piety* (sometimes translators of this dialogue call it *holiness*). Nowadays, these ideas are perhaps less centrally important than in other times. But might the central question in this dialogue be revised to center around other concepts, perhaps of more relevance to us?

6. Socrates raises, as an analogy, the idea expressed by the saying "Where there is fear there is respect" (12b). What is the point here? Give an outline of Socrates' reasoning around this point.

Apology

Introduction

The *Apology* is so called not because Socrates is the least bit apologetic (in the modern sense), but as a transliteration of the Greek word *apologia*, which means a speech in defense of one's beliefs or behavior. It is Plato's depiction of the speech that Socrates made at his trial, in response to accusations of impiety and the corruption of the youth of Athens.

It has three parts. The first is Socrates' speech in his own defense. Socrates was unsuccessful, and the jury voted to convict him. The second speech is Socrates' proposal for what his punishment should be (see the general introduction for more information on Athenian trial procedures). In this he also fails to persuade the jury, and he is sentenced to death. The final speech—which would not have been part of the court procedure—comprises Socrates' reflections to his friends before he is led off to await his execution.

Cast of Characters

Anaxagoras of Clazomenae: A precursor of Socrates (he died in about 428 BCE), Anaxagoras was born in the area that is modern-day Turkey and is sometimes credited with being the first person to bring philosophy to Athens. He developed a sophisticated cosmology—which in some ways was the distant ancestor of modern atomic theory—and for his pains he was tried for impiety and forced into exile.

Anytus: One of Socrates' prosecutors. A wealthy democrat, he had been a not-very-successful general during the wars with Sparta and had escaped punishment for his failures by bribing the courts. He hated the Sophists and, probably influenced by Aristophanes' play *Clouds* (originally produced in 423 BCE), associated Socrates with them.

Apollodorus of Phaleron: A volatile, aggressively loyal, and wealthy man who was another prominent student of Socrates. He is not portrayed as an independent thinker but as someone who uncritically and fervently accepted Socrates' views.

Chaerephon: A charismatic, impetuous, popular "man about town" or socialite, Chaerephon is mentioned (unflatteringly) in no fewer than three of Aristophanes' comedies. Both Aristophanes and Xenophon describe him as one of Socrates' closest companions, and he appears in three Platonic dialogues.

Crito: By the end of Socrates' life, Crito was his most loyal and closest friend. He was about Socrates' age and grew up with him in the same deme. However, he is portrayed in contemporary accounts as being more pragmatically than philosophically inclined.

Critobulus: Crito's eldest son and, like his father, a wealthy farmer rather than a philosopher.

Gorgias: Nicknamed "the nihilist," Gorgias was a prominent Sophist from Sicily who settled in Athens as an old man and became extremely popular and in great demand as a teacher of wealthy young men. When he died he was rich enough to commission a gold statue of himself for a public temple.

Lycon: Little is known about Lycon, Socrates' third accuser, although he is referred to as "an orator," perhaps implying a politician who uses his skill with rhetoric to influence the democratic masses in order to gain power and fame for himself. If so, Socrates and he would have been natural enemies.

Meletus: The main presenter of the case against Socrates. He was a fairly young man and a religious zealot who had previously been involved in bringing legal charges of impiety.

Apology

17a How you were affected, men of Athens,[1] by my accusers, I do not know. But I, even I myself almost forgot who I was because of them, so persuasively did they speak. And yet they have said practically

1 *men of Athens* The proper form of address is "judges" or "gentlemen of the jury," which Socrates uses later. (See 40a.)

nothing true. I was especially amazed by one of the many lies they told, the one in which they said that you should take care not to be deceived by me because I am a skilled speaker. Their lack of shame— b
since they will be exposed immediately by what I do, when I show myself not to be a clever speaker at all—this seems to me to be most disgraceful of them. Unless of course they mean to call "clever" someone who speaks the truth. Because if they mean this, then I would indeed admit—not in the way they do—that I am an orator.

So, as I say, these men have said little or nothing that is true, whereas from me you will hear the whole truth. Not, by Zeus, beautified speeches like theirs, men of Athens, and not ornamented with fine c
phrases and words, but you will hear me say the words that come to me spoken at random—for I believe what I say is just—and let none of you expect otherwise. After all, it would surely not be fitting, gentlemen, for someone of my age to come before you composing speeches, as it might be for a young man. And this most of all, men of Athens, I beg and request of you: if in these speeches you hear me defending myself in the language I also typically use in the marketplace by the tables, where many of you have heard me, as well as elsewhere, don't be surprised and don't make a disturbance because of it. Because this is ex- d
actly how it is: I have now come before the court for the first time, at seventy[1] years of age. So I am simply a stranger to the manner of speech here. And so, just as you would certainly have sympathy for me if I actually happened to be a stranger and spoke in the accent and manner in which I had been raised, I now particularly ask you for this just request, 18a
at least as it seems to me, to disregard my manner of speech—maybe it's better, maybe it's worse—and to consider only the following and pay attention to it: whether I say just things or not. For this is the virtue of a judge, while of an orator it is to speak the truth.

It is right for me to defend myself, men of Athens, first against the earliest untrue accusations made against me and the earliest accusers, and then against the later accusations and the later accusers. For many b
of my accusers came to you many years ago now, saying nothing true, and I fear these more than Anytus and his friends,[2] though indeed they are dangerous too. But these men are more dangerous, gentlemen, the

---

1 *seventy* The year is 399 BCE, which puts Socrates' birth at 469 BCE. Other references to Socrates' age are made by him at 17c, 25d, 34e, 37d, *Crito* 43b, 49a, 52e.

2 *Anytus and his friends* His friends were Meletus and Lycon; the three of them were prosecuting. The leader of the prosecution was Meletus, a young man who probably held a grudge against Socrates; Anytus hated the Sophists and probably regarded Socrates as one of them; Lycon was a rhetorician. Anytus is mentioned in particular because he was the most politically influential of these, having played an important part in the restoration of Athenian democracy.

ones who, taking most of you aside from childhood, influenced you and made accusations against me that are not in fact true: that there is a certain Socrates, a clever man, a student of things in the sky who has investigated everything under the earth, and who makes the weaker
c speech the stronger. These people, men of Athens, having spread this allegation, are my fearsome accusers, for those who have heard them think that the people who study these things do not acknowledge the gods either. Moreover, these accusers are numerous and have been making accusations for a long time now. And what's more, they spoke to you at an age when you would be liable to believe them—some of you being children and youths—crudely making accusations against an absent person with no one else to make a rebuttal.

d What is most unreasonable is that one can't know and name the names of these people, except if one happens to be a comic playwright.[1] These people who misled you with envy and slander—and others who, having themselves been persuaded, then persuade others—all of these are hardest to deal with. For it is not possible to summon them here to court or to cross-examine any of them, but it is necessary to defend myself just as if shadow-boxing, and conduct a cross-examination without anyone responding. So you too must accept that my accusers are twofold, as I said, those who accused me re-
e cently and those whom I mentioned from long ago, and believe that I must first defend myself against the latter. For you heard their accusations against me earlier and much more often than those of the later people.

Well then. I must make a defense, men of Athens, and in such a
19a short time must try to banish this prejudice from you that you have held for a long time. I would like it to turn out this way—that I will succeed in defending myself—if that would be better for both you and me. But I think this is difficult, and just what it is I'm attempting doesn't escape me at all. Nevertheless, let the case proceed in whatever way the god favors; I must obey the law and make my defense.

Let us consider, then, from the beginning, what the accusation is,
b from which the prejudice against me arose that Meletus believed when he brought this charge against me. Well then. What precisely did the accusers say when they accused me? Just as if they were charging me, it is necessary to read out their indictment: "Socrates is guilty of med-

---

1 *a comic playwright* In his play *Clouds* of 423, Aristophanes had portrayed a Socrates who was head of a "Thinkery" of students engaged in natural science and cosmological speculation, as well as in argumentation. Aristophanes is named in 19c. His caricature of Socrates seems to combine two types: the natural scientist and the sophist.

dling, of inquiring into things under the earth and in the heavens, of
making the weaker speech the stronger, and of teaching these very c
things"—something like this. For even you yourselves have seen these
things in the comedy of Aristophanes, a certain Socrates being carried
around up there,[1] insisting that he walks on air and spouting off a lot
of other nonsense that I do not claim to know anything about, either
great or small. I don't speak in order to dishonor such knowledge, if
someone is wise about such things—I hope I am not somehow prose-
cuted by Meletus on such great charges—but in fact I have nothing to
do with them, men of Athens, and I call on the majority of you as wit-
nesses, and I expect you to teach and inform one another, those of you d
who have ever heard me in conversation—and this includes many of
you. Tell one another if any of you heard me ever discussing such
things, either a lot or a little. And from this you will realize that the
same is true of the other things that the many say about me.

But in fact none of them is the case. And indeed, if you have heard
from anyone that I endeavor to teach people and make money, this is e
not true. Though again, I think that it is a fine thing if an individual is
able to teach people,[2] such as Gorgias of Leontini and Prodicus of
Chios and Hippias of Elis. For each of these people, gentlemen, going
into each of the cities, to the young—who could associate with
whomever they want from their own citizens for free—they convince
them to leave their company and join them, paying them money, and 20a
to feel grateful besides!

For that matter, there is currently another wise man, from Paros,
whom I have discovered is in town because I happened to meet a man
who has paid more money to sophists than all the others combined,
Callias, son of Hipponicus. So I asked him—because he has two
sons—"Callias," I said, "If colts or calves had been born to you as
sons, we could find and hire a trainer who would make them well-bred b
with respect to the appropriate virtue; he would be some horse-trainer
or farmer. But as it is, since they are humans, whom do you have in
mind to hire as a trainer for them? Who is knowledgeable about such
virtue, of the human being and of the citizen? Because I assume you
have looked into it, since you have sons. Is there someone," I said, "or
not?" "Certainly," said he. "Who?" I said, "and where from? And for
how much does he teach?" "Evenus, Socrates," he said, "from Paros,

---

1 *Socrates being carried around up there* In the play, the satire of Socrates' desire to inquire into higher things is given physical form through the depiction of Socrates in a hanging basket.

2 *able to teach people* All three individuals named are sophists (20a).

for five mina."[1] And I considered Evenus blessed, if he really has this
c skill and teaches for such a sweet-sounding price. I at any rate would be proud of myself and be boastful, if I knew these things. But in fact I don't know them, men of Athens.

Perhaps some one of you might respond, "But Socrates, what is *your* profession? Where have these slanders against you come from? For surely it's not by busying yourself with the usual things that so much hearsay and talk has arisen, but by doing something different from most
d people. Then tell us what it is, so that we don't judge your case rashly." The person who says this seems to me to speak justly, and I will try to show you what it is, precisely, that won me this reputation and notoriety.

Listen, then. And while I will perhaps appear to some of you to be joking, rest assured that I will tell you the whole truth. For I, men of Athens, have acquired this reputation due to nothing other than a certain wisdom. What sort of wisdom is this? Quite likely it is human wisdom. There's a good chance that I actually have this kind of wis-
e dom, while those men I was speaking of just now might perhaps be wise with a wisdom more than human—or I don't know how I should put it, for I certainly don't have it, and whoever says so is lying and is saying it to slander me. But don't interrupt me, men of Athens, not even if I strike you as talking big. The story I will tell you is not my own, but I will refer you to a trustworthy source for what I say, because regarding whether it is wisdom of a sort and of what sort it is I will present to you as my witness the god in Delphi.[2]

21a You know Chaerephon, I presume. He was a companion of mine from youth and a comrade of yours in the democracy and joined you in the recent exile[3] and returned with you. And you know how Chaerephon was, how zealous he was about whatever he pursued, and so for example when he went to Delphi he was so bold as to ask this—and, as I say, don't interrupt, gentlemen—he asked if there was anyone wiser than me. The Pythia then replied that no one was wiser. And his brother here will bear witness to you about these things, since he himself has died.

---

1 *five mina* (See also 38b for "a mina of silver.") A mina was 100 silver drachmas (see 26e, 36b), and a drachma was equivalent to 6 obols. Daily earnings ranged from 2 to 6 obols. Admission to the theater was 2 obols. Pay for being a judge (jury duty) was 2 obols.

2 *the god in Delphi* At Delphi one could ask questions of the god Apollo via his oracle, a priestess known as the Pythia.

3 *in the democracy ... the recent exile* Athens was subject to violent political turmoil between rival factions who wanted to restrict the ruling positions to a small number (oligarchs) or broaden it to more (democrats). See also 32c. For details of the exile and return, see the Introduction, pp. 14–16.

Think about why I am bringing this up: it's because I'm going to b
teach you where the prejudice against me came from. Because when
I heard this I pondered in the following way: "Whatever does the god
mean? And what riddle is he posing? For I am not aware of being wise
in anything great or small. What in the world does he mean, then, when
he says that I am wisest? For certainly he does not lie; he is not per-
mitted to." And for a long time I puzzled over his meaning.

Then, very reluctantly, I embarked on a sort of trial of him. I went
to one of the people who are thought to be wise, hoping to refute the
oracle there if anywhere, and reply to its pronouncement: "This man c
here is wiser than me, though you said I was." So, scrutinizing this
fellow—there's no need to refer to him by name; he was one of the
politicians I had this sort of experience with when I examined him,
men of Athens—in talking with him it seemed to me that while this
man was considered to be wise both by many other people and espe-
cially by himself, he was not. And so I tried to show him that he took
himself to be wise, but was not. As a result I became hated by this man d
and by many of those present.

And so, as I was going away, I was thinking to myself, "I am at least
wiser than this man. It's likely that neither of us knows anything worth-
while, but whereas he thinks he knows something when he doesn't know
it, I, when I don't know something, don't think I know it either. It's likely,
then, that by this I am indeed wiser than him in some small way, that I
don't think myself to know what I don't know." Next, I went to another
one of the people thought to be wiser than him and things seemed the same e
to me, and so I made an enemy of that man as well as of many others.

So, after this, I now went to one after another, realizing with pain
and fear that I was becoming hated. But nevertheless I thought it nec-
essary to consider the god's oracle to be of the utmost importance, so
I had to continue going to all of the people thought to know something,
investigating the meaning of the oracle. And by the dog, men of Athens,
because I must tell you the truth, my experience was really something 22a
like the following: in my divine search those held in highest esteem
seemed to me to be lacking just about the most, while others thought to
be poorer were better men as far as wisdom is concerned.

I have to represent my wanderings to you as though I were under-
taking various labors[1] only to find that the oracle was quite irrefutable.
After the politicians I went to the poets, including those of tragedies
and those of dithyrambs[2] and others, so that there I would catch my- b

---

1 *labors* Alluding to the labors of Heracles, a series of difficult tasks the mythological hero performed as penance.

2 *dithyrambs* Hymns to the god Dionysus, sung by a chorus.

self being more ignorant than them. Reading the works which I thought they had really labored over, I would ask them what they meant, so that at the same time I might also learn something from them. I am ashamed to tell you the truth, gentlemen, but nevertheless it must be told. Practically anybody present, so to speak, could have better explained what they had written. And so, as before, I quickly re-
c alized the following about the poets: that they do not write what they write because of their wisdom but because they have a certain nature and are possessed, like the seers and fortune-tellers, who also say many fine things but know nothing about what they're saying. It seemed clear to me that the poets had had a similar experience. And at once I understood that, because of their writing, they thought themselves to be the wisest of all men even about other things, but they weren't. And so I departed from them thinking that I was superior to them in the same way as I was to the politicians.

So finally I went to the crafters, because I was aware that while I
d knew practically nothing, I knew that I would find that they knew many fine things. And in this I was not mistaken—they knew things I didn't and in this they were wiser than me. But, men of Athens, the noble crafters seemed to me to have the same flaw that the poets also had. Because each of them performed his craft well, he considered himself to be most wise about the greatest things—and this sour note
e of theirs overshadowed their wisdom. And so I asked myself on behalf of the oracle whether I would prefer to be just as I am—neither being at all wise in the ways that they are wise nor ignorant in the ways they are ignorant—or to be both, as they are. And I answered myself and the oracle that it would be best for me to be as I am.

23a As a result of this quest, men of Athens, a lot of hatred developed against me, and of the most difficult and oppressive kind, such that from it many slanders arose, and I gained this reputation for being wise. For on each occasion the bystanders thought that I myself was wise about the subject on which I was examining the other person. But in fact it's likely, gentlemen, that in truth the god is wise, and by this pronouncement he means the following: that
b human wisdom is worth little or nothing. And he appears to be using me as an example, speaking of this man Socrates and even using my name, just as if he said, "Human beings, he among you is wisest who knows like Socrates that he is actually worthless with respect to wisdom." That's why, both then and now, I go around in accordance with the god, searching and making inquiries of anyone, citizen or stranger, whom I think to be wise. And if I then learn that he isn't, I assist the god and show him that he is not wise. And because of this busyness I lack the time to participate in any public

affairs worth mentioning or any private business, but I am in great
poverty because of my service to the god.[1] c

Furthermore, the young people follow me around of their own ac-
cord, those with the most leisure, the sons of the very wealthy. They
delight in hearing me examine people and they often imitate me, hav-
ing a go at examining others afterwards. And, I think, they discover a
great number of people who think they know something but know lit-
tle or nothing. As a result, the people who are examined by them then
grow angry with me, but not themselves, and they say that Socrates is d
a most vile person and corrupts the young. And whenever anyone asks
them, "By doing what and by teaching what?," they have nothing to
say and do not know, but, so as to not appear at a loss, they say these
things that are handy against all philosophers, about "the heavenly
things and the things under the earth" and "not acknowledging the
gods" and "making the weaker speech the stronger." I believe it's be-
cause they don't want to tell the truth, that they are obviously pre-
tending to know something even though they know nothing. Since e
they are ambitious and impetuous, I think, and there are many of them
and they speak about me ruthlessly and persuasively, they have filled
up your ears, badmouthing me violently for a long time. On the
strength of this, Meletus attacked me along with Anytus and Lycon,
Meletus complaining on behalf of the writers, Anytus on behalf of the
crafters and the politicians, and Lycon on behalf of the orators. 24a

And so, as I said in the beginning, I would be amazed if I could rid
you of this slander in such a short time, since it has become so pow-
erful. This, I assure you, men of Athens, is the truth, and in speaking
I conceal nothing, either big or small, nor hold anything back. Indeed
I am quite aware that I am hated on account of these very things, which
is an indication that I tell the truth, and that this is the slander against
me and that these are the causes. And if you inquire into these things,
either now or later, this is what you'll find. b

Concerning the charges of my initial accusers, let this defense be-
fore you be enough. Next I will try to defend myself against Meletus,
the good and patriotic man, as he says, and the later accusers. And
once more, as though they are different accusers, let's take up their in-
dictment in turn. It goes something like this: he says Socrates is guilty
of corrupting the young and not acknowledging the gods that the city
does, but other strange spiritual things. The complaint is something c
along these lines. Let's examine this complaint point by point.

---

1 *I am in great poverty ... to the god* The five mina charged by Evenus of Paros to teach a single student, mentioned above, is about equal to the total value of Socrates' worldly possessions, according to his contemporary Xenophon (*Oeconomicus* 2.3).

He says that I am guilty of corrupting the young. But I say, men of Athens, that Meletus is guilty, that he jokes in earnest, carelessly bringing a person to trial, pretending to be serious about and to trouble himself over various matters, none of which was ever an interest of his. This is how it is, as I will try to demonstrate.

d Socrates: Here, Meletus, do tell me: don't you take making the young as good as possible to be your highest priority?

Meletus: I certainly do.

Socrates: Come now, tell these men, who makes them better? It's clear that you know. It's certainly a concern of yours, since upon discovering the one who corrupts them—me, as you claim—you bring me in front of these people here and accuse me. Come, state who is the one who makes them better and reveal to them who it is.... You see, Meletus, that you are silent and unable to speak? Doesn't it seem shameful to you, and sufficient proof of exactly what I'm claiming, that it meant nothing to you? So tell us, my good man, who makes them better?

Meletus: The laws.

e Socrates: But that's not what I'm asking, best of men, but what man, whoever knows this very thing—the laws—in the first place?

Meletus: These men, Socrates, the judges.

Socrates: What do you mean, Meletus? These men can educate the young and make them better?

Meletus: Definitely.

Socrates: All of them, or some can and others can't?

Meletus: All of them.

Socrates: Well done, by Hera! And what a great number of benefactors
25a you speak of. What next? Do these listeners[1] make them better or not?

Meletus: These too.

---

1 *these listeners* Those attending Socrates' trial; ordinary Athenian citizens.

Socrates: Who else? The councilors?

Meletus: The councilors too.

Socrates: Well then, Meletus, surely those in the assembly, the assemblymen, they don't corrupt the young people? So do they all make them better, too?

Meletus: These too.

Socrates: Every Athenian, it seems, makes them fine and good except for me, and I alone corrupt them. Is this what you mean?

Meletus: That's exactly what I mean.

Socrates: You charge me with a great misfortune. But answer me: do
you think it's like this with horses? That everyone makes them better, b
while one person is their corrupter? Or isn't it the complete opposite of this: one individual can make them better—or very few, the horse-trainers—while the many corrupt the horses if they deal with them and use them? Isn't this how it is, Meletus, concerning both horses and every other animal? ... It certainly is, whether you and Anytus agree or disagree. It would be a great blessing for the young if only a single person corrupted them, and all the others benefited them. But, Mele-
tus, you have sufficiently demonstrated that you never before cared c
about the young, and you clearly reveal your indifference in that you have given no thought at all to the matters you indict me on.

Still, before Zeus, Meletus, tell us whether it is better to live among good citizens or wicked ones? ... Answer, my good man—I'm not asking anything difficult, you know. Don't the wicked always do something bad to those who are constantly closest to them, while the good do something good?

Meletus: Certainly.

Socrates: But is there anyone who wishes to be harmed by those he as- d
sociates with rather than to be helped? ... Keep answering, my good man, for the law also requires you to answer. Is there anyone who wants to be harmed?

Meletus: Of course not.

Socrates: Come then, do you bring me here on charges of intentionally or unintentionally corrupting the young and making them worse?

Meletus: Intentionally, I say.

Socrates: What then, Meletus? Are you so much wiser at your age than I am at mine that you know that the wicked always do something bad
e to those who are very close to them, and the good do good, while I, on the other hand, have fallen into such great ignorance that I don't also know this—that if I make one of my associates bad, I risk being harmed by him? And so I would do this great evil intentionally, as you claim?

I don't believe you, Meletus, and I think that no one else does. And
26a either I do not corrupt, or if I do corrupt, I do so unintentionally, and so you are lying either way. If I corrupt unintentionally, the procedure is not to prosecute me here for such offenses, but to take me aside privately and teach and admonish me, since it is clear that if I learn, I will cease doing what I do unintentionally. You, however, fled from me and were unwilling to associate with me and teach me, but prosecuted me here, where the procedure is to prosecute those who need punishment rather than instruction.

And so, men of Athens, what I was saying is now clear, that Mele-
b tus never troubled himself about these matters in the slightest.

Nevertheless, tell us, Meletus, how do I corrupt the young, according to you? Or rather, isn't it clear from the indictment you wrote that I corrupt them by teaching them not to acknowledge the gods that the city recognizes, but other strange spiritual things? Don't you say that I corrupt them by teaching these things?

Meletus: That's absolutely what I'm saying.

c Socrates: But by the gods, Meletus, the very gods that the discussion is currently about, speak even more clearly to me and these people here, because I can't tell whether you mean that I teach the young to believe that there are some gods—and so I believe there are gods and am not entirely godless nor guilty of this—not, however, the gods that the city believes in but others, and this is what you prosecute me for, that they are different, or, whether you mean that I do not acknowledge gods at all, and teach this to others?

Meletus: That's what I mean, that you don't acknowledge the gods at all.

d Socrates: Incredible Meletus, why do you say that? I don't believe the sun, or even the moon, to be gods,[1] like other men do?

---

1 *I don't believe ... to be gods* Sun and moon worship were common in Greece.

Meletus: No, by Zeus, judges, since he says that the sun is a stone and the moon is earth.

Socrates: Do you think you are prosecuting Anaxagoras, my dear
Meletus? Do you have so much contempt for these men, and think
them to be so unfamiliar with literature that they do not know that the
books of Anaxagoras of Clazomenae are full of such claims? And
what's more, do you think that the young learn these things from me,
which they can buy sometimes for a drachma, at most, on the floor of e
the agora and can mock Socrates for, if he pretends they are his, es-
pecially when they are so distinctive? By Zeus, is this how I appear to
you? Believing that there are no gods?

Meletus: You certainly don't, by Zeus; none whatsoever.

Socrates: You are unbelievable, Meletus, and are so even to yourself,
I think. For the man seems to me, men of Athens, to be exceedingly ar-
rogant and uncontrolled, and clumsily lodged this indictment out of
hubris and lack of discipline and youthful zeal. He appears to be test-
ing me, as though setting a riddle: "Will the wise Socrates realize that 27a
I am being facetious and contradicting myself, or will I deceive him
and the other listeners?" For it looks to me as though he is saying con-
tradictory things in his indictment, just as if he said "Socrates is guilty
of not acknowledging the gods, and of acknowledging the gods." This
is just like a riddler.

Now join me in examining, gentlemen, in what way he seems to
be saying these things. And you, Meletus, answer us. And as I begged b
of you all at the beginning, remember not to interrupt if I speak in my
customary way.

Is there anyone, Meletus, who believes there are human matters,
but does not believe in humans? ... Gentlemen, make him answer and
not digress about other things. Is there anyone who does not believe
there are horses, but believes there are equestrian matters? Or that there
are not flute-players but there are flute-playing matters? ... There is
not, best of men—since you are unwilling to answer I will answer on
behalf of you and these others. But at least answer the next question:
Is there anyone who believes there are spiritual matters but does not c
believe there are spirits?

Meletus: There is not.

Socrates: How delightful, that you answered reluctantly when compelled by these men. And so you say that I acknowledge and teach

about spirits, and whether they be novel or old I at any rate believe in
spiritual matters, according to your accusation, and you even swear
this in the indictment. But if I believe in spiritual matters, surely it is
unavoidably necessary that I believe in spirits too. Isn't that so? ... Of
course it is. I take it that you agree, since you're not answering. Now,
d don't we think the spirits are either gods or the children of gods? Do
you agree or not?

Meletus: Yes indeed.

Socrates: Well then, since I believe in spirits, as you say, then if, on the one hand, the spirits are gods of some sort, this would be what I am claiming you are riddling and being facetious about, saying that while I don't believe in gods, at the same time again I do believe in gods, since I indeed believe in spirits.

If, on the other hand, the spirits are certain illegitimate children of
gods—either by nymphs or by some others that they're said to come
from—who among men would think the children of gods exist, but
e not gods? Similarly, it would be strange if someone believed in the
children of horses, or of asses too, namely mules, but did not believe
in horses and asses.

And so, Meletus, it must be that you brought this indictment in
order to test us about these things, or were at a loss as to what true
crime you might charge me with. How you could persuade anyone
with even a little intelligence that the same man does not believe in
28a both spiritual and divine matters, or again, that this same man believes
in neither spirits nor gods nor heroes—it's not possible!

And so, men of Athens, it seems to me that it doesn't take much of
a defense to show I am not guilty of what Meletus charges me with,
and even this is enough. What I said earlier, on the other hand—that I
incurred a great hatred and from many people—you know well to be
true. This is what convicts me, if indeed it convicts me, and not Mele-
tus or Anytus, but the slander and malice of many people. And I know
that these people have convicted, and will convict, many other good
b men; there is no fear that they will stop with me.

Perhaps then someone might say, "Aren't you ashamed, Socrates,
that you engaged in the kind of practice that now places you at risk of
dying?" In reply to this I would justly say, "You do not speak well, Sir,
if you think a man who is worth anything should take the risk of liv-
ing or dying into account, rather than looking only to this: whether
when he acts he acts justly or unjustly, and does the deeds of a good
c man or a bad one." For those demigods who met their ends in Troy

would be fools according to you, especially the son of Thetis,[1] who
thought so little of the risk in comparison with enduring some disgrace
that, when his mother, a god, told him, when he was eager to kill Hec-
tor, something like this, as I recall: "Son, if you avenge the slaying of
your comrade Patroclus[2] and kill Hector, you will be killed—because
immediately after Hector," she said, "your fate is at hand"; he, hear-
ing this, belittled death and the danger and feared much more living as d
a coward and not avenging his friends. He said, "May I die at once,
having served justice to the unjust, and not remain here, a laughing
stock by the curved ships, a burden upon the Earth." Do you think he
cared about death or danger?

This is how it is, men of Athens, in reality. Wherever someone po-
sitions himself, thinking it to be for the best, or is positioned by his
commander, he must, it seems to me, remain there and face the dan-
ger, and not put death or anything else ahead of disgrace. I would have
done a terrible thing, men of Athens, if, when positioned by the offi- e
cers, those whom you elected to command me at Potideia and Am-
phipolis and Delium,[3] I remained where these men stationed me and
risked dying, just like anyone else, but when stationed by the god, as
I believed and accepted—required to live my life seeking wisdom and
examining both myself and others—I had abandoned my station for 29a
fear of death or anything else. That would be terrible, and truly under
such circumstances someone could justly bring me to court for not be-
lieving that there are gods, defying the oracle and fearing death and
thinking myself to be wise when I am not.

Indeed, to fear death, gentlemen, is nothing other than to regard
oneself as wise when one is not; for it is to regard oneself as knowing
what one does not know. No one knows whether death is not the great-
est of all the goods for man, but they fear it as if they knew it to be the
greatest of evils. And indeed, how could this ignorance not be re- b
proachable, the ignorance of believing one knows what one does not
know? But I, gentlemen, am perhaps superior to the majority of men
to this extent and in this regard, and if indeed I seem to be wiser in
any way than anyone, it would be in this, that I am not so certain about
how things are in Hades and I do not think that I know.

---

1 *son of Thetis* The son of Thetis is Achilles. His reply to his mother's prophecy is from *Iliad* 18.98.

2 *Hector ... Patroclus* In the *Iliad*, Hector is a prince of Troy who kills Achilles' comrade, Patroclus, in battle.

3 *Potideia and Amphipolis and Delium* Part of the Peloponnesian War (431–404 BCE) between the Athenian empire and a league led by Sparta, these were battles in which Socrates fought as a citizen-soldier.

But wrongdoing and defiance of one's superiors, whether god or
man, *that* I know to be evil and shameful. So I will never fear nor flee
things that for all I know could turn out to be good, rather than the evils
c that I know to be evil. So if you now acquitted me—rejecting Anytus,
who said that either I should not have been brought here to trial in the
first place, or, now that I have, executing me is unavoidable, and who
tells you that if I were acquitted, your sons, practicing what Socrates
teaches, will at once be thoroughly corrupted—if, referring to this, you
said to me, "Socrates, we are not at present persuaded by Anytus and we
acquit you but on the following condition, namely that you no longer
spend your time on this quest and search for wisdom, and that if you are
d caught still doing this, you will die"—if, as I was saying, you were to ac-
quit me on these conditions, I would say to you, "I cherish and love you,
men of Athens, but I am more obedient to the god than to you, and so
long as I have breath and am able I will not cease seeking wisdom and
appealing and demonstrating to every one of you I come across, saying
my customary things: Best of men, you are an Athenian, of the greatest
and most renowned city in regard to wisdom and power. Are you not
ashamed that you care about how you will acquire as much money as
e possible, and reputation and honor, while you do not care or worry about
wisdom and truth and how your soul might be as good as possible?"

And if one of you disputes this and says that he does care, right
away I will not let him go or leave him but will question and cross-ex-
amine and refute him, and if he does not appear to possess virtue, but
30a he says he does, I will reproach him for considering the most valuable
things to be of the least importance and the most worthless to be of the
greatest importance. I will do this for anyone I meet, young and old,
stranger and citizen, though more for the citizens, insofar as they are
closer to me in blood.

Rest assured that the god commands this, and I believe there has
never been a greater good for the city than my service to the god. For
I go around doing nothing other than persuading you, both young and
b old, not to care for your wealth and your bodies ahead of, or as in-
tensely as, caring for how your soul might be as good as possible, say-
ing that virtue does not come from wealth, but from virtue come
wealth and all other human goods, both private and public. So if I cor-
rupt the young by saying these things, they would be harmful; but if
anyone claims that I say anything different from this, he is talking non-
sense. "Men of Athens," I would say, "either be persuaded by Anytus
or not, or acquit me or not, in light of the fact that I would not act dif-
c ferently, not even if I am destined to die again and again."

Do not create a disturbance, men of Athens, but keep to what I
begged of you, not to make a disturbance at what I say and to listen,

since I think by listening you might even be helped. For I am about to
say a few other things to you at which you will perhaps cry out; but
don't do this, no matter what. Rest assured that if you kill me for being
the kind of person I describe, you will not harm me more than your-
selves. Neither Meletus nor Anytus can do me any harm; it is not pos-
sible, since I think it is not permitted[1] for a better man to be harmed by d
a worse one. Perhaps he will kill or exile or disenfranchise me, but
while he and many others probably think that these are somehow great
evils, I do not. It is a much greater evil to do what this man here is
doing at this moment, attempting to put a man to death unjustly.

Indeed, men of Athens, I am making a defense hardly at all for my
own sake, as one might suppose, but for yours, so you will not com-
mit a wrong concerning the god's gift to you by condemning me. If e
you were to execute me you would not easily find another person like
me, who is—although it is rather funny to say—attached to the city by
the god just as though to a great and noble horse that's somewhat slug-
gish because of its size and needs to be provoked by a gadfly.[2] This is
just the way, I think, the god attached me to the city, the sort of per-
son who never ceases provoking you and persuading you and re-
proaching each one of you the whole day long everywhere I settle. 31a
You won't easily get another person like this, gentlemen, and if you
are persuaded by me, you will spare me. Or, being annoyed just like
people roused from sleep, you might perhaps swat me, and persuaded
by Anytus would put me to death without a second thought. And then
you could live out your days in slumber, unless out of his concern for
you the god sends you someone else.

You can tell from the following that I am the kind of person who
is given by the god to the city: it is not human to disregard all my af- b
fairs and to endure the neglect of my household for so many years now
but always be acting for your sake, going to each person privately just
like a father or elder brother, urging you to pay attention to virtue. If
I had gained something from these actions and received payment for
inciting you in this way, they would make some sense. But you your-
selves see now that my accusers, while so shameless in every other
charge, lacked the audacity to present a witness to the effect that I ever c
charged anyone a fee or asked for one. For I believe I provide ade-
quate witness that I am telling the truth: my poverty.

Perhaps it might be thought strange that I go around giving advice and getting myself involved privately, while I do not dare go to our as-

1 *not permitted* In the sense of being impossible—roughly, perhaps, a less wise person can't force someone who is wiser than them to become less wise.

2 *gadfly* A fly that bites livestock, such as a horse fly.

sembly to advise the city publicly. The reason for this is something
d you have heard me say often and in many places: that something di-
vine and spiritual comes to me, which Meletus jokingly included in
the indictment. This has been coming to me as a kind of voice, begin-
ning in childhood, and, whenever it comes, it always diverts me from
what I am about to do but never toward anything. This is what pre-
vented me from doing anything political, and I think it was entirely
right to oppose me. Rest assured, men of Athens, if long ago I had
tried my hand at political matters, long ago I would have perished and
e benefited neither you nor myself. And do not be offended by my
telling the truth; there is no man who could save himself from you or
any other populace while honestly opposing you and preventing many
32a unjust and unlawful things from happening in the city. Rather, some-
one who genuinely fights for what is just, if he wishes to survive even
for a short time, must act privately and not engage in public life.

I will provide you with ample evidence for this—not words, but
what you admire, deeds. Listen to what happened to me, so that you
may know that I did not yield to anyone, fearing death over justice,
even though I might then have lost my life by not yielding. What I will
b relate is tiresome and lawyerly, but true. I, men of Athens, never held
any office in the city apart from being on the council. And it so hap-
pened that our tribe, Antiochis, was presiding when you resolved to try
as a group—contrary to law, as you all came to realize later—the ten
generals[1] who did not rescue the people forsaken in the naval battle.
At that time I alone of the committee members was opposed to you
doing anything contrary to the laws and I voted against it. With the
orators ready to indict and arrest me, and you inciting them and rais-
c ing a ruckus, I thought it more important for me to risk everything with
law and justice on my side than to side with you for fear of imprison-
ment or death, when you were contemplating unjust actions.

This was when the city was still a democracy. But again, when the
oligarchy came to power, the Thirty summoned me and four others
into the Rotunda and ordered us to bring Leon the Salaminian[2] from

1 *the ten generals* After the successful battle of Arginusae (406 BCE), the Athenian generals tasked with retrieving survivors at sea were unable to do so because of a violent storm. Many Athenians were outraged, and the generals were tried as a group and sentenced to death. Socrates opposed the decision on the grounds that Athenian law prohibited a group trial for those accused of a capital crime.

2 *Leon the Salaminian* Leon was an Athenian commander and war hero. The Rotunda or town hall was the home of the presidents of the council and assembly, which had been taken over by the tyrants. Its occupants were fed meals at the public expense (see 36d below, where Socrates proposes this be his penalty for being convicted).

Salamis for execution; they made many such demands of a lot of other
people, in order to tarnish as many as possible with their guilt. Then
once again I demonstrated, not in speech but in action, that I couldn't d
care less about death, if it's not too crude to put it that way, but I care
the world about this: that I avoid doing anything unjust or unholy. That
regime did not intimidate me into doing something unjust, even though
it was so powerful. And so when we exited the Rotunda, the other four
left for Salamis and brought back Leon, but I left and headed home.
And I might have been put to death for this, if the regime had not been
overthrown soon after. There are many who will bear witness to these e
events before you.

Do you think I would have lasted for so many years if I had en-
gaged in politics and, acting in the manner worthy of a good man, I
came to the aid of the just decisions and rightly made them my utmost
concern? Far from it, men of Athens, and neither would any other man.
Throughout my whole life, I have shown myself to be the same sort of 33a
man in public—if I did anything at all—as in private, never joining
anyone in anything illegal—neither those whom they say—slander-
ing me—are my students, nor anyone else.

I have never been anyone's teacher, but if anybody desired to lis-
ten to me talking and fulfilling my mission, whether young or old, I
never rejected anyone. Nor do I converse if I receive money but refuse b
to if I don't, but I allow rich and poor alike to question me, and like-
wise if anyone wishes to hear whatever I have to say in reply. And if
any of them turn out to be good, or not good, I cannot justly be held
responsible, since I never promised any instruction to any of them nor
did I teach them. And if someone says that he learned anything from
me or heard privately something all the others did not hear, rest as-
sured that he is not speaking the truth.

But why then do people enjoy spending a lot of time with me? You c
have heard why, men of Athens—I told you the whole truth. It is be-
cause they enjoy hearing me expose those who think themselves wise
but are not, for it is not unpleasant. I was commanded to do this, as I
say, by the god, both in oracles and dreams and in every way that any
divine fate at all ever ordered a man to do anything whatsoever. This
is the truth, men of Athens, and easily tested. Because if I am indeed
corrupting some of the young and have corrupted others, then surely d
if any of them realized when they were older that I recommended
something evil at some point when they were young, they should have
come forward just now to accuse me and avenge themselves. If they
themselves were reluctant, someone from their family—a father or
brother or some other relative—should call it to mind and take re-
venge, if they ever suffered any evil at my hands.

In any case, many of them are present here, whom I can see. First
there is Crito here, who is my contemporary and from my district and
e the father of this man, Critobulus. Next there is Lysanias of Sphettus,
father of Aeschines here. Also, this here is Antiphon of Cephissos, fa-
ther of Epigenes. These others have brothers who spent their time in
this way: Nicostratus son of Theozotides, brother of Theodotus—
Theodotus who died, which means that he could not have begged him
not to testify—and Paralios here, son of Demodocus, whose brother
34a was Theages. And here is Adeimantus, son of Ariston, the brother of
Plato here, and Aeantodorus, brother of this man, Apollodorus. I have
many others I could mention to you, some of whom Meletus certainly
should have brought forth as a witness during his own presentation. If
he forgot then, let him call them now—I yield my time—and let him
speak if he has anyone of this kind.

Instead you will find the complete opposite of this, gentlemen; they
are all ready to help me, the corruptor, the one who harms their kin, as
b Meletus and Anytus claim. Those who were corrupted perhaps would
have a reason to help me. But the uncorrupted, who are already old
men and who are their relatives, do they have any other reason for
helping me except the right and just one, that they know just as well
as Meletus does that he is lying, while I tell the truth?

Well then, gentlemen. What *I* would say in my defense is this and
c maybe other similar points. One of you, perhaps, might then be angry
when he is reminded of his own conduct—if, when contesting a lesser
charge than this one, he begged and beseeched the judges with many
tears, bringing forth his children so that they would pity him even
more, with other members of his family and many friends, whereas I
will do none of this, even though I run, I might suppose, the ultimate
risk. Someone who brought this to mind might be more hard-hearted
towards me and, feeling resentful, might cast his vote in anger. If this
d is really how any of you feel—I don't expect that it is, but if so—it
seems reasonable for me to say to that person, "I, Sir, have a family,
you know, and was not born 'from oak or from rock'—this is again an
expression of Homer[1]—but from human beings, so that I have a fam-
ily too, and indeed sons, men of Athens, three of them, one already a
teenager and two who are children. But nonetheless I will not beg you
to acquit me by bringing any of them here."

So why then won't I do any of these things? Not out of stubborn-
e ness, men of Athens, nor out of disrespect for you. Whether or not I am
confident in the face of death is another story, but with respect to my
good name, and yours and the whole city's, I don't think it's right for

1 *an expression of Homer* From *Odyssey* 19.163.

me to do any of these things at my age and with my reputation. Be it
true or false, people have at any rate decided that Socrates is superior 35a
to most men in some respect, and if any of you who are reputed to be
superior in wisdom or courage or any other virtue acted like that, it
would be shameful. I have often seen people like this when they are on
trial, men of some reputation but carrying on remarkably, as though
they thought that something terrible will happen if they die, as if they
would be immortal if you did not kill them.

I think these people bring shame upon the city, so that some
stranger might think that the foremost of the Athenians in virtue, b
whom the Athenians nominate ahead of themselves for offices and
other honors, they are no better than women. Those of you who are re-
puted to be something in any way whatsoever, men of Athens, should
not do these things, and if we do them you should not permit it but be
very clear about it, that you will more readily convict a person who
puts on these miserable theatrics and makes a laughingstock of the city
than one who holds his peace.

Apart from reputation, gentlemen, I do not think it is right to beg the c
judges nor to be acquitted by begging, but to teach and persuade in-
stead. The judge does not sit for this reason—to hand out justice as a
gift—but for the purpose of judging the case. He did not swear to do
favors for whomever he feels like, but to judge according to the laws.
We should not accustom you to breaking your oath and neither should
you accustom yourselves; neither of us would then be acting piously.
Do not, then, men of Athens, expect that I should act towards you in
a way that I think is neither fine nor just nor holy, especially when, by d
Zeus, I am charged precisely with impiety by Meletus here. Clearly,
if by begging I persuaded and convinced you who had sworn an oath,
I would be teaching you to not believe that the gods exist, and in de-
fending myself I would stupidly be accusing myself of not believing
in the gods. But this is not at all how things are, since I do believe in
them, men of Athens, unlike all of my accusers. And I trust you and
the god to decide my case in whatever way you think is best both for
me and for you.

[The judges vote and Socrates is found guilty by 280 votes to 220. The next stage of the trial involves each side proposing a penalty. The prosecution proposes the death penalty. Socrates must respond with a proposal of his own.]

Many things contribute to my lack of anger, men of Athens, over what e
has just happened—that you found me guilty. And I am not surprised 36a
that what happened happened. Indeed, I am much more amazed at the

final tally of each of the votes, since I, at least, did not think the difference would be so small, but larger. It now appears that if only thirty votes had changed sides, I would have been acquitted. I myself think that I was acquitted of Meletus' charges, and not just acquitted, as it is clear to everyone that if Anytus and Lycon had not joined him in ac-
b cusing me, he would have owed a thousand drachmas for not receiving a fifth of the votes.[1]

The man proposes death as my penalty. Well then. Shall I make a counterproposal to you,[2] men of Athens? Or is it clear what I deserve? What, then? What do I deserve to suffer or pay, knowing that I have not gone about quietly throughout my life but, paying no attention to what the masses care about—money and estate and generalships and political power and other offices and clubs and political parties present in the city—and realizing that in reality I am too honorable a per-
c son to pursue these things and survive, I did not pursue the affairs that it would likely have helped neither you nor myself for me to get into, but I set out to accomplish the greatest good, as I declare, by going to each of you privately, trying to persuade each one of you not to put concern for any of his own affairs ahead of concern for how he himself might be as good and wise as possible, nor to put the affairs of the city ahead of the city itself, and to care for other things in the same
d way—what do I deserve for being such a person? Something good, men of Athens, if I must indeed make a proposal truly in accordance with merit. And more than that, some good which is fitting for me. What then is fitting for a poor man, a benefactor who needs to be at leisure to instruct you? There is nothing more fitting, men of Athens, than to feed such a man in the town hall, even more so than when one of you has won a race at Olympia[3] on a single horse or in a two- or four-horse chariot. For while he makes you think that you are happy, I make you so, and while he does not need the nourishment, I do. So if I must propose a penalty according to justice based on merit, I pro-
37a pose this: dinners in the town hall.

Perhaps in saying this I seem to be speaking to you in much the same way as I spoke about pitying and imploring—out of arrogance.

---

1 *a fifth of the votes* Because it was considered a matter of public interest to punish impiety, Socrates' accusers would not have had to pay any court fees. To discourage frivolous suits, however, Athenian law levied a substantial fine against plaintiffs who failed to obtain at least one in five of the jury's votes.

2 *Shall I make a counterproposal to you* No penalty was specified by law for some crimes, including the crime of which Socrates has been convicted. Instead, the prosecution and defendant both proposed a penalty and the jurors had to decide which of the two recommended penalties to impose.

3 *at Olympia* At the Olympic Games.

But it is not that, men of Athens, but rather because of the following sort of thing: I am convinced that I wrong no man willingly. But I cannot convince you of this, since we have been talking it over with each other for only a short time, whereas, I think, if your practice was the same as other people's, to deliberate about death penalty cases not just for one day but for many, you would be convinced. But, as it stands, b
it's not easy to demolish great prejudices in a short time.

Since I am convinced that I never do wrong, I certainly won't wrong myself and say against myself that I deserve something bad and proposing something of the sort for myself. Why should I? Because I'm afraid of something? So that I can avoid what Meletus proposes for me, when I claim not to know whether it is good or bad? Should I choose something that I am sure is something bad instead of this, and propose it as a penalty? What? Prison? And why must I live in the c
prison, enslaved to the Eleven[1] who are appointed to the office at the time? Then how about a fine, with imprisonment until I have paid it? But in my case this is the same as what I just said, since I don't have any money to pay with.

Well then, shall I propose exile? You would probably accept this. But I would have an excessive love of life, men of Athens, if I were so stupid as to be unable to see that when you, my fellow citizens, could not bear my discussions and speeches, but they became so bur- d
densome and so resented that you now seek to be free of them—would others willingly put up with them? Far from it, men of Athens. It would be a fine life for me, a man going into exile at my age, to spend my life being driven out and traipsing from one city to another. I'm quite sure that wherever I might go, the young will listen to me speak, just like here. And if I drive them away, they themselves will persuade their elders to drive me away; and if I don't drive them away, their fathers e
and relations will do so on their behalf.

Perhaps someone might say, "Can't you live quietly and peacefully in exile, Socrates, for our sake?" This is the hardest thing of all to make some of you believe. For if I say that this would be to disobey the god and so, because of this, I cannot live peacefully, you would think I was being ironic and not believe me. If instead I say that in fact this is 38a
the greatest good for a man, to talk every day about virtue and the other things you hear me converse about when I examine both myself and others, and that the unexamined life is not worth living for a man, you would believe this even less if I said it. As I say, this is how things are, gentlemen; but it is not easy to persuade you.

---

1 *the Eleven* Elected officials in charge of prisons, executions, and confiscations. See *Athenian Constitution* 52.

And besides, I am not accustomed to thinking of myself as worthy
b of anything bad. If I had money, I would have proposed as much money as I could pay, since it wouldn't have harmed me at all. But as it is I can't, unless you are willing to demand of me as much as I can pay. And perhaps I could somehow pay you a mina of silver. So I propose that amount....

Plato here, men of Athens, and Crito and Critobulus and Apollodorus, they order me to propose thirty minas, and they guarantee it. So I propose that amount, and these men will be dependable guarantors of your silver.

[The jury votes in favor of the death penalty, 360 to 140.[1]]

c Men of Athens, among those who wish to criticize the city you will gain the reputation and take the blame for putting to death Socrates, a wise man—they will say I am wise, even if I am not, those people who wish to rebuke you—for the sake of a little time, because if you had waited a short while, this would have happened for you of its own accord, since you see that I am already advanced in years and that death is near.

d I say this not to all of you, but to those who voted to execute me. And I say the following to those same people: perhaps you think, men of Athens, that I was condemned because I lacked the words that would convince you, as if I thought I must do and say everything possible to escape the charge. Far from it. I was condemned by a lack, certainly not of words, but of audacity and shamelessness and by my unwillingness to say to you what would be sweetest for you to hear—me lamenting and wailing and doing
e and saying many other things that, as I say, are unworthy of me, which you are used to hearing from other people. But I did not think at the time that I must do anything slavish on account of the danger.

Nor do I now regret how I defended myself—I would much rather choose to die having made this kind of defense than live having made
39a the other kind. Neither on trial nor in war should I or anyone else contrive to avoid death by doing everything possible. Indeed, in battles it often becomes clear that a man could escape death by throwing aside his arms and begging his pursuers for mercy, and there are many other ways of fleeing death in each dangerous situation, provided one has the shamelessness to do and say anything.

---

1 *360 to 140* Notice that this is a larger majority in favor of the death penalty than the original vote to convict.

It's not that it's not difficult to escape death, gentlemen, but it's
much harder to escape wickedness, since it runs faster than death.
And now, because I am a slow old man, I am being overtaken by the b
slower of the two, and my accusers, because they are clever and
keen, by the swifter, by evil. And I am going away now, having
been condemned to death by you, while they have been condemned
by the truth to depravity and injustice. And both I and they will keep
to our punishment. Perhaps this is how it had to be, and I suppose
it's appropriate.

Next, I want to foretell the future to you my condemners, since I c
am now at the moment when men especially prophesy: whenever
they are about to die. I declare that retribution will come to you
swiftly after my death, you men who have killed me, and more trou-
blesome, by Zeus, than the retribution you took when you sentenced
me to die. You have done this just now by trying to avoid giving an
account of your life, but I think the complete opposite will happen:
you will have more prosecutors—whom I was holding back until d
now, though you did not notice—and as they are younger they will
be more troublesome, and you will be more enraged. If you think
that killing people will prevent anyone from rebuking you for not
living properly, you are not thinking straight, since this escape is nei-
ther scarcely possible nor noble, whereas escape from the other is
noblest and easiest: not by cutting down others but equipping oneself
so that one can be as good as possible. With this prophecy to you
who sentence me, I depart.

I would gladly converse with those who acquitted me, concerning e
what has come to pass, while the officials are busy and I am not yet on
my way to the place where I must die when I arrive. Wait with me,
gentlemen, for that long, since nothing prevents us from chatting to-
gether while we can. Since you are my friends, I want to show to you 40a
the meaning of what has just happened to me.

Something surprising happened to me, judges—and by calling
you "judges" I would be using the word appropriately.[1] Always in
the past my usual divine prophetic sense was very strong and would
even oppose me on detailed points if I was about to do something
improper. And what happened to me just now, as you see your-
selves, was what people might think, and do think, to be the worst
of evils. And yet the sign of the god has not opposed me, not when b
I left home at dawn, nor when I arrived here in court, nor at any
point during my speech when I was about to say something, whereas

1 *using the word appropriately* In voting to acquit Socrates they (according to Socrates) dispensed justice correctly, as a judge should.

in many other speeches it has often stopped me, right as I was speaking. But now in this affair it has not been opposed to anything I have said or done.

So what do I take to be the cause of this? I will tell you. There's a good chance that what has happened to me is a good thing and that we
c understand death incorrectly, those of us who think death is something bad. I have strong evidence for this, since it is impossible that my customary sign would have failed to oppose me, unless I was about to do something good.

Let us also consider how there is great hope that it's a good thing in the following way: Now, death is one of two things, since it's either a kind of not being and the dead person has no perception of anything, or, according to what is said, it is a certain change and migration of the soul from its place here to another place.

d And if it is the absence of perception and the kind of sleep when someone sleeps without having any dreams, death would be a wonderful gift—because I think if someone had to pick out the night when he slept so soundly that he did not have a dream and compared the other nights and days of his life with this night, and after considering them he had to say how many days and nights he had lived in his life that were better and more sweet than this night, I think that he—not
e only a private citizen but the great king—would find it easy to count them in comparison with other days and nights. If death is like this, I say it is a gift, since all of time would seem to be nothing more than a single night.

If, in turn, death is a kind of migration from here to another place, and what's said is true and perhaps all of the dead are there, what greater good could there be than this, judges? If someone who ar-
41a rives in Hades, having moved on from these so-called judges here, finds those who were truly judges, who are said to act as judges there—Minos and Radamanthus and Aeacus and Triptolemus and as many other demigods who were judges in their own lifetimes—would it be unpleasant to depart? Or to spend time with Orpheus and Musaeus and Hesiod and Homer, how much would any of you give? I am willing to die many times if this is true, since I person-
b ally would find life there to be most amazing, if I could meet with Palamedes and Ajax son of Telamon, and anyone of the ancients who died as a result of an unjust decision, and measure my experience against theirs. I think it would not be unpleasant. And the greatest thing would be examining them and finding out which of them is wise and who thinks so but isn't, just like I do to people here.

How much would you give, judges, to quiz the leader of the great army against Troy, or Odysseus, or Sisyphus,[1] or many others one c
might mention, both men and women there whom it would be indescribably marvelous to debate and pass the time with and question? I should certainly hope that the people there would not put someone to death for that, since the people there are not just immortal for the rest of time but happier than those here in other respects, if what is said is true.

And so you too must be optimistic about death, judges, and hold this one thing to be true, that for a good man there is nothing evil in d
either living or dying. And neither do his deeds go unnoticed by the gods. My actions just now did not happen by themselves, but it is clear to me that it was to my advantage to die now and be released from my troubles. Because of this, my sign never deterred me. And I am not at all angry at those who voted against me and not much at my accusers—though they did not vote against me or accuse me with this in mind, but instead did so intending to harm me, and they deserve to be e
blamed for this.

Nonetheless, I beg them for this much: revenge yourselves on my sons, when they have grown, gentlemen, by giving them the same trouble I gave you, if they seem to prioritize money or anything else ahead of virtue or if they think themselves to be something that they are not. Reproach them as I reproached you, for not caring about what they ought to and for thinking that they are something when they are worth nothing. If you would do this, I will have been served justice by you, 42a
and my sons, too.

But now it really is time to depart, I to die and you to go on living. But which of us goes to a better life is unclear to everyone except to the god.

---

1 *Minos ... Sisyphus* Most of the figures mentioned in this passage are mythological: Minos, Radamanthus, and Aeacus were mortal sons of Zeus, rewarded with the position of judges of the dead because they had established the first just laws on earth; Triptolemus was a demigod who brought agriculture to earth and was also a central figure of the Eleusinian Mysteries, which promised mysterious benefits to initiates after their death; Orpheus was a singer and a poet, and founder of the Orphic religious cult; Musaeus was a producer of sacred poetry and oracles; Palamedes was a clever inventor; Ajax was a king and Greek hero in the Trojan War, and "the leader of the great army against Troy" was Agamemnon; Odysseus was a cunning and eloquent Greek hero of the Trojan War, and protagonist of the *Odyssey*; Sisyphus was a king punished in the underworld by having perpetually to push a rock uphill. Possibly real figures were two revered Greek poets: Homer, author of the *Iliad* and the *Odyssey*, and Hesiod, whose only surviving works are *Works and Days* and the *Theogony*.

Suggestions for Critical Reflection

1. How does Socrates defend himself? Why does he not argue directly that he and his followers were models of civic virtue and respectful of the traditional gods?

2. Socrates is depicted as going to some lengths to differentiate himself from the Sophists. Why do you think he does this?

3. Socrates says, "either I do not corrupt, or if I do corrupt, I do so unintentionally" (26a). What is his argument for this claim, and how persuasive is it?

4. When Socrates, perhaps unwisely, says, "Rest assured that if you kill me for being the kind of person I describe, you will not harm me more than yourselves" (30c), what do you think he means?

5. In the final section of the *Apology*, Socrates argues that death may well be a good thing. What are his arguments for this? What do you think of them?

Crito

Introduction

In this dialogue, which takes place while Socrates is in prison awaiting execution, one of his best friends, Crito, tries to persuade him to escape while Socrates gives his reasons for refusing to do so.

Ancient Greek executions normally took place only a day or two after conviction, but Socrates' death was unusually delayed for religious reasons. No executions were permitted while the city was purified for the annual holy festival for the god Apollo—the god, incidentally, who is described in the *Apology* as having given Socrates his divine mission through the oracle at Delphi. The dates of this festival were marked by the departure and return of a special holy ship that traveled between Athens and Apollo's sacred island of Delos. The ship had left Athens the day before Socrates' trial and normally would have been gone for a couple of weeks, but this year contrary winds kept it away for thirty days. For this reason, Socrates had not only a month to languish in prison—where he was kept in chains overnight to discourage his escape—but also extra time to indulge in his favorite activity: having philosophical discussions with his friends.

The main topic of *Crito* is whether it is ever permissible to do anything unjust. Socrates argues that it would be unjust for him to disobey the laws of Athens, and that therefore he will not do so on this occasion, even though on the face of it doing so would be in his own interests (and would benefit others and cause no one any particular harm).

Cast of Characters

Cebes of Thebes: A friend of Simmias and like him a philosophical follower of Socrates.

Crito: By the end of Socrates' life, Crito was his most loyal and closest friend. He was about Socrates' age and grew up with him in the same deme. However, he is portrayed in contemporary accounts as being more pragmatically than philosophically inclined.

Simmias of Thebes: A disciple of Socrates but also a philosopher in his own right who wrote a score of dialogues, none of which have survived.

Crito

43a Socrates: Why have you come at this hour, Crito? Or isn't it still early?

Crito: It certainly is.

Socrates: About what time is it?

Crito: Just before dawn.

Socrates: I'm surprised that the prison guard was willing to let you in.

Crito: He is used to me by now, Socrates, since I visit here so often. And besides, I have done him a good turn.

Socrates: Did you get here just now or a while ago?

Crito: Quite a while ago.

b Socrates: So how come you didn't wake me up immediately, but sat by in silence?

Crito: By Zeus, no, Socrates. I wish I myself were not so sleepless and sorrowful, and so I have been marveling at you, when I see how peacefully you've been sleeping. I deliberately didn't wake you so that you would pass the time as peacefully as possible. And indeed, many times before I have thought you fortunate in your demeanor towards your entire life, and even more so in your present misfortune, so easily and calmly do you bear it.

Socrates: It's because it would be out of tune, Crito, to be angry, at my age, if I must finally die.

c Crito: And yet others of your age, Socrates, have been caught up in such misfortunes, but their age does not prevent them from being angry at their fate.

Socrates: That's true. But why did you come so early?

Crito: Carrying troubling news, Socrates—though not for you, as it appears—but deeply troubling for me and all of your friends, and I, it seems, am among the most heavily burdened.

Socrates: What is it? Has the ship arrived from Delos, upon whose ar- d
rival I must die?

Crito: No, it hasn't arrived, but it looks like it will arrive today, based on the report of some people who have come from Sounion[1] and who left when it was there. It's clear from this that it will arrive today, and you will have to end your life tomorrow, Socrates.

Socrates: May it be for the best, Crito. If this pleases the gods, so be it. However, I don't think it will come today.

Crito: Where do you get your evidence for this? 44a

Socrates: I will tell you. I must be put to death sometime the day after the ship arrives?

Crito: That's what the authorities in these matters say, at least.

Socrates: In that case, I don't think it will arrive this coming day, but the next. My evidence is something I saw in a dream a little while ago during the night. It's likely that you chose a very good time not to wake me.

Crito: Well, what was the dream?

Socrates: A woman appeared, coming towards me, fine and good-
looking, wearing white clothing. She called to me and said, "Socrates, b
you shall arrive in fertile Phthia on the third day."[2]

Crito: What a strange dream, Socrates.

---

1 *Sounion* The tip of Attica; a headland 200 feet above sea level, bearing a temple to Poseidon, where ships headed for Athens could be sighted early.

2 *fertile Phthia ... third day* In the *Iliad* 9.363, Achilles threatens to leave Troy and return home, saying "in three days shall I be in Phthia," but instead chooses to stay to avenge the death of his childhood friend Patroclus, which ultimately leads to his own death. A reference to this is made in the *Apology* (28c).

Socrates: But obvious, at least as it appears to me, Crito.

Crito: Too obvious, perhaps. But, my supernatural Socrates, even now listen to me and be saved. If you die, for me it won't be just one misfortune: apart from being separated from the kind of friend the likes of which I will never find again, many people, moreover, who do not
c know me and you well will think that I could have saved you had I been willing to spend the money, but that I didn't care to. And wouldn't this indeed be the most shameful reputation, that I would seem to value money above friends? For the many will not believe that it was you yourself who refused to leave here, even though we were urging you to.

Socrates: But why, blessed Crito, should we care so much about the opinion of the many? The best people, who are more deserving of our attention, will believe that the matter was handled in just the way it was.

d Crito: But surely you see, Socrates, that we must pay attention to the opinion of the many, too. The present circumstances make it clear that the many can inflict not just the least of evils but practically the greatest, when one has been slandered among them.

Socrates: If they were of any use, Crito, the many would be able to do the greatest evils, and so they would also be able to do the greatest goods, and that would be fine. But as it is they can do neither, since they cannot make a man either wise or foolish, but they do just whatever occurs to them.

e Crito: Well, let's leave that there. But tell me this, Socrates. You're not worried, are you, about me and your other friends, how, if you were to leave here, the informers would make trouble for us because we stole you away from here, and we would be compelled either to give up all our property or a good deal of money, or suffer some other pun-
45a ishment at their hands? If you have any such fear, let it go, because it is our obligation to run this risk in saving you and even greater ones if necessary. So trust me and do not refuse.

Socrates: I certainly am worried about these things, Crito, and lots of others too.

Crito: Well don't fear them. Indeed, some people only need to be given a little silver and they're willing to rescue you and get you out of here.

And on top of that, don't you see how cheap those informers are and
that we wouldn't need to spend a lot of money on them? My money is b
at your disposal, and is, I think, sufficient. Furthermore, even if, because of some concern for me, you think you shouldn't spend my money, there are these visitors here who are prepared to spend theirs. One of them has brought enough silver for this very purpose, Simmias of Thebes, and Cebes too is willing, and very many others. So, as I say, don't give up on saving yourself because you are uneasy about these things.

And don't let what you said in the court get to you, that you wouldn't know what to do with yourself as an exile. Wherever you go, there
are places they will welcome you. And if you want to go to Thessaly, c
I have some friends there who will think highly of you and provide you with safety, so that no one in Thessaly will harass you.

What's more, Socrates, what you are doing doesn't seem right to me, giving yourself up when you could be saved, ready to have happen to you what your enemies would urge—and did urge—in their wish to destroy you.

I also think you are betraying your sons, whom you could raise and d
educate, by going away and abandoning them, and, as far as you are concerned, they can experience whatever happens to come their way, when it's likely that as orphans they'll get the usual orphans' treatment of orphans. One should either not have children or endure the hardship of raising and educating them. But it looks to me as though you are taking the laziest path, whereas you must choose the path a good and brave man would choose, especially when you keep saying that you care about virtue your whole life long.

So I am ashamed both on your behalf and on behalf of us, your e
friends, that this whole affair surrounding you will be thought to have happened due to some cowardice on our part: the hearing of the charge in court, that it came to trial when it need not have,[1] and the legal contest itself, how it was carried on, and, as the absurd part of the affair, that by some badness and cowardice on our part we will be thought to
have let this final act get away from us, since we did not save you, nor 46a
you save yourself, when it was possible and we could have done so if we were of the slightest use. So see, Socrates, whether this is both evil and shameful, for you and for us as well. Think over—or rather, there's no longer time for thinking but only for deciding—this one consideration, because everything must be done this coming night; if we hang

1 *when it need not have* Socrates could have left the country and so avoided the trial.

around any longer it will be impossible and we'll no longer be able to. So in every way, Socrates, believe me and do not refuse.

b Socrates: My dear Crito, your eagerness would be worth a lot if it were
in pursuit of something righteous, but the more it is not, the more dif-
ficult it is to deal with. We must therefore examine whether we should
do this or not, because as always, and not just now for the first time, I
am the sort of person who is persuaded in my soul by nothing other
than the argument which seems best to me upon reflection. At present
I am not able to abandon the arguments I previously made, now that
this misfortune has befallen me, but they appear about the same to me,
c and I defer to and honor the ones I did before. If we have nothing bet-
ter than them to offer under the present circumstances, rest assured
that I will not agree with you, not if, even more so than at present, the
power of the multitude were to spook us as though we were children,
imposing chains and deaths and monetary fines upon us.

What's the most reasonable way we can examine this matter? By
first resuming this argument that you give about reputations. Was it
d correct on each occasion when we said that one must pay attention to
the opinions of some people and not to others'? Was this the correct
thing to say before I had to die, whereas now it has become obvious
that it was said only for the sake of argument and was actually just
child's play and hot air?

I am determined to examine this together with you, Crito, whether
it appears different when I consider it in this condition, or the same,
and whether we should ignore it or be persuaded by it. It is always put
like this, I think, by people who think there is something in it, the way
e I put it just now: that it is necessary to pay serious attention to some
of the opinions that men hold and not to others. By the gods, Crito,
doesn't this seem correct to you? Because you, as far as any human can
47a tell, are in no danger of being executed tomorrow and the present mis-
fortune should not lead you astray. Have a look, then. Is it fair enough
to say that one should not value every human opinion but only some
and not others? And not the opinions of everyone but of some and not
others? What do you say? Isn't this right?

Crito: Yes, that's right.

Socrates: Shouldn't we value the good opinions, and not the worthless ones?

Crito: Yes.

Socrates: Aren't the good ones the opinions of the wise, while the worthless ones come from the ignorant?

Crito: Of course.

Socrates: So then, what did we say, again, about cases such as this:
should a man in training, who takes it seriously, pay any heed to the b
praise and blame and opinion of everyone, or only to one person, the
one who is a doctor or a trainer?

Crito: Only to the one.

Socrates: So he should fear the criticisms and welcome the praises of that one person, and not those of the many?

Crito: Clearly.

Socrates: He must practice and exercise, and eat and drink, in the way that seems best to that one person, the trainer and expert, more than to all the others together.

Crito: That's right.

Socrates: Well then. If he disobeys this one man and dishonors his c
opinion and his praises and instead honors those of the many who
know nothing, won't he suffer harm?

Crito: How could he not?

Socrates: What is this harm, and what does it tend to do, and in what part of the disobedient person?

Crito: It's clear that it's in the body, since this is what it destroys.

Socrates: Well said. Isn't it the same with the other things—not to go over
them all, but in particular justice and injustice and shameful and fine things
and good and bad, which are what our current discussion is about—
whether we must follow the opinion of the many and fear it or instead the d
opinion of the one person, if there is someone who has knowledge, whom
we must defer to and fear more than all the others together? If we do not
heed his opinion we will corrupt and harm that part of us which becomes
better with justice and is destroyed by injustice. Or don't you think so?

Crito: I do indeed, Socrates.

Socrates: Tell me, if we do not follow the opinion of the person who knows and so destroy that part of us which is improved by what is wholesome and corrupted by what sickens, is life worth living when
e that part is ruined? This is the body, I suppose, isn't it?

Crito: Yes.

Socrates: Then is life worth living with a wretched and corrupt body?

Crito: Not at all.

Socrates: And is life worth living after the part of us which injustice injures and justice benefits has been corrupted? Or do you think this is unimportant in comparison with the body, this part of us, whatever
48a it is, that injustice and justice affect?

Crito: Not at all.

Socrates: But more valuable?

Crito: Much more.

Socrates: So, best of men, we must not pay much heed to what the many will say to us, but to what the one who knows about just and unjust things will say—to that one person, and to the truth itself. So you were wrong, at the beginning, to bring this up, that we must heed the opinion of the many concerning just things and noble things and good things and their opposites. "But in spite of that," someone might declare, "the many can put us to death."

b Crito: That too is obvious. For someone might say so, Socrates. You're right.

Socrates: But, you wonderful fellow, it seems to me that the following statement, which we have been over before, remains just the same as before. So examine again whether or not it still holds true for you, that it's not living that should be our priority, but living well.

Crito: Why, of course it's still true.

Socrates: And that this is living well and finely and justly, does that remain true or not?

Crito: It remains true.

Socrates: Therefore, based on what you've agreed, we must consider
the following: whether it is just or unjust for me to try to leave here,
when I was not acquitted by the Athenians. And if it seems just, let's c
try it, and if not, let's abandon it. As for the points you make about
spending money and reputation and the upbringing of children, Crito,
I suspect that these are really questions belonging to people who would
casually put someone to death and resurrect him, if they could, without any thought—to the members of the multitude.

As for us, since the argument requires it, I suppose we should examine precisely what we just mentioned: whether we will act justly
by giving money and thanks to those who will get me out of here— d
both you in the lead and me being led—or whether we will in fact act
unjustly by doing all of this. If we think that we're acting unjustly by
doing these things, I don't think we should take into consideration
whether we will die if we hold our ground and keep our peace, or anything else we will suffer—only whether we're acting unjustly.

Crito: I think you put that well, Socrates. See what we should do, then.

Socrates: Let's look together, my good man, and if at any point you
have an objection to what I am saying, make it and I will persuade
you; if not, you blessed man, finally quit saying the same thing over e
and over, that I have to get out of here against the will of the Athenians. I think it is most important to act with your consent and not against
your will. See, then, that the starting point of the inquiry is laid down
to your satisfaction and try to answer the questions in the way you 49a
think best.

Crito: I shall certainly try.

Socrates: Do we say that we should never willingly act unjustly, or
that we should in some instances and not in others? Or is acting unjustly never good or noble, as we often agreed on previous occasions?
Or have all our previous agreements been overturned in these last few
days, and did we fail to notice long ago, Crito, that when we have serious discussions with one another, we ourselves, at our age, are no b
different from children? Or more than anything isn't what we used to

say still true? Whether the many agree or not, and whether we must also suffer harsher things than these or gentler, nevertheless acting unjustly is evil and shameful in every way for the person who does it. Do we say this or not?

Crito: We do.

Socrates: And so one must never act unjustly.

Crito: By no means.

Socrates: And so one should not repay an injustice with an injustice, as the many think, since one should never act unjustly.

c Crito: It appears not.

Socrates: What next? Should one cause harm, Crito, or not?

Crito: Presumably not, Socrates.

Socrates: And then? Is returning a harm for a harm just, as the many say, or not just?

Crito: Not at all.

Socrates: Because harming a man in any way is no different from doing an injustice.

Crito: That's true.

Socrates: One must neither repay an injustice nor cause harm to any
man, no matter what one suffers because of him. And see to it, Crito,
d that in agreeing with this you are not agreeing contrary to what you be-
lieve, because I know that few people believe it or will believe it. And
so there is no common ground between those who hold this belief and
those who don't; when they see each other's positions they are bound
to despise one another. So think carefully about whether you yourself
agree and believe, and let us begin thinking from here: that it is never
right to act unjustly, or to return an injustice, or to retaliate when one
has suffered some harm by repaying the harm. Do you reject or ac-
e cept this starting principle? For it still seems good to me now, as it did
long ago, but if it seemed some other way to you, speak up and edu-

cate me. If you're sticking to what we said before, listen to what comes next.

Crito: I do stick to it, and I accept it. Go ahead.

Socrates: Here in turn is the next point. Or rather, I'll ask you: when someone has made an agreement with someone else, and it is just, must he keep to it or betray it?

Crito: He must keep to it.

Socrates: Observe what follows from this. If we leave here without
having persuaded the city, are we doing someone a harm—and those 50a
whom we should least of all harm—or not? And are we keeping to the just agreements we made, or not?

Crito: I'm unable to respond to what you're asking, Socrates; for I do not know.

Socrates: Well, look at it this way. If the laws and the community of the city came to us when we were about to sneak away from here—or whatever it should be called—and, standing over us, were to ask, "Tell me, Socrates, what are you intending to do? By attempting this deed,
aren't you planning to do nothing other than destroy us, the laws, and b
the civic community, as much as you can? Or does it seem possible to you that any city where the verdicts reached have no force but are made powerless and corrupted by private citizens could continue to exist and not be in ruins?"

What will we say, Crito, to these questions and others like them? Because there's a lot more a person could say, especially an orator, on behalf of this law we're destroying, which makes sovereign the ver-
dicts that have been decided. Or will we say to them, "The city treated c
us unjustly and did not decide the case properly"? Will we say this or something like it?

Crito: By Zeus, that's what we'll say, Socrates.

Socrates: What if the laws then said, "Socrates, did we agree on this, we and you, to honor the decisions that the city makes?" And if we were surprised to hear them say this, perhaps they would say, "Socrates, don't be surprised at what we're saying, but answer, since you are accustomed to using questions and answers. Come then, what
reason can you give us and the city for trying to destroy us? Did we d

not, to begin with, give birth to you?[1] And wasn't it through us that your father married your mother and conceived you? So show those of us, the laws concerning marriages, what fault you find that keeps them from being good?" "I find no fault with them," I would say.

"What about the laws concerning the upbringing and education of children, by which you too were raised? Or didn't those of us, the laws established on this matter, give good instructions when they directed
e your father to educate you in the arts and gymnastics?" "They did," I would say.

"Well, then. Since you have been born and brought up and educated, could you say that you were not our offspring and slave from the beginning, both you and your ancestors? And if this is so, do you suppose that justice between you and us is based on equality, and do you think that whatever we might try to do to you, it is just for you to do these things to us in return? Justice between you and your father, or your master if you happened to have one, was not based on equality, so that you could not do whatever you had suffered in return, neither
51a speak back when crossed nor strike back when struck nor many other such things. Will you be allowed to do this to your homeland and the laws, so that, if we try to destroy you, thinking this to be just, you will in return try to destroy us the laws and your homeland with as much power as you have and claim that you're acting justly in doing so—the man who truly cares about virtue?

"Are you so wise that it has slipped your mind that the homeland deserves more honor and reverence and worship than your mother and father and all of your other ancestors? And that she is held in higher esteem
b both by the gods and by men of good sense? And that when she is angry you should show her more respect and compliance and obedience than your father, and either convince her or do what she commands, and suffer without complaining if she orders you to suffer something? And that whether it is to be beaten or imprisoned, or to be wounded or killed if she leads you into war, you must do it? And that this is just, and that you must not be daunted or withdraw or abandon your position, but at
c war and in the courts and everywhere you must do what the city and the homeland order, or convince her by appealing to what is naturally just? And that it is not holy to use force against one's mother or father, and it is so much worse to do so against one's homeland?" What will we say to this, Crito? That the laws speak the truth? Or not?

---

1 *give birth to you* Socrates appears to be suggesting that without the civic structures—laws—governing marriage and families he would not have been born (at least, not as an Athenian citizen).

Crito: It looks so to me.

Socrates: "Consider, then, Socrates," the laws might say, "if what we
say is true: that it is not just for you to try what you're now attempt-
ing to do to us. For we gave birth to you, brought you up, educated
you, and gave you and all the other citizens every good thing we could, d
and yet even so we pronounce that any Athenian who wishes, once he
has been admitted as an adult and sees the affairs of the city and us the
laws, has the power, if he is not pleased with us, to take his possessions
and leave for wherever he wants. And if any among you wants to live
in a colony because we and the city do not satisfy him, or if he wants
to go somewhere else and live as a foreigner, none of us laws stands
in the way or forbids him from taking his possessions with him and
leaving for wherever he wants.

"But whoever remains with us, having observed how we decide e
lawsuits and take care of other civic matters, we claim that this man by
his action has now made an agreement with us to do what we com-
mand him to do, and we claim that anyone who does not obey is guilty
three times over: he disobeys us who gave birth to him; and who raised
him; and because, despite agreeing to be subject to us, he does not
obey us or persuade us that we are doing something improper. And
we give him an alternative and don't angrily press him to do what we 52a
order; and although we allow either of two possibilities—either to per-
suade us or to comply—he does neither of these.

"We say that you especially will be liable to these charges,
Socrates, if indeed you carry out your plans, and you not least of the
Athenians but most of all." If, then, I would say, "How do you mean?,"
perhaps they would scold me justly, saying that I most of all among the
Athenians have made this agreement. They might say, "Socrates, we b
have great evidence for this, that we and the city satisfy you. For you
would never have spent more of your life here than all of the other
Athenians unless it seemed particularly good to you. You never left the
city for a festival, except once to the Isthmus, but never went any-
where else except on military duty, nor did you ever make another trip
like other Athenians do, nor did any urge seize you to get to know a
different city or other laws, but we and our city were sufficient for
you. So decidedly did you choose us and agree to be governed by us c
that, among other things, you had children in it, because the city was
satisfactory to you.

"Moreover, at your trial you could have proposed exile, if you had
wished, and what you're now trying to do to the city without her con-
sent, you could have done then with her consent. At the time, you
prided yourself on not being angry if you had to die, and you chose

death, you said, in preference to exile. But now you neither feel shame in the face of those words nor have you any respect for us the laws. By
d trying to destroy us you are doing what the most despicable slave would do, trying to run away contrary to the contract and the agreement by which you agreed to be governed by us. So answer us first on this particular point: do we speak the truth when we say that you agreed to be governed by us in deed and not merely in words?" What can we say to this, Crito? Mustn't we agree?

Crito: We must, Socrates.

e Socrates: "Aren't you," they might say, "going against your contracts and agreements with us, which you were not forced to agree to, nor deceived about, nor compelled to decide upon in a short time, but over seventy years, in which time you could have gone away if we did not satisfy you and these agreements did not appear just to you? You did not prefer Lacedaemon[1] or Crete, each of which you claim is well-
53a governed, nor any of the other Hellenic cities or the foreign ones, but you left her less often than the lame and the blind and the other disabled people. Evidently the city and also we the laws were so much more pleasing to you than to other Athenians, for is a city pleasing to anyone without its laws? Now then, won't you keep to what you agreed? You will, if you are convinced by us, at any rate, Socrates; and at least you won't make yourself ridiculous by leaving the city.

"Just think about what good will it do you and your friends if you break them and do wrong in one of these ways. It's pretty clear that
b your friends will risk exile along with you and disenfranchisement from the city and confiscation of their property. And if you first go to one of the closest cities, to Thebes or to Megara—since both are well-governed—you will come as an enemy, Socrates, of those governments, and everyone who cares about their cities will regard you suspiciously, thinking that you are a destroyer of the laws.[2] And you will confirm the opinion of the judges, so that they will think they
c judged the case correctly, since whoever is a destroyer of the laws would certainly be considered in some way a destroyer of young and foolish men.

---

1 *Lacedaemon* Sparta.

2 *Thebes or to Megara ... destroyer of the laws* These were oligarchical states neighboring Athens. Socrates would be seen as an enemy because he was a law-breaker. When Socrates says 'well-governed,' he means that they operate by a strict rule of law (by contrast, perhaps, with Thessaly, mentioned below at 53d), not necessarily the same or as good laws as Athens.

"Will you flee, then, from well-governed cities and from the most
civilized people? Is it worth it to you to live like this? Will you asso-
ciate with them, Socrates, and feel no shame when talking with them?
What will you say, Socrates? What you said here, that virtue and jus-
tice are of the greatest value to humans, and along with lawfulness and
the laws? And you don't think the conduct of such a Socrates will ap-
pear shameful? One should think so. d

"But will you leave these places and go to Crito's friends in Thes-
saly.[1] There is plenty of disorder and disobedience there and they
might listen with pleasure to you, about how you amusingly ran away
from prison wearing some costume or a peasant's vest or something
else of the sort that runaways typically dress themselves in, altering
your appearance. But still, will no one say that an old man, who prob-
ably only has a short time left in his life, was so greedy in his desire
to live that he dared to violate the greatest laws? Perhaps not, if you do e
not annoy anyone. But if you do, Socrates, you will hear many dis-
honorable things about yourself. You will surely spend your life suck-
ing up to everyone and living like a slave. What else will you do in
Thessaly but feast, as though you had traveled to Thessaly for dinner?
And those speeches, the ones about justice and the other virtues, where 54a
will they be?

"Is it for the sake of your children that you want to live, so that you
can raise and educate them? What are you going do, in that case?
You'll raise and educate them by bringing them to Thessaly and mak-
ing them outsiders, so that they will enjoy that benefit too? Or if not
that, will they grow up better if they are raised and educated with you
away from them but alive, because your friends will take care of them?
But is it that if you go to Thessaly, they'll look after them, whereas if
you go to Hades, they won't? If those who claim to be your friends are
any good, you must believe they will. b

"So be convinced by us who brought you up, Socrates, and do not
put children or life or anything else ahead of justice, so that when you
go to Hades you will be able to provide all this as your defense to those
who rule there. Since neither in this world, nor in the next when you
arrive, will this action be thought better or more just or more pious for
you and your friends to do. But as it is you leave us, if indeed you de-
part, having been done an injustice not by us, the laws, but by men. If c
you return the injustice, however, and repay the harm and flee in
shame, having violated your agreement and contract with us and
harmed those who least of all should be harmed—yourself, your

1 *Thessaly* The Athenians associated this place with gluttony and debauchery.

friends, your homeland, and us—we will make life hard for you while you're alive, and then our brothers, the laws in Hades, will not receive you favorably, knowing that you tried to destroy us too, as far as you
d were able. So do not be persuaded by Crito to do what he says instead of what we say."

Rest assured, my dear friend Crito, that this is what I seem to hear, just as the Corybants[1] seem to hear the pipes, and the echo from these words resonates within me and makes me unable to hear anything else. So know that, based on my current beliefs, at least, if you speak against them you will speak in vain. Nevertheless, if you honestly think you can achieve anything more, speak.

Crito: No, Socrates. I am unable to speak.

e Socrates: Then let it be, Crito, and let us act in this way, since this is where the god leads us.

Suggestions for Critical Reflection

1. Socrates represents the city of Athens as saying to its citizens, "whoever remains with us, having observed how we decide lawsuits and take care of other civic matters, we claim that this man by his action has now made an agreement with us to do what we command him to do" (51e). How does Socrates argue that the city may be right to say this? If true, what are the implications of this claim?

2. Socrates argues that, since he could not persuade the citizens of Athens to spare him, he must accept their judgment and agree to die. Yet he also argues passionately, especially in the *Apology*, that he cannot accept that any human being has the right to prevent him from doing his god-given duty of philosophizing and teaching others to philosophize: that is, he argues that there are limits to what a law can impose on its citizens. There seems to be a tension between these two positions. What do you think? Is Socrates really contradicting himself?

3. Socrates holds that wisdom contributes to genuine self-interest: that doing the right thing is always in one's own best interests. Yet, in the end, he is executed for his behavior and because he has refused

1 *Corybants* Priests of the Asiatic goddess Cybele, and also sometimes the infant Dionysus. The rites of the Corybants were accompanied by wild music and trance-like dancing.

to do the things that might have saved him (such as giving up doing philosophy, or accepting Crito's help to flee from Athens). What are we to make of this?

4. Socrates holds that one should not retaliate against people who do one harm. What are his reasons? Do you agree? Why or why not?

5. Socrates says that he has a contract with his city that he must obey. Do you think that you are under contract with your society and/or its government? Did you agree to anything like this arrangement? Do you have any duties toward society or its government? Why or why not?

Phaedo

Introduction

This dialogue is set sometime after Socrates' death. Phaedo, one of Socrates' younger friends, is depicted as describing Socrates' final hours to a group in Phlius, a Greek city that was allied with Sparta. The dialogue begins with Socrates' description of the truly good life—the life of the true philosopher—which concentrates on real knowledge and contemplation of the eternal things—things "of the soul"—and despises bodily matters such as pleasure and wealth. The best life, therefore, involves freeing the soul from the injurious distractions of the body; but this is what happens in death. Therefore, he reasons, a true philosopher should not be afraid of death: in fact, death should be welcomed.

In response to his friend Cebes' fear that the soul may die with the body, Socrates offers a number of considerations. Opposites come from their opposite, he points out; the dead, as we know, come from the living, so the living must come from the dead. Thus, he concludes, souls must exist before they are united with a body. In response to the fear that nevertheless souls may die with their bodies, Socrates claims that this would mean that eventually no souls would be left.

In addition to these arguments, Socrates briefly recounts the reasons to believe that real knowledge is not learned but is recollected (see *Meno* for more on this). This must mean that the soul pre-exists the body. Furthermore, we can be assured that those souls who are least polluted with bodily matters will have the reward of the best afterlife. And he claims that the soul resembles or incorporates the form of life—that is, the form of existence—and so it is the essence of souls to be immortal, and contradictory to imagine them perishing.

Next, Socrates gives a speculative account of the passage of the soul to the afterlife, which includes a theory of the structure of the Earth and its regions.

The final scene is a description of Socrates' words and demeanor as he carries out his own execution by drinking a cup of poison. There has been much debate as to whether a potion made of hemlock would have the relatively peaceful lethal effects that are depicted here. It used to be thought that Plato was exercising poetic license, but recent research[1] suggests that the particular species of hemlock found near ancient Athens would in fact have acted in just the way that Plato describes.

Cast of Characters

Anaxagoras of Clazomenae: A precursor of Socrates (he died in about 428 BCE), Anaxagoras was born in the area that is modern-day Turkey and is sometimes credited with being the first person to bring philosophy to Athens. He developed a sophisticated cosmology—which in some ways was the distant ancestor of modern atomic theory—and for his pains he was tried for impiety and forced into exile.

Apollodorus of Phaleron: A volatile, aggressively loyal, and wealthy man who was another prominent student of Socrates. He is not portrayed as an independent thinker but as someone who uncritically and fervently accepted Socrates' views.

Cebes of Thebes: A friend of Simmias, and like him a philosophical follower of Socrates.

Crito: By the end of Socrates' life, Crito was his most loyal and closest friend. He was about Socrates' age and grew up with him in the same deme. However, he is portrayed in contemporary accounts as being more pragmatically than philosophically inclined.

Critobulus: Crito's eldest son and, like his father, a wealthy farmer rather than a philosopher.

Echecrates of Phlius: A Pythagorean philosopher who held Socrates in high regard, and the person to whom Phaedo is depicted as describing Socrates' final hours.

Euenus of Paros: Represented as Socrates' poetry instructor, Euenus was therefore presumably contemporaneous with him. Some poetry surviving today is attributed to him.

1 See Enid Bloch, "Hemlock Poisoning and the Death of Socrates: Did Plato Tell the Truth?," *The Trial and Execution of Socrates*, ed. T.C. Brickhouse and N.D. Smith (Oxford: Oxford UP, 2001), pp. 255–78.

Phaedo of Elis: A philosopher who was captured in war as a young man and held as a slave by a wealthy Athenian until he was freed by Socrates (or rather by a rich friend of Socrates—perhaps Crito—at his request), and who took Socrates as his mentor.

Simmias of Thebes: A disciple of Socrates but also a philosopher in his own right who wrote a score of dialogues, none of which have survived.

Phaedo

Echecrates: Were you there with Socrates in person, Phaedo, on the 57a
day he drank the poison in the prison, or did you hear about it from
someone else?

Phaedo: In person, Echecrates.

Echecrates: Then what did the man himself say before his death? And
how did he die? I would be glad to hear what happened, since pretty
much none of the Phliasian citizens goes to Athens these days, and no
visitor has come from there in a long time who could tell us anything b
clearly about the events, except of course that he died by drinking poi-
son. Beyond that they have nothing to report.

Phaedo: Did you not learn about what happened with the trial? 58a

Echecrates: Yes, someone told us about that, and we were curious that, even though it took place a while ago, it seems he died much later. Why was this, Phaedo?

Phaedo: He had some good luck, Echecrates. It happened that on the day before the trial the prow of the ship that the Athenians send to Delos had been garlanded.

Echecrates: What is this, exactly?

Phaedo: This is the ship in which, according to the Athenians, The-
seus once went off to Crete, taking with him the famous 'twice seven'
and saved them, and he too survived.[1] And, it is said that back then b

1 *Theseus ... survived* Athens was obliged periodically to send seven boys and seven girls to Crete, there to be eaten by the Minotaur, a bull-headed monster. Theseus accompanied the "twice seven" on one voyage, and slayed the monster.

they had vowed to Apollo that, should they be saved, they would bring a mission back to Delos every year. And so, from then on, even up to the present day, they always send a mission to the god on each anniversary. Now their custom is that once the mission starts, they keep the city pure from then on and don't put anyone to death until the ship gets to Delos and arrives back again. This sometimes takes
c a long time, when headwinds arise. The beginning of the mission is when the priest of Apollo garlands the stern of the ship and this occurred, as I said, the day before the trial took place. And so this is the reason Socrates spent a long time in the prison between the trial and his death.

Echecrates: What about the details of his death, then, Phaedo? What was said and done, and who from among his friends was in attendance, or did the officials not allow them to attend and he died deprived of friends?

d Phaedo: Not at all—some were present; many, in fact.

Echecrates: Keep going: tell us everything, as clearly as possible, unless there is some business pressing you.

Phaedo: Yes, I have the time and will certainly try to describe it for you, since remembering Socrates—both by speaking of him and hearing others—always brings me the greatest pleasure of all.

Echecrates: Well, Phaedo, your listeners are just like you. So, try as much as you can to go over everything as accurately as possible.

e Phaedo: Okay. Well, being there was a strange experience for me. Pity did not cross my mind, as when I am present at the death of a friend, because he appeared to me to be a happy man, Echecrates, both in behavior and in speech. He was approaching his end so fearlessly and nobly that it occurred to me that, although he was going to the land of Hades,[1] he was going with a share of the divine and that he would fare
59a well when he got there, if indeed anyone ever does! For this reason I did not feel pity at all, as would likely be appropriate for a person attending a mourning, but on the other hand I didn't feel any of the usual pleasure from our philosophizing, either—for such was our talk, in fact—but I experienced an absolutely strange feeling, some strange

1 *land of Hades* The underworld, where all souls go after death. Not a place just for evil, as is the Christian hell, but merely of continued existence.

combination of pleasure mixed together with pain, when it really sank in that he was about to meet his end. And more or less everyone who was there was affected the same way, sometimes laughing, sometimes crying, one of us in particular, Apollodorus—you know the man, of b
course, and what he's like.

Echecrates: Of course.

Phaedo: Well, he was suffering in exactly this way, and I myself was mixed up, and the others, too.

Echecrates: Who was in fact there, Phaedo?

Phaedo: Of the locals, Apollodorus, of course, and Critobulus and his father,[1] and then Hermogenes and Epigenes and Aeschines and Antisthenes; there was also Ctessipus from Paianieus[2] and Menexenus and some others from the area. Plato, I think, was sick.

Echecrates: Were any visitors present?

Phaedo: Yes, Simmias the Theban and Cebes and Phaedondes, and c
from Megara Euclid and Terpsion.

Echecrates: And what about Aristippus and Cleombrotus, were they present?

Phaedo: Definitely not; they were said to be in Aegina.

Echecrates: Was anyone else there?

Phaedo: I think these are about it for the attendees.

Echecrates: Very well, then. Will you go over the conversation?

Phaedo: I will try to report everything to you from the beginning.

So, then. On the previous days we always used to go and visit d
Socrates, both me and the others. We used to gather in the court where the trial itself took place, since it was close to the prison. And each day we used to hang around until the prison was opened, passing the time together, because it was not opened early. But whenever it was

1 *his father* Crito.

2 *Paianieus* An eastern suburb of Athens.

opened, we would go in to Socrates and often times would spend the day with him.

On that particular day, we came together even earlier, since on the
e previous day when we left the prison in the evening we learned that the
ship had returned from Delos. So we told each other to get to the usual
spot as early as possible. We got there and the jailer came out to us, the
one who usually acknowledged us, to tell us to wait and not to proceed
until he gave the word. "The Eleven,"[1] he said, "are releasing Socrates
and giving directions for his execution today." But after a short wait
60a he came and bade us go in. So we went in and came upon Socrates,
who had just been released, and sitting beside him was Xanthippe[2]—
you're familiar with her—holding his young child. Well, when Xan-
thippe saw us she cried aloud and said the kind of thing that women
usually say: "Socrates, this is the very last time that your friends will
speak to you and you to them." And Socrates looked over at Crito and
said, "Crito, have someone take her home." And one of Crito's peo-
b ple led her away, wailing and beating herself.

Sitting down on the bench, Socrates bent up his leg and rubbed it
with his hand. And while he was rubbing it said, "How strange it seems
to be, gentlemen, the thing that men call 'pleasure'. And how curi-
ously it is related to its apparent opposite, the painful: the two of them
don't want to arise in a person at the same time, but if someone pur-
sues the one and gets a hold of it, it is pretty much always necessary
that he grasps the other one too, as if they are joined together at the
c head, even though they are two. It seems to me," he said, "that if
Aesop[3] had thought of these things, he would have composed a story
about how god wanted to reconcile these warring parties, but when he
could not, he joined them by their heads into a single thing, and that's
why when one of them arises in a person it is next followed by the
other, just as seems to be the case with me: after my leg was in pain
because of my bonds, the pleasant seems to have come following
along."

Well, then Cebes interrupted and said, "By Zeus, Socrates, it's good
d you made me remember. I mean about the lyric poetry[4] that you com-
posed, putting the stories of Aesop into meter, and the hymn to Apollo;
some other people were asking me, like Euenus the day before yes-

---

1 *The Eleven* Elected officials in charge of prisons, executions, and legal confiscations.

2 *Xanthippe* Socrates' wife.

3 *Aesop* Legendary author of famous fables, thought to have lived in the sixth century BCE.

4 *lyric poetry* This form of metrical poetry was sometimes sung, with or without accompaniment.

terday, whatever put it into your head, when you came here, to compose them, when you hadn't composed any previously. So if you care that I can answer Euenus whenever he asks me again—for I know full well that he will ask—tell me what I should say."

"Well, tell him the truth, Cebes," he said, "that I composed them not because I wished to compete with him or his poems—I knew that would not be easy—but to test what certain dreams might mean, and to satisfy my conscience in case, by chance, they were ordering me to make this music. They were something just like this: the same dream often came to me in my former life, appearing sometimes in different guises but saying the same thing; 'Socrates,' it said, 'compose lyrics and devote yourself to it.' And I supposed, up until now at least, that it was encouraging me and cheering me on in what I was doing, and just like those who encourage runners, in my case too the dream was cheering on what I was doing, making music, since philosophy is the greatest music and this was what I was doing.

"But now, when the trial had finished and the festival of the god was delaying my execution, I thought that if, by chance, the dream was indeed ordering me to 'make music' in the popular sense, I should not disobey but do it, since it was safer not to depart[1] before satisfying my conscience by composing lyric poems and obeying the dream. And so I composed first for the god for whose festival was ongoing, and after the god, I thought that a poet—if he really intends to be a poet—should compose lyrics for the stories rather than their lessons,[2] and since I was not a story-maker myself, I thus took the stories that were ready to hand and which I knew—those of Aesop—and I composed lyrics for the first of these that I happened upon. Well then, Cebes, tell Euenus this, and 'farewell,' and, if he is wise, to follow me as soon as possible. I, it seems, will depart today—so the Athenians have ordered."

And Simmias said, "What a thing this is to recommend to Euenus, Socrates! I have met the man many times already and from what I have seen of him, he is entirely unlikely to heed your advice willingly."

"What's that?" said he. "Is Euenus not a philosopher?"

"I think so," said Simmias.

1 *depart* To Hades.

2 *lyrics for the stories rather than their lessons* Two distinct ways of discussing a topic are, on the one hand, using argument and logic and organizing propositions, and, on the other, telling stories and conjuring feelings. We might think we take away the moral or the lesson of one of Aesop's fables, but the stories are vivid illustrations that perhaps get at something the reasoning cannot capture. After all of the argumentation, *Phaedo* will end with a story (110b).

"Then even Euenus will be willing, as will anyone who is worthy of sharing in this undertaking. Though perhaps he will not harm himself, since they say this is not permitted."

d And as he said these words he lowered his legs to the ground and spent the rest of the discussion sitting in this position. So then Cebes asked him, "What do you mean, Socrates, that it is not permitted to harm himself, even though the philosopher is willing to follow after the dying man?"

"What's that, Cebes? Have you and Simmias not heard about such things in your conversation with Philolaus?"

"Not clearly, at any rate, Socrates."

"I'm speaking about these things from hearsay, of course, but there's no harm in saying what I happen to have heard. For it is per-
e haps especially fitting for me, going away as I am to that other place, to analyze and mythologize about what we think the time spent there will be like. Indeed, what else should one do during the time until the sun sets?"

"Well then, why exactly do they say that it is not permissible to kill oneself, Socrates? For what you said just now I previously heard Philolaus say, when he was living among us, and from various others too, that we must not do this. But I never heard anything clear about these things from anyone."

62a "You must keep at it," he said, "and maybe you will hear. But perhaps it seems remarkable to you that this doctrine, out of all the others, is absolute, and it is never true in the case of a human—as it is with other things—that there is an occasion and people for whom it is better to die rather than to live; and yet, for the people for whom it is better to die—perhaps it seems remarkable to you—that it is not holy for them to do a good thing for themselves, but they must wait for something else to help."

And Cebes, chuckling softly, said, "May Zeus know it," speaking in his own dialect.[1]

b "It would certainly seem strange," Socrates said, "if it were like this. But no, perhaps there is some sense to it. The doctrine that is given in secret about this matter—that we are men in some sort of prison who must not free themselves or run away—seems to me to be something big and not easy to figure out. But the following, I think, is well said, at least, that the god is our guardian and that men are one of the possessions of the gods. Doesn't it seem so to you?"

"Yes, it does," said Cebes.

---

1 *in his own dialect* The form of Greek then spoken in Boeotia, a region of central Greece which includes Thebes.

"And so," said he, "in the case of your own property[1] too, if some one of them killed himself when you had not indicated that you wished for him to die, you would be hard on him and if you could punish him, you would." c

"Definitely," he said.

"Then perhaps, in this way, it is not unreasonable that he must not kill himself until a god sends him some imperative, just like the present situation we now have."

"This, at least" said Cebes, "seems likely. As you were saying just now, Socrates—that philosophers would easily be willing to die—that seems strange, if what we were saying just now is reasonable, that god is our guardian and we are his possessions. It makes no sense that the d
wisest men would *not* be upset when they leave their service,[2] when the best overseers of beings, the gods, oversee them, since there's no way this man thinks he will be a better caretaker of himself than the gods, once he becomes free. A foolish man perhaps thinks this, that he must flee from his master, not because he reasons that he must not flee a good master but instead should definitely stay, but because he flees when he is irrational, whereas the person of sense always desires to be alongside what is better than him. In this way, then, Socrates, the opposite of what we were just saying is likely: it is appropriate for wise men to be upset at dying, while the foolish rejoice."

Hearing this, Socrates was pleased, it seemed to me, at Cebes' thor- 63a
oughness, and looking over towards us he said, "Cebes is always going over the arguments and is unwilling to believe right away anything someone says.

And Simmias said, "But surely, Socrates, at the moment, at least, I think Cebes has a point: Why would truly wise men flee masters who are better than them and lightly wish to be free of them? And I think Cebes is directing the argument at you because you are bearing so lightly your departure from us and from good rulers, as you yourself agreed—the gods.

"You are both making just accusations and I think you are saying b
that I have to defend myself against these charges as if at trial."

"Yes, absolutely," said Simmias.

"Come, then," said he, "Let me try to mount a more persuasive defense than I did before the jurors. For if I did not believe, Simmias and Cebes," he said, "that I will reach, firstly, other wise and good gods and, secondly, dead men better than those here, I would be wrong not to be upset at death. But rest assured that I hope, at present, to arrive c

1 *your own property* I.e., his slaves.

2 *their service* I.e., their status as servants to the gods.

among good men, though I wouldn't strongly assert this. But that I will reach gods who are very good masters, however, rest assured that were I to insist on any statement of this sort, this would be it! And so, for this reason I am not upset in that way but I am hopeful that there is something more for the dead and—as has long been said, at least—that it is much better for the good than for the bad."

"Well, then, Socrates," said Simmias, "do you intend to keep this
d thinking to yourself as you depart, or might you share it with us? Because it certainly seems, to me at least, that it would be to our advantage to share in it too, and at the same time it would be your defense, if you convince us of what you say."

"Yes, I will try," he said. "But first, let's see what it is Crito here has been wanting to say for a while, I think."

"Oh, Socrates," Crito said, "it's just that for a while the man who will be giving you the poison has long been saying that I should tell you to talk as little as possible. He says that those who talk become
e warmer and nothing like that should come in contact with the poison; otherwise, people who act in this way sometimes have to drink twice or three times."

And Socrates said, "Tell him to go and just get ready to do his job and give it twice, or three times, even, if he has to."

"That's pretty much what I thought," said Crito, "but he has been pestering me for a while."

"Send him off," he said. "But to you, my jurors, I want to present, right away, my argument for why it seems to me that a man who has really spent his life on philosophy should reasonably be confident
64a when he is about to die, and be hopeful of winning there the greatest goods after he has died. How exactly this might be, Simmias and Cebes, I will try to demonstrate.

"It's likely that other people aren't aware that those who truly undertake philosophy practice nothing other than dying and being dead. If this is true, it would certainly be strange to be eager for nothing other than this, for their whole lives, but, when it has come, to be upset at what they had been anticipating and practicing for so long."

b And Simmias burst out laughing and said, "By Zeus, Socrates, you made me laugh even though I'm not at all in a laughing mood right now. For I think that most people who hear this would think that it is very well said, with regard to philosophers, and the people where we're from[1] would agree completely that philosophers really do want to die and are quite aware that this is what they deserve to suffer."

---

1 *where we're from* Thebes (which the Athenians would have looked down on as a bit of a cultural backwater).

"And they would be speaking the truth, Simmias, except about being 'quite aware,' for they aren't aware in what way those who are truly philosophers want to die, and in what way they deserve death, and what sort of death. So, let us discuss these things among ourselves c
and ignore these people. Do we think that there is such a thing as death?"

"Definitely," said Simmias in reply.

"And that it is nothing other than the separation of the soul from the body? And that the following is what death is: the body exists separately, itself by itself, set free from the soul, and the soul, set free from the body, exists itself by itself. Is death anything other than this?"

"No, it's exactly this," he said.

"Then, see if the following seems right to you, as it does to me, for d
on this basis I think we will know more about what we're looking into. Does it seem to you that it belongs to a man of philosophy to pay attention to the so-called pleasures, such as eating and drinking?"

"Least of all, Socrates," said Simmias.

"What about the pleasure of sex?"

"Not at all."

"And what about the other cares of the body? Does it seem to you that such a man thinks highly of them, possessing distinctive clothes and shoes and other adornments of the body? Do you think he honors or dishonors them to the extent that there is no great necessity to par- e
take in them?

"I think he dishonors them," he said, "the man who is truly a philosopher, that is."

"Therefore, in general," he said, "don't you think that the business of such a person has nothing to do with the body, but that as much as possible he keeps away from it and turns toward the soul?" "I do."

"So, first of all, in such matters it is clear that the philosopher dif- 65a
fers from other men by separating the soul as much as possible from associating with the body?"

"It seems so."

"And it certainly seems to most people, Simmias, that a person who takes no pleasure from these and does not partake in them does not deserve to live, and the person who pays no mind to the pleasures that come from the body is, in a way, as good as dead."

"You've got that right!"

"But what about this next point: the acquisition of prudence. Is the body an impediment whenever someone brings it along as a partner on the search, or not? I mean this kind of thing: do the sight and hearing b
of men have any truth, or aren't they the sort of thing that the poets are

always going on about to us, that we neither hear nor see anything accurately? And if these, out of all the perceptions by the body, are not accurate or clear, the others will scarcely be, for they are all inferior to them. Don't you think so?"

"Absolutely," he said.

"Well, then," said he, "when does the soul grasp the truth? For whenever it tries to examine something with the body, it's obviously deceived by it."

c "You're right."

"Well, then, is it not by reasoning, if at all, that something about the real things becomes discernible to it?"

"Yes."

"And it reasons most finely when it is not diverted by any of these things—not hearing or sight, none of the pains nor any pleasure—and instead, whenever it is by itself as much as possible and ignores the body and, as much as it can, does not associate with it and is not bound to it, it reaches out for what is real."

"That's how it is."

d "So in this too, the soul of the philosopher greatly dishonors the body and flees from it, but it seeks to be by itself?"

"It appears so."

"Well, then, what about this sort of thing, Simmias? Do we say there is something that is, by itself, just, or not?"

"We certainly do, by Zeus!"

"And further, something beautiful? And something good?"

"Of course."

"And up to now, have you ever seen anything of this sort with your eyes?"

"Not at all," he said.

"And would you grasp them by means of any other sense that uses the body? I am talking about all of these things, such as size, health,
e strength, and in a word, the essence of all these others, that each happens to have. Or isn't this how it is: the person among us who has prepared to consider as carefully and precisely as possible each essence of the things he examines, this man would come closest to knowing each of them?"

"Absolutely."

"And the person who would do this most thoroughly is the one who approaches each thing with the mind, isolated as much as possible and
66a not bringing any sight into the consideration or adding any other sense to his reasoning, but using reasoning, by itself and unmixed, tries to pursue each thing, by itself and unmixed, among the things that are, letting go as much as possible of eyes and ears and the whole body, so

to speak, so that, by not allowing the soul to be troubled, he acquires
truth and prudence whenever the soul shares in them. Isn't it this man,
Simmias, who will hit upon what is, if anyone does?"

"It is remarkable how truly you speak, Socrates," Simmias said.

"And so for all these reasons a belief like this must occur to legitimate b
philosophers,[1] with the result that they also say to one another something
of the following sort: 'Look, it's likely some narrow path, as it were, will
see us through, with the help of reason, in the inquiry, because as long as
we have a body, and our soul is kneaded together with this evil thing, will
we never sufficiently possess what we desire, which is, we say, the truth.
For the body provides us with countless tasks because of its need for sus- c
tenance, and moreover, if some diseases befall it, they impede our hunt
for what is. With lusts and desires and fears and all kinds of illusions and
a lot of nonsense it fills us up, so that, as the saying goes, it is really and
truly impossible to think anything whatsoever because of it. Of wars and
factions and battles there is no other cause than the body and its desires.
All wars are produced by the acquisition of money, but money is what we d
are compelled by the body to acquire, being enslaved to servicing it, and
on top of that we have no leisure time for philosophy, for all these reasons.
And to cap it all, if one of us actually does get leisure from it and we turn
to examining something, the body once more intrudes everywhere upon
our inquiries, causing disruption and disturbance and distracting us, so
that it is impossible to behold the truth because of it. And really it be-
comes clear that if we intend to ever know anything plainly, we must rid e
ourselves of it and must look into the things themselves by means of the
soul alone. And the time, as it seems, when we will have what we desire
and prudence—is when we are dead, or so the argument indicates, and not
when we are living. For if the body prevents us possessing it in a pure
state, then one of these must be true: we can possess it either never, or only
when dead, for then the soul will be by itself and separate from the body, 67a
and not before. And while we are alive, we would come closest to know-
ing, it seems, by not interacting or associating with the body at all, unless
completely necessary, and by not being infected by its nature but by keep-
ing clean and clear of it until god himself frees us. And cleansed in this
way by being set free from the foolishness of the body, we will likely
exist alongside other such souls, and know for ourselves everything that
is pure. And this is perhaps the truth, since the impure would not be al- b
lowed to attain the pure.' Such, I think, Simmias, must be what they say
to each other and what all those who are properly lovers of learning think.
Or don't you think so?"

---

1 *legitimate philosophers* Genuine lovers of wisdom, *philo-sophoi*.

"More than anything, Socrates."

"Well, then," said Socrates, "if these things are true, my friend, I
have great hope that, when I arrive at the place I am traveling to, I will
sufficiently possess, there if anywhere, the thing for the sake of which
c our mighty labors have been in the life gone by, so that the journey
abroad that I am now ordered to make is indeed taking place with good
hope, as it does for every man who thinks his mind has been pre-
pared—purified, even."

"Absolutely," said Simmias.

"And doesn't this purification happen to be what was said a while
back during our discussion, the separation of the soul from the body
as much as possible and to accustom it to collecting and assembling it-
self by itself from all the parts of the body, and to live alone by itself
d as much as it can, both now and in the future, set free from the body
as if from chains?"

"Absolutely," he said.

"Well, then, this is what is called 'death', the releasing and separation of the soul from the body?"

"Precisely," he said.

"And those who philosophize truly are always eager to release it, as we maintain, especially and only them, and this is what philosophers practice: the release and separation of the soul from the body. Or is it not?

"It seems so."

"And I was saying in the beginning, wouldn't it be laughable for a
e man who is accustoming himself, throughout his life, to living as close
as possible to being dead to then be upset when it comes to him?"

"It would be laughable, of course."

"In reality, then, Simmias, those who philosophize correctly are prac-
ticing dying, and death is least frightening to them of all men. Consider
it on these grounds: if they resented the body in every way and wanted
to have the soul itself by itself, but they were afraid and upset when this
68a happens, would it not be very irrational, if they would not gladly go to
the very place where those arriving can hope to achieve what they were
yearning for throughout life—they were yearning for prudence—and of
freedom from being yoked to the thing they resented? Many people have
willingly gone to the land of Hades[1] in pursuit of the beloved fellows or
wives or sons who have died, driven by the hope of there seeing and
being with what they desire. But someone who truly loves prudence and
b holds tightly to that same hope, that they will not find it anywhere else

1 *Many ... Hades* In Greek mythology, mortals who have visited Hades include Orpheus, Odysseus, Heracles, Sisyphus, Psyche, Theseus, and Pirithous.

in any form worth mentioning except in the land of Hades, will he be upset when he dies, or rather, won't he gladly go to that very place? We must think he will, if indeed he really is, my friend, a philosopher, because he believes this very much, that nowhere else but there will he encounter prudence in its pure form. But if he believes this, then, as we were saying previously, would it not be irrational if such a man were frightened of death?"

"Very much so, by Zeus," he said.

"Well, then, is this sufficient proof for you," he said, "that the man who privately is aggrieved at the prospect of dying is not a 'lover of c
wisdom' but some sort of lover of the body? This same man is likely some kind of money-lover and honor-lover—certainly one of these, or perhaps both."

"It certainly is as you say," he said.

"And so, furthermore, Simmias," he said, "doesn't what is called 'bravery' belong especially to those who are in this state of mind?"

"Absolutely," he said.

"And self-control, too, which even most people call 'self-control,' not being agitated by the desires but holding them in contempt and regulating them, doesn't it belong only to these people, the ones who think especially little of the body and live philosophically?"

"Necessarily," he said. d

"If you care," said he, "to consider the bravery and self-control of other men, it will seem strange to you."

"How so, Socrates?"

"You know," said he, "that everyone else thinks that death is among the great evils?"

"Very much so," he said.

"And so the brave, when they stand their ground in the face of death, stand their ground because of a fear of greater evils?"

"So they do."

"All others except the philosophers are brave because they are afraid and because of fear, but it's nonsensical, surely, to be brave because of fear and cowardice."

"Absolutely." e

"What, then, about the orderly people among them? Don't they suffer in the same way: because of some sort of self-gratification they are self-controlled? Of course, we say that this is impossible but nevertheless this is what their experience of their simple-minded self-control is like, for they fear that they will be deprived of other pleasures and, from their desire for these, they give up on some because of those
others that they are ruled by. And while they do call being ruled by 69a
pleasures 'self-gratification,' it nevertheless happens that when they

are mastered by pleasures, they master other pleasures, which is similar to what was said just now, about how they are self-controlled because of self-gratification."

"Apparently so."

"Blessed Simmias, this is probably not the right exchange to make for excellence, to exchange pleasures for pleasures and pains for pains and fear for fear and greater for less, as if they were currency. Perhaps this one thing—prudence—is the correct coin, for which all of these
b things should be exchanged, and everything that is bought and sold for this and with this would actually exist, and bravery and self-control and justice and, in sum, true excellence, exist with prudence, with pleasures and fears and all the other things of this sort being added and subtracted, and when they are separate from prudence and exchanged for one another, that sort of virtue is, perhaps, some counterfeit, that, in fact, would be slavish and lacking health or truth, while
c true virtue—self-control and justice and bravery—would actually be a purifying away of all such things, and prudence itself would be the purifier.

"Moreover, it looks as though the people who established our initiation ceremonies[1] for us were not some simple men, but have long been saying, in riddles, that whoever arrives in the land of Hades uninitiated and incomplete will lie down in filth, while he who has been purified and perfected will live with the gods when he arrives there. For, as the people concerned with ceremonies say, 'the narthex-
d bearers are many but the Bacchoi are few,'[2] and the latter, in my opinion, are none other than those who have philosophized correctly. And I in my life, as much as possible, have left nothing undone and have striven in every way to become one of them. Whether I have been right in my striving and we have accomplished something important, we will know the definitive answer when I arrive there, if god wills it, in just a little while, I think.

"So this, Simmias and Cebes," he said, "I put forward as a defense, in order to show how reasonable it is for me not to find it difficult nor
e be upset as I leave you and the rulers here, believing that there, no less than here, I will encounter good rulers and companions. In most peo-

---

1 *initiation ceremonies* Into the secretive "mystery cults" of religious groups.

2 *the narthex-bearers ... Bacchoi are few* Narthex is giant fennel, the staff of which was wrapped in ivy and topped with a pine cone to form a *thursos*, which was carried by those being initiated into the rites of Dionysus. Plato here suggests that the originators of the rites knew that not everyone who carried the fennel-wand was truly among the Bacchoi (those who reached the frenzied state). This aspect of the worship of Dionysus was incorporated into Roman mythology and the god Bacchus is named after it.

ple this produces disbelief; so if you find me a bit more convincing in my defense than the Athenian jurors, that would be good."

When Socrates was done saying all this, Cebes replied by saying, "Socrates, I think the other things you said were fine but matters con- 70a
cerning the soul produce a lot of disbelief among men, for fear that when it departs the body it is no longer anywhere, but is destroyed and ceases to exist on the day a man dies, as soon as it is separated from the body, and that as it exits, it is dispersed like breath or smoke being emitted and goes away, vanishing and no longer anywhere. If it were somewhere just by itself, gathered together and separated from those evils that you were going over just now, there would be a great and fine hope, Socrates, that what you are saying is true, but this probably b
requires a great deal of encouragement and persuasion, to show that a soul from a dead man exists and still has some capacities and prudence."

"Your words are true, Cebes," said Socrates, "but what should we do? Do you want to keep discussing these matters and whether or not they are likely to be as we say?"

"I, at least," said Cebes, "would be glad to hear your opinion on them."

"I certainly do not think," said Socrates, "that anyone who heard us now, even if he were a comic poet,[1] would say that I am chatting idly c
and arguing about things that are none of my business. So, if it seems good to you, we must look into them.

"Let's examine it something like this: are the souls of dead people in the land of Hades or not? There is certainly that old account[2] that we are reminded of, that they arrive from here, exist there, and come back here again and are reborn from the dead. And if this is the case, that the living come into being again from those who died, is there any option but that our souls would exist there? For they could not somehow d
be born again without existing, and I suppose this would be sufficient proof that things are this way, if it really were clear that the living are born from nowhere else except from those who have died. But if it is not, a different account would be needed."

"Absolutely," said Cebes.

"And indeed, look not just at humans," said he, "if you want to learn more easily, but also at all animals and plants, and let's look in general at everything that has a birth to see whether they all come to e
be in precisely the following way, as opposites from opposites—for those that have an opposite, such as the noble is the opposite of the

1 *comic poet* Authors of comic plays sometimes included cruel caricatures of Socrates. Aristophanes' play *Clouds*, in particular, is supposed to have played a major part in turning the public away from him.

2 *that old account* Socrates has in mind the views of Pythagoras and his followers.

shameful in some way, and the just of the unjust, and thousands of other opposites like these. Let us look into this, whether it is necessary for things with an opposite to come into being from nowhere else than from its opposite. For example, whenever something comes to be greater, must it somehow be from previously being less that it subsequently becomes greater?"

"Yes."

"And even if it should become less, it is from previously being
71a greater that it will become less later on?"

"That's how it is," he said.

"And surely from being stronger comes the weaker and from the slower the faster?"

"Certainly."

"What else? If a thing becomes worse, is it not from being better, and if more just, from being more unjust?"

"Of course."

"So, we have sufficiently grasped," he said, "that everything comes to be in this way, from the opposites come the opposite things?"

"Certainly."

"What next? Is there also something like this sort in them, I mean, in all these opposites something between both of them, two types of
b becoming—since there are two of them—from one to another and in turn from the other back again to the one? Between a greater thing and a lesser there is augmentation and reduction, and we thus call the one 'augmenting' and the other 'reducing'?"

"Yes," he said.

"And similarly, there's breaking up and combining, and cooling and heating, and everything like this. And even if we don't have the words in some cases, in practice mustn't it be like this in every case, that they come to be from one another and there is a process of generation of each of them into the other?"

"Absolutely," he said.

c "Well, then," he said, "is there an opposite to being alive, in the same way that being asleep is the opposite to being awake?"

"Absolutely," he said.

"What?"

"Being dead," he said.

"And these come to be from one another, since they are opposites, and the processes of generation between them are two, since there are two of them?"

"Of course."

"I will tell you about one of the pairs I mentioned just now," Socrates said, "both the pair and its generating processes, and then you

can tell me about the other one. I say that there is being asleep and being awake, and from being asleep comes being awake and from being awake comes being asleep, and the generating processes of the d
two are on the one hand, falling asleep, and, on the other, waking up. Is that enough for you, or not?"

"Absolutely."

"Okay, then you tell me in the same way," he said, "about life and death. For wouldn't you say that being dead is the opposite of being alive?"

"I would."

"And they come to be from one another?"

"Yes."

"And so what comes to be from the living?"

"The dead," he said.

"And what," he said, "from the dead?"

"I have to concede that it's the living?"

"From the dead, Cebes, come both living things and living people?"

"It seems so," he said. e

"And our souls," he said, "exist in the land of Hades."

"Apparently."

"And then, concerning the processes of generation related to these, isn't one of them obvious? For dying is certainly obvious, isn't it?"

"Absolutely," he said.

"And how," he said, "will we proceed? Will we not balance it with the opposite process of generation, but instead say that nature is defective in this regard? Or must we give some process as the opposite of dying?"

"By all means," he said.

"What is it?"

"Rebirth."

"Well, then," he said, "if rebirth does exist, it would be a process 72a
from those who have died to those who are alive, rebirth?"

"Indeed."

"So, then, in the same way we also agree that the living come from the dead no less than the dead from the living, and that since this is so, it seems to be sufficient proof that the souls of those who are dead exist in some place, from where they once again come into being."

"I think, Socrates," he said, "that, based on what we have agreed, that's how it must be."

"Look at it like this, too, Cebes," he said, "to see that we were not incorrect in our conclusion, in my opinion. If one side did not always repay the other by becoming, like going around in a circle, but instead b generation was something from one of them straight toward the direct opposite without bending back again to the other and it did not 'turn at the post,'[1] everything, you know, would end up in the same form and would reach the same condition and cease generating."

"How do you mean?" he said

"I don't mean anything difficult to understand," he said, "just, for example, that if falling asleep exists, but waking up did not repay it by
c coming to be from falling asleep, then everything would end up showing that Endymion wasn't unique—he would then be an 'also ran'[2] because everything else is already doing the same thing as him, sleeping. And if everything is mixed together and not separated, the saying of Anaxagoras would quickly come true: 'everything together.'[3] And similarly, my dear Cebes, if everything died that has life, but the dead, having died, remained in that state and were not again reborn, isn't it
d completely necessary that everything would end up dead and not living? For if the living come to be from other things but the living die, by what mechanism would anything not wind down into death?"

"I can't think of any, Socrates," said Cebes, "and I think you are speaking the absolute truth."

"I think it is, Cebes," he said, "more than anything at all, and we are not deceived into agreeing to this but being reborn really exists, and the
e living come to be from the dead, and the souls of the dead exist."

"And it certainly is," said Cebes, following up, "according to the argument that you often give, Socrates, if it is true that learning, for us, is nothing other than recollection,[4] and so we must have at a pre-
73a vious time somehow learned what we now recollect. This is impossible unless our souls exist somewhere prior to coming into being in this human form. And so, in this way too, the soul seems to be immortal."

"But Cebes," said Simmias in reply, "how are these claims demonstrated? Remind me, for I don't remember them very well just at the moment."

---

1 *turn at the post* In Greek horse races, a post marked the place where horses were to turn around and come back.

2 *showing ... also ran* Endymion was a mythological youth who was distinguished from other humans by spending most of his life asleep (as a punishment, or gift, from Selene the goddess of the moon). "Also ran" (literally, "appears nowhere" or "is a no-show") is another reference to horse-racing (after "turn the post" in 71b): in modern horse-racing, after the top finishers are named, the number of horses in a race that "also ran" is given.

3 *everything together* Anaxagoras was a pre-Socratic philosopher who held that the universe was an undifferentiated and uniform mass (separated into distinct forms by mind).

4 *learning ... recollection* See the *Meno*.

"One very beautiful argument," said Cebes, "is that when men are being questioned, if someone questions them well, they can say for themselves how everything is, but if the understanding and the correct argument did not happen to be within them already, they could not do this. And if you bring in diagrams or anything of this sort, too, b
you will most confidently declare that this is so."

"And if you are not persuaded by this, Simmias," Socrates said, "see if you agree when you look at it something like the following, since you are disbelieving about how what is called 'learning' is recollection."

"Disbelieve you? No!" Simmias said. "It's just," he said, "that I want to experience the very thing the discussion was about: recollection. And based on what Cebes tried to explain I pretty much already remember and am convinced. Even so, I would still hear how you were trying to explain it."

"For me, it's like this," he said. "We certainly agree that if some- c
one is to recollect something, he must know it at some previous time."

"Indeed," he said.

"And then we also agree to this, that whenever knowledge is produced in this way, that's recollection? I mean in a way something like this: if someone, when he sees something or hears or grasps it by some other sense, not only knows that thing but also has in mind something else, of which the knowledge is not the same but different, don't we justly say that he has recollected the thing he thought of?" d

"How do you mean?"

"Such as the following: there is different knowledge of a man and of a lyre."[1]

"Of course."

"And don't you know that lovers, whenever they see a lyre or cloak or something else that their beloved boy would customarily use, they have the following experience: they have knowledge of the lyre *and* in their mind they grasp the form of the boy whose lyre it was? This is recollection, just like someone seeing Simmias is often reminded of Cebes, and there might be thousands of other such cases."

"By Zeus, thousands more," said Simmias.

"Well, then," said he, "is this kind of thing recollection of a sort? e
And especially when someone has this experience about something that he has forgotten, because he hasn't observed it for a while?"

"Absolutely," he said.

"And what about the case" said he, "when someone who sees a picture of a horse or a picture of a lyre recalls a man, or from seeing a picture of Simmias recalls Cebes?"

---

1 *lyre* A stringed musical instrument.

"Indeed."

"Or from seeing a picture of Simmias recalls Simmias himself?"

74a "It is, certainly," he said.

"And based on all of these, recollection can be from similar things and also from dissimilar?"

"It can."

"But when someone recollects something similar to a present thing, isn't it necessary that he also experiences this: he has in mind whether the present thing is exactly similar to the recollected thing or not?

"Necessarily," he said.

"See, then," said he, "if the following is the case. We say that something equal exists, I don't mean a log equal to a log or a stone equal to a stone, but something else of a different kind, something beyond all of these, the equal itself. Shall we assert that *this* exists, or not?"

b "Let us assert it, by Zeus," said Simmias, "with wonder."

"And we know *what* this is?"

"Indeed," said he.

"From where did we grasp the knowledge of it? Was it not from what we mentioned a moment ago, by seeing equal logs or stones or whatever else, from these we brought to mind that other thing, different from them? Or does it not seem to you to be different? Look at it this way, too. Do not equal stones or logs, although the same, sometimes appear equal to one person but to another do not?"

"Absolutely."

c "But what about this: is there ever an occasion when the equal itself appears unequal to you, or when equality appears to be inequality?"

"At no time whatsoever, Socrates."

"So they are not the same," he said, "those equals and the equal itself."

"They seem not at all the same to me, Socrates."

"And yet it was from those equals," he said, "even though they are different from the equal, that you nevertheless brought to mind the knowledge of equality itself and grasped it?"

"You are entirely correct," he said.

"And either it is similar to them or dissimilar?"

"Indeed."

d "It makes no difference," said he. "As long as from the appearance of one thing that you see you bring to mind another, whether similar or dissimilar, that must," he said, "be recollection."

"Absolutely."

"What next?" said he. "Do we experience anything of this sort concerning the equals in the logs and the equals in what we were just talking about? Do *they* appear to be equal to us in the same way that the equal itself is equal or do they lack something compared to it, as far as being of the same sort as the equal, or nothing?

"They lack a lot," he said.

"So, we agree that whenever someone who sees something thinks,
'What I now see aims at being like some other of the beings, but falls e
short and is unable to be an equal in the way it is, but is inferior,' the person who thinks this must know in advance the thing which he says it resembles, though quite deficiently?"

"Necessarily."

"Well, then, did we experience something of this sort, or not, concerning the equal things and the equal itself?"

"Undoubtedly."

"Then we must have known in advance the equal before the time 75a
when, upon seeing the equals, we thought 'All these things are aiming to be like the equal but are falling short.'"

"That is so."

"But surely we also agree to this: from nowhere else this is brought to mind—nor *can* it be brought to mind—except by seeing or touching or one of the other senses; I'm taking all of these to be the same."

"They are the same, Socrates, at least with respect to what the argument is trying to show."

"And of course it must be through our sensations that we bring to
mind that all the things in our sensations strive for the thing that *is* b
equal and are quite lacking compared to it. Or how should we put it?"

"Like that."

"Before we began to see and hear and to perceive in other ways, we must have somewhere acquired the knowledge of the equal itself and what it is, if we were going to compare the equals from our sensations to that one."

"This follows necessarily from what we said before, Socrates."

"And immediately from birth we were seeing and hearing and using the other senses?"

"Indeed."

"And it is necessary, we claim, to have acquired the knowledge of c
the equal before them?"

"Yes."

"So it seems we must have acquired it before being born."

"Apparently."

"If we acquired it before being born and were born possessing it, then we had the knowledge even before being born and immediately upon birth—and not just the equal and the more and the less but everything of the sort? For our present discussion is not just about the equal
d any more than it is about the noble itself and the good itself and the just and the holy and, as we said, about everything we label 'the ___ itself' in both our questions, when asking questions, and in our answers, when answering. And so we must have acquired the knowledge of all these before being born."

"That is so."

"If, once acquired, we *don't* forget them at any point, we would always be born knowing them and know them always throughout life. For this is what knowing is: to hold onto the knowledge we have acquired and to not have lost it. Or isn't that what we call forgetting, Simmias, the loss of knowledge?"

e "Completely right, Socrates," he said.

"But if, I think, we possess it before being born but *lose* it when being born, and then later, by use of the senses, we re-acquired the knowledge that we previously possessed, wouldn't what is called learning be the re-acquisition of our own knowledge? If we named this something like 'recollection', wouldn't we be naming it properly?"

"Indeed."

76a "For it seems possible that by perceiving something—either by seeing or hearing or using any other sense—a person may bring to mind, based on that perception, some other thing that had been forgotten but which was associated with the perception, whether dissimilar or similar. So, as I was saying, one of two things is the case: either we are born knowing and know throughout our whole life or, after birth, those whom we say learn, these people are just recollecting, and learning would be recollection."

"Very much so, Socrates."

b "So, which do you choose, Simmias? Are we born knowing or do we later recollect the things that we had previously come to know?"

"At present, Socrates, I am unable to choose."

"Well, then, perhaps you can make a choice about the following, and something will suggest itself to you about it: whenever a man has knowledge, is he able to give an account of what he knows, or not?"

"He really must, Socrates," he said.

"And does everyone in fact seem to you to be able to give an account of the matters we were discussing just now?"

"I wish they could," said Simmias, "but I'm afraid it's much more likely that by this time tomorrow there won't be a single human who is up to the task."

"So then in your opinion," he said, "does everyone have knowl- c
edge of these things?"

"Not at all."

"So, they are recollecting what they once learned?"

"Necessarily."

"When did our souls acquire the knowledge of these things? It certainly can't be after we became human."

"Certainly not."

"Then it was before."

"Yes."

"So the souls also existed before, before taking human form, separate from the body, and possessing prudence."

"Unless we acquired these truths at birth, Socrates—that time still remains a possibility."

"But, then, my friend, at what other time do we lose them? For we d
are not born possessing them, as we agreed just now. Or do we lose them at the same time as we acquire them? Or is there some other time you can mention?"

"Not at all, Socrates. I didn't notice I was talking nonsense."

"So, is this how we think things are, Simmias?" he said. "If the things that we're always going on about exist—a thing that is noble, and a good, and each such essence—and we compare all of the things
from our sensations to this—it is available from before and we dis- e
cover again that it is ours and compare these things to that—it must be that, just as these things in fact exist, our soul likewise exists, even before we were born? And if these do not exist, this argument would have been given in vain? Is this how it is, that it is equally necessary that these things exist and our souls exist, even before we are born, and if these did not, neither did they?"

"This necessity seems overwhelming to me, Socrates," said Sim-
mias, "and the argument reaches the fine conclusion that our soul ex- 77a
ists before we are born and likewise the essence which you now mention. There's nothing that seems more obvious to me than this does, that all such things exist to the fullest extent, the noble and the good and all of the others that you were mentioning just now. The matter seems to have been sufficiently proven to me."

"And to Cebes?" said Socrates. "Cebes must be convinced too."

"It's enough," said Simmias, "even though he is the most stubborn of people when it comes to believing arguments. But I think he is suf-
ficiently convinced of this, that before we were born our soul existed. b
However, that it will still exist whenever we die, I don't think has been proved, Socrates, and what Cebes mentioned just now still stands in the way, the common fear that at the same time as we die the soul scat-

ters from the body and this is the end of its existence. For what prevents it from coming to be and being put together from some other place, and existing even before it takes on a human body, but then, when it leaves and escapes it, it too meets its end and is destroyed?"

c "Well put, Simmias," said Cebes. "It appears that only half of what is needed has been proved, that before we are born our soul existed. But it also needs to be proved that even when we die it will exist no less than before birth, if the proof is going to be complete."

"It has already been proved, Simmias and Cebes," Socrates said, "if you are prepared to put this argument together with the one that we agreed upon earlier, that all living things are born from the dead. For if
d the soul exists previously and it must enter life and be born from nowhere else but from death and being dead, must it not also exist after death, since it has to be born again? So what you mentioned just now has been proved. Nevertheless, I think that you and Simmias would gladly continue discussion of this claim still further and fear, as children do, that
e when it departs the body the wind truly does disperse and scatter it—especially whenever a person dies not in calm weather but in a great gust!"

Cebes laughed and said, "Try to convince us, Socrates, as if we did have this fear, or rather, not as though *we* were afraid but as though there is perhaps within us a child who has these fears. So, try to coax him into not fearing death as if it were a bogeyman."

"Well, then, it is necessary to sing to him every day until he is charmed out of it."

78a "So where," he said, "will we find a good singer of such charms, Socrates, since *you*," he said, "are leaving us?"

"Greece is large, Cebes," he said, "and somewhere in it there are good men. And many also are the races of foreigners, all of which must be examined thoroughly in pursuit of such a charmer, sparing neither money nor effort, as there is nothing more critical to spend your money on. You yourselves must make the search, with each other, as perhaps you would not easily find anyone more capable of this task than yourselves."

b "Well, that certainly will be done," said Cebes, "but let's go back to where we left off, if that's okay with you."

"I am happy to, of course."

"You are quite gracious," he said.

"Well, then," Socrates said, "mustn't we ask ourselves things like this: 'What is the kind of thing that undergoes this experience, scattering, and what sort of thing should we be afraid for, in case it undergoes it, and to what is not that kind of thing?' and beyond this, we must in turn examine to which the soul belongs, and based on this we should be confident or fearful for our souls?"

"That's true," he said.

"Now a compounded and composite thing is naturally inclined to c
undergo this, to be divided in the very way it was compounded. And if something happens to be uncompounded, this alone, if anything, is not the kind of thing to undergo it."

"That's the way it seems to me," said Cebes.

"And whatever is always the same and in the same way, these are especially likely to be the uncompounded things, whereas what changes across time and is never the same, these are compounds?"

"It seems so to me, at least."

"So, let us turn to 'the same things' from our earlier discussion. Is d
the essence itself—whose being we give an account of by questioning and answering—always in the same way and the same, or does it vary with time? The equal itself, the noble itself, each thing itself, *being*: are these capable of any change at all? Or is each of them always what it is, having a single form, itself by itself, remaining the same thing in the same way, and incapable of any change at any time, in any respect or by any means?"

"It must be in the same way and the same thing, Socrates," said Cebes.

"What about the many beautiful things, such as men or horses or e
cloaks or whatever else of this sort, or equal things, or everything that has the same name as those? Do they remain the same, or entirely opposite to those? Are they, so to speak, "no-when and no-way" the same, either with respect to themselves or to each other?"

"They, in turn, are like this," said Cebes, "they never stay the same way."

"And these you can touch and see and perceive with the other 79a
senses, while the things that are the same, there is nothing by which they can be grasped except the reasoning of the mind, as such things are invisible and cannot be seen?"

"You are completely right," he said.

"Is it your wish that we assume there are two forms of beings, one visible and the other invisible?"

"Let us assume them," he said.

"And that the invisible always remains the same, while the visible is never the same?"

"Let us assume that too," he said.

"Come, now," he said, "is there anything more to us than the body, b
on the one hand, and the soul, on the other?"

"Nothing else," he said.

"Which form would we say that the body is more similar to and closer to?"

"It's obvious to everyone," he said, "that it's to the visible."

"And what about the soul? Visible or invisible?"

"Not by humans, anyway, Socrates," he said.

"But we, at any rate, were calling things visible and invisible in relation to the nature of humans? Or were you thinking of some other way?"

"To the human."

"And what do we say about the soul? Is it visible or not visible?"

"It is not visible."

"Invisible, then?"

"Yes."

"Soul is then more similar to the invisible than the body, and the body to the visible."

c "That's entirely necessary, Socrates."

"And so we were saying just this a while ago, that the soul, whenever it uses the body for investigating something, whether by seeing or by hearing or by some other sense—for doing it 'by means of the body' is to investigate something by the senses—it is drawn by the body towards things that are never the same, and the soul itself wanders about and is stirred up and becomes dizzy, as if it were drunk, to the extent that it latches onto such things?"

"Indeed."

d "But whenever this investigates by itself, it goes to the place of the pure and constant being that persists without dying and change, and since it is kin to this, it always becomes one with it, whenever it is by itself and allowed to do so, and it ceases its wandering, and when around these objects it always remains the same, and in the same way, so long as it is united with such things, and this condition is called 'prudence'?"

"Your words, in every way," he said, "are fine and true, Socrates."

"Which form, then—based on what we were saying both previously
e and now—do you think the soul is more like and closer to?"

"I think everyone would agree," he said, "even the slowest learner, that, based on this inquiry, the soul is wholly and completely like what is always the same, rather than what is not."

"And what about the body?"

"Like the other kind."

80a "Look at it in this way, too, that whenever soul and body are in one thing, nature establishes one to be slave and be ruled, and the other to rule and be master. So, again, which one in this case seems to you to be similar to the divine and which to the mortal? Or don't you think that the divine by nature rules and leads, while the mortal is ruled and serves?"

"I think so."

"So, which is the soul like?"

"It's clear, Socrates, that the soul is like the divine and the body is like the mortal."

"Well then, Cebes," he said, "see if, from all that has been said, this b
is how things stand: to the divine and the undying and the intelligent and the uniform and the indissoluble and to what always is as it is and remains the same as itself, soul is most similar, but to the human and the dying and the multiform and unintelligent and dissoluble and to what never remains the same as itself, body is in turn most similar. Do we have something else to say beside this, dear Cebes, according to which this is *not* how things are?"

"We do not."

"What next? With these things being so, isn't it fitting that the body soon disintegrates, but for soul to be completely indissoluble, or something close to it?"

"Of course." c

"Consider, then," he said, "that when a man dies, the visible part of him, the body, which lies in the visible—the very thing we call 'a corpse'—and which is the kind of thing that unravels and crumbles and blows away, does not undergo any of these right away, but as is reasonable continues on for quitc a while, and even for a long time, if a person dies with the body in fine condition and in the prime of life. A body shrunken and embalmed, as is the practice in Egypt, remains
almost whole for an extraordinary length of time, and even if it rots, d
some parts of the body—bones and sinews and so on—are nonetheless immortal, so to speak. Or not?"

"Yes."

"But the soul, the invisible, that goes to some other place that is noble and pure and invisible, to the true land of Hades, alongside the good and wise god—to where, if god wills it, my soul must presently go—is *this*, being of this kind and having this nature, immediately dis-
persed and destroyed when it escapes from the body, as many men e
say? Not at all, my dear Cebes and Simmias! In all probability it's like this: if it escapes cleanly, dragging with it nothing from the body, since it voluntarily has nothing in common with it during life, but avoids it and keeps itself to itself, and this is always its focus—and this, inci-
dentally, is precisely philosophizing correctly and really practicing to 81a
bear being dead lightly—or would this not be practicing for death?"

"Undoubtedly, yes."

"Then, in that case, it departs into the invisible, which is like it, divine and undying and wise, and arriving there it can be happy, set free from wandering and madness and fears and strong desires and the

other evils of humankind, as is said about the initiates,[1] and in truth
spends the rest of time with the gods. Is this how we should put it,
Cebes, or in some other way?"

"Like this, by Zeus," said Cebes.

b "But if, I suppose, it is tainted and impure when it is set free from
the body, insofar it always went along with the body, and served and
loved it, and was put under its spell by desires and pleasures, so that
nothing seemed real to it but the bodily—whatever a person can touch
and see and drink and eat and use for sexual pleasure—whereas what
is obscure and invisible to the eyes, though intelligible and under-
standable to philosophy, it has been trained to hate and shun and flee
c from, do you think that in this case the soul would escape itself by it-
self and unmixed?"

"Not at all," he said.

"In fact, won't it be riddled with the bodily, which the association and companionship of the body made natural to it, by constantly being together and giving it a lot of attention."

"Indeed."

"Moreover, my friend, we must suppose that this is cumbersome
and heavy and earthly and visible, and such a soul, by bearing this
very thing, is weighed down and dragged back into the visible place
d by fear of the invisible and of the land of Hades, and, as it is said, it
rolls around among the memorials and graves, around which in fact
have been seen some shadowy apparitions of souls, the kind of phan-
toms produced by souls that were not cleanly set free but had a share
of the visible, which is why they are seen."

"That is quite likely, Socrates."

"Likely indeed, Cebes. And also that it's not the souls of good peo-
ple but of bad people that are compelled to wander around such places,
paying the price for their previous evil way of life. And they wander
e about until they are again bound to a body by the desire of the thing
accompanying them: the bodily. And they are bound, it is likely, to
things of such character as they happened to pursue during life."

"What kind do you mean, Socrates?"

"For example, those who focused on gluttony and violence and
drunkenness, and were not on guard against them, are likely to enter
82a the species of mules and other such beasts. Or do you think not?"

"What you say is very likely."

"Indeed. And the unjust and the tyrannical and those who focused on stealing go into the species of wolves and hawks and kites. Or where else should we say such souls go?"

1 *initiates* New members of a religious cult.

"Without a doubt," said Cebes, "into these."

"So," said he, "it's clear that each of the others too would enter whatever is similar to their focus?"

"Clearly," he said. "Of course."

"And the most fortunate of these," he said, "and those entering the best place, are those who pursued popular and social virtue, so-called b
'moderation' and 'justice', produced by habit and practice without philosophy and thought?"

"In what way are these most fortunate?"

"Because they probably come again into some kind of social and civilized species, bees perhaps, or wasps or ants, or even the same as before, into the human race once more—and from them decent men are born."

"Probably."

"Yes, and those who did not philosophize and were not completely c
purified are not permitted to enter into the race of gods when they leave, but only the lover of learning. It's for *this* reason, my friends Simmias and Cebes, that those who correctly philosophize stay away from all of the bodily desires and stay strong and don't give themselves over to them—not because they fear the waste of resources and poverty, as do the many who love money, nor again out of a fear of dishonor and bad reputation, like those who love power and repute, since they stay away from those."

"That would not be suitable, Socrates," said Cebes.

"Not at all, by Zeus!" said he. "And it's for that very reason that all d
those who prioritize their souls, Cebes, and do not live nourishing their bodies, bid farewell to such people, and they do not travel in the same direction as people who do not know where they are going, but thinking that they must not do anything opposed to philosophy, with its deliverance and purification, they turn and follow *it*, wherever it leads."

"How, Socrates?"

"I will tell you," he said. "The lovers of learning know," said he, e
"that philosophy, taking the soul under its wing when it is absolutely bound fast and stuck to the body and is compelled to consider reality by means of it, as if through a cage, and not on its own and in its own way, and is rolling around in complete ignorance, and further, realizing that what is most terrible about the cage is that it results from desires, and so the imprisoned soul[1] could be the primary accomplice in the imprisonment—the lovers of learning, as I say, know 83a
that when philosophy takes on their soul in this state it gently encourages it and tries to free it, pointing out that inquiry by means

1 *the imprisoned soul* The soul when it desires bodily things. See 83d.

the eyes is full of deceit—as it likewise is by means of the ears and the other senses—persuading it to pull back from these, at least to the extent that it is not necessary to use them, and recommending that it gather itself by itself and to collect itself, and to
b trust nothing but itself, believing only the thing itself by itself—of the things that are—that it can apprehend itself by itself; and to think that whatever it might look into through other modes—different for different things—is untrue, and that such things are perceptible and visible, whereas what the soul sees is intelligible and invisible. The soul of the true philosopher, thinking that he must not oppose this deliverance, abandons the pleasures and the desires and pains and fears as much as possible, reasoning that whenever someone strongly feels pleasure or fear or pain or desire, he
c suffers not just the kind of evil one might suppose—being sick or using something up because of desires—but suffers what is the greatest and the ultimate of all evils, and without taking it into account."

"What is that, Socrates?" said Cebes.

"That the soul of every man must, at the same time as it experiences extreme sensation or is pained by something, think, concerning what it is greatly being affected by, that it is most clear and most true, even though it is not. Visible things especially, or not?"

"Indeed."

d "And in this experience especially, soul is imprisoned by the body?"

"How so?"

"Because each pleasure and pain is like a nail in attaching and fastening it to the body and making it bodily, thinking that whatever the body says is true. For from its agreement with the body and its delighting in the same things, it must, I think, come to be of the same breed and the same breeding, so that it never makes a clean getaway to the land of Hades but always exits filled with the body, so that it
e soon falls again into another body, implanted like a seed being sown, and because of this does not share in the divine and the pure and uniform."

"Your words are most true, Socrates," said Cebes.

"It is for these reasons, Cebes, that those who rightly pursue learning are moderate and brave, and not for what the many say. Or do you think so?"

84a "I certainly do not."

"No, the soul of a philosophical man reasons rather in this way: it would not consider using philosophy to free it and then, having freed itself, giving itself back to pleasures and pains to bind itself

again, performing the never-ending task of a Penelope putting her hand to the loom[1] in reverse. Instead, remaining calm, following reason and always keeping to it, and targeting the true and the divine and the factual, and being nourished by this, it thinks that it must b
live in this way for as long as it lives, and when it reaches its end, it stays away from human evils and departs into what is related and similar to it. Based on this upbringing, there is no risk that it would be afraid of being pulled apart in the departure from the body, blown in different directions by the winds, and go flying off and no longer exist anywhere."

For quite a while after Socrates had said these things there was si- c
lence and Socrates himself was preoccupied with what had been said, or so it seemed by looking, as were most of us, too, though Cebes and Simmias were talking quietly together. And seeing them, Socrates asked, "What's that? No doubt you think what was said was not sufficiently argued? There are certainly still many doubts and weak spots, if someone wishes to go over these matters thoroughly. If you two are considering something else, I will move on, but if you have any difficulties with them, don't hold back from stating them and discussing them, if it some- d
how seems that anything better could have been said, and bring me along too, if you think you will fare somewhat better with me."

And Simmias said, "Of course, Socrates. I will tell you the truth. For a long time, each of us in puzzlement has been pushing the other forward and bidding him to ask a question, wanting to hear but hesitating to make trouble, in case it prove troublesome for you because of your present situation."

When he heard this, he laughed gently and said, "Uh-oh, Simmias, it will surely be difficult to persuade other men that I do not think my e
present situation is a misfortune when I can't even persuade you two, and instead you are afraid that I am somewhat more touchy now than previously in my life. And, it appears, you think I am worse at prophesying than the swans who, when they realize that they must die, even though they sing throughout life, then sing most abundantly and most 85a
earnestly, overjoyed that they are about to go away to be with the god whose servants they are.[2] Men, however, because of their own fear of death, misrepresent the swans and say that they sing out in pain and are bewailing death, and they do not take into account that no bird sings

---

1 *Penelope ... loom* In Homer's *Odyssey*, Penelope was the wife of Odysseus, remaining true to him while he was away for 20 years, discouraging numerous suitors by telling them to wait until she'd finished her weaving while by night ripping out what she had woven by day.

2 *the swans who ... servants they are* This myth is the origin of the phrase 'swan song,' i.e., a final effort before death or retirement.

when it is hungry or cold or experiencing any other pain, not the
nightingale itself, nor the swallow, nor the hoopoe, which they say
b sing a dirge in pain. But these don't seem to me to sing in pain, and
neither do the swans, but rather, I think, because they are birds of
Apollo, they are prophets, and knowing the good things to come in the
land of Hades, they sing and enjoy that day in a way different than any
before. And I think myself a fellow-servant of the swans, an initiate of
the same god, and have received from the master the ability to proph-
esy just as well as they can, and am being released from life with no
more melancholy than them. But as far as this is concerned, you must
speak and ask whatever you want, for as long as the Eleven of Athens
permit."

c "You speak well," said Simmias, "and I will tell you what is puz-
zling me, and then he in turn will say why he does not accept what
was said. I think, Socrates, as perhaps you do too, that it is impossible
or extremely difficult to gain clear knowledge of these matters in this
life, but having said that, if someone refuses to examine what is said
about them by every means and without giving up before considering
them in every way, he is a very faint-hearted man. For it is necessary
to carry out, concerning these, at least one of the following: either to
learn or discover how things are or, if these are not possible, to sail
through life by taking hold of the human account that is best and most
d resistant to refutation and riding upon it as if defying danger on a raft,
unless he is able to travel more safely and with less risk, either in a
more secure vehicle or with the assurance of some god. And especially
now I am not ashamed to ask, since even you say to do so, nor will
later blame myself for not saying what I think now. For, when I ex-
amine, Socrates, either by myself or with Cebes, what was said, it
e doesn't seem quite sufficient."

And Socrates said, "Perhaps, my friend, the truth appears to you.
But say in what way it is insufficient."

"In the following way, at least to me," said he, "The same argu-
ment might be made about harmony and a lyre and its strings, that the
harmony is invisible and lacks a body and is something very beautiful
86a and divine in the tuned lyre, while the lyre itself and the strings are
bodies, and bodily and composite and earthy and related to the mor-
tal. And so whenever someone shatters the lyre or cuts through and
breaks the strings, if he should conclude by the same argument as
yours that the harmony must still exist and not have died—since it
does not allow for any mechanism by which the lyre, on the one hand,
could still exist after the strings are broken, as they have a mortal form,
b while the harmony, which is of the same nature and related to the di-
vine and undying, has died and died before the mortal strings—he

might claim that it is somehow necessary that the harmony still exists
and that the wood and the strings rot away long before anything hap-
pens to the harmony, and in fact, Socrates, I think—and you yourself
have also pondered on this—that we actually understand the soul to be
something of this sort: our soul is a tautness of our body, held together
by heat and cold and dry and wet and so on, a blending and a harmony c
of these very things, when they are blended together well and propor-
tionately, and so if the soul is a certain harmony it is clear that, when-
ever our body is disproportionately loosened or overly tightened by
disease or other evils, the soul must immediately die, even though it
is a most god-like thing, just as happens to other harmonies such as in
vocal cords and in all of the works of craftsmen, while the remains of
each body stick around for a long time, until they are either burnt or d
rot away; see what we will say to this argument, if someone thinks the
soul, as a blending of things in the body, is first to be destroyed in
what is called 'death'."

Socrates looked straight at us, as he often did, and smiling, said,
"Simmias certainly has a fair point. If any of you is more resourceful
than me, why doesn't he respond? For, in fact, he seems to have a
strong hold on the argument. But before responding I think we should
listen to Cebes, to what objection he has to the argument, so that there e
will be some time to consider how to respond, and when we have lis-
tened, we can either agree with them if they seem to be singing in tune,
or if not, at that point we can advocate for the argument. Come then,
Cebes, tell us, what is troubling you?"

"I will certainly tell you," said Cebes. "It seems to me that the ar-
gument is still in the same place, and the same objection that we made
before still holds. That our soul existed even before coming into this 87a
form, I do not deny to have been shown very elegantly and, if it is not
arrogant to say, most satisfactorily. But not, it seems to me, that it still
exists somewhere when we have died, in the following way: I do not
agree with Simmias' objection that soul is not stronger and longer-
lasting than body, since I think that it is far superior in all those re-
spects. 'But why, then,' the argument might say, 'do you still doubt,
when you see that after a man dies the weaker part still exists? You
don't think that the longer-living part must still be preserved during b
this time?' See whether I'm saying anything with the following; it
seems that, like Simmias, I too need an image. I think these matters can
be described in the same way as how someone might say about an old
weaver who died, that the man had not been destroyed but is safe and
sound somewhere, and provide as evidence the cloak that he wove and
wrapped around himself which was safe and sound and not destroyed,
and if someone disbelieves him, he could ask whether humans are c

longer-lasting than cloaks that are being used and worn, and when it is answered that the man lasts longer, he would think it proven more than anything else that the man is safe, since the shorter-lived one had not been destroyed. But this is not so, Simmias, if you'll think about what I say. Anyone could reply that a person who says this speaks foolishly. For this weaver wore out many such cloaks, and after weav-
d ing all of them he died, I suppose, before the last one, but for that reason a man is in no way worse or weaker than a cloak. And this same image works for soul's relationship to body and someone saying the same thing about them would seem to me to be speaking reasonably, that the soul is long-lasting and the body is weaker and shorter-lasting, since it seems that each soul wears out many bodies, especially if it lives for years and years. So, if the body changes and is destroyed
e while the man goes on living but the soul always re-weaves what has been worn out, when the soul is destroyed it must have on the final cloak and it is destroyed prior to this one only, though at the moment the soul is destroyed the body shows its weak nature and quickly rots and disappears. So, it is not yet appropriate to confidently accept this
88a argument that when we die our soul still exists somewhere. For if someone should add more to the argument than what you said, granting to it not only that our souls exist in the time before we come to be but also that nothing that prevents that when we die the souls of some people still exist and will exist and many times come to be and die—for in this way it is by nature stronger, such that the soul survives being born many times—granting these one might further *not* agree that it does not suffer in all of the comings-to-be and it is finally completely
b destroyed in one of the deaths, even though, he might say, no one knows which death and separation of the body brings the destruction of the soul, since that is impossible for any of us to perceive. If this is how things are, anyone who is confident about death is foolishly confident, if he is unable to show that soul is *completely* immortal and indestructible. If not, the person approaching death must always be afraid that his soul will be completely destroyed in its forthcoming unharnessing from the body."

c All of us who heard them speak were pained—as we later discussed with each other—having been thoroughly convinced by the preceding argument; they seemed to have upset us and cast us back down again into disbelief, not only about the initial arguments, but also as to what could be said going forward, afraid that we were not worthy judges, or even that these things were themselves not trustworthy.

Echecrates: By the gods, Phaedo, I have sympathy for you all. For now
d that I have listened to you it occurs to me too to say something like

'What argument shall we believe? How thoroughly convincing was the argument that Socrates gave! But now it has collapsed into doubt.' For both now and always, this very argument has captivated me remarkably—that our soul is some kind of harmony—and so when it was brought up it reminded me that I previously held these ideas too. And so I greatly need some other argument that will convince me again, as though from the beginning, that upon dying the soul doesn't die too. So tell me, by Zeus, how did Socrates take up the argument?
And also was *he*, as you said you all were, visibly distressed in any e
way, or was he not, and calmly came to the help of the argument? And was his help sufficient or lacking? Go over everything for us as accurately as possible!

Phaedo: Of course, Echecrates. I have been amazed by Socrates many times but I have never marveled at him more than when I was along-
side him then. That he had something to say is no surprise, but I was 89a
especially impressed by this about him: first, at how sweetly and gently and respectfully he received the arguments of the young men, and next, how keenly he sensed how we had been affected by the arguments, and further, how well he cured us; just as if he were presenting a defense in court in response to a suit, he rallied us when we were defeated and urged us to accompany him in examining the argument.

Echecrates: How?

Phaedo: I will tell you. It happened that I was sitting at his right next b
to the bench on a low stool, and he was much higher up than me. He caressed my head and pressed the hair around my neck together—he used to tease me about my hair at every opportunity—and said, "Tomorrow, perhaps, you will cut off this beautiful hair,[1] Phaedo."

"Probably, Socrates," I said.

"Not if I can convince you, at least."

"Well, when, then?"

"Today," he said, "I'll cut my hair and you'll cut yours, if our ar-
gument is finished and we cannot revive it. I would, if I were you, and c
the argument was escaping me, take an oath, like the Argives[2] do, not to let my hair grow long until I was victorious after renewing the battle against the argument of Simmias and Cebes."

"But," I said, "they say that Heracles is not strong enough against two enemies."

1 *cut off ... hair* As a traditional mark of mourning.

2 *Argives* Men of Argo, who were defeated by the Spartans and took an oath not to cut their hair until they were avenged.

"Just call on me," he said, "as your Iolaus, while there is still light."

"I call on you, then," I said, "not that I am Heracles, but as Iolaus[1] calling upon Heracles."

"It makes no difference," he said. "But first let's take precautions that we don't succumb to a particular danger."

"What sort?" I said.

d "That we do not become," said he, "misologists, just as some people become misanthropes,[2] since there is," he said, "no greater evil that a person could suffer than the hatred of argument. Misology and misanthropy develop in the same way. Misanthropy comes from earnestly believing someone, but without skill, thinking that everything a man says is true and sound and trustworthy, but then finding out a little later that it is wretched and untrustworthy; and then the same thing happens with other people, and whenever someone experiences this many times, and especially with those whom he
e thought his closest relatives and dearest friends; and, clashing with them many times, in the end he hates them all and thinks there is nothing sound about anyone at all. Or don't you yet believe that this happens?"

"Indeed," I said.

"Well," said he, "isn't it an obvious disgrace that such a person, without any skill regarding human beings, tries to deal with others? If he were somehow to deal with them intelligently, he would know how
90a things are: that good and bad people are each exceedingly few and that those in the middle are many."

"How do you mean?" I said.

"Just like," said he, "with the exceedingly small and large. Do you think it's quite rare to find something that is either exceedingly large or exceedingly small, whether a man or a dog or anything whatever? Or again, fast and slow, or shameful and noble, or light and dark? Or have you not noticed that in all of these cases the utmost extremes are rare and few, while those in between are abundant and many?"

"Indeed," said I.

b "Don't you think," he said, "that if a competition in wickedness were proposed, there too, very few would appear exceptional?"

"Quite likely," I said.

"Likely indeed," he said. "But in this regard arguments are not like men—I followed after you as you led the way—but rather they're alike

---

1 *Heracles ... Iolaus* In Greek mythology, Heracles was assigned twelve labors; he could not achieve the second one, to kill the many-headed monster Hydra, because whenever he cut off one of the monster's heads, two new ones immediately grew back in its place. He succeeded only with the help of his charioteer and companion Iolaus, who prevented the new heads from growing.

2 *misologists ... misanthropes* Misology is the dislike or hatred of reason or argument, while misanthropy is the dislike or hatred of humanity.

in that, when someone without expertise in arguments trusts some ar-
gument as true and then a little later it seems false to him, and some-
times it is and sometimes it's not, and then there's another one and
another one, and especially those who have spent time with contra- c
dictory arguments, you know, they end up thinking that they are most
wise and that they alone have figured out that nothing whatsoever is
sound and firm, neither things nor arguments, but that everything is as
though it were in the Euripus,[1] turning up-stream and down-stream
and never staying in any place for any length of time."

"Absolutely," I said. "You are right."

"And so, Phaedo," he said, "it would be a regrettable experience,
if, although there is indeed some truth, and clarity of argument, and
understanding is possible, due to encountering such arguments as d
those—that seem sometimes true and sometimes not—a person does-
n't fault himself or his lack of expertise, but in the end, because of the
pain he feels, readily casts the blame from himself onto the argu-
ments, and spends the rest of his life hating and bad-mouthing argu-
ments, and being deprived of the truth and the knowledge of the
things that are."

"By Zeus," said I, "regrettable indeed."

"First, then," he said, "let's beware of this and not let it enter our e
souls that there is a risk of arguments not being sound, but much more
that *we* are not yet sound, and must be brave and eager to become
sound, you and the others for the sake of your entire life to come, and
me for the sake of my death itself, since I risk not being philosophical 91a
about the matter in the present situation, but instead being intent on
victory, like very uneducated people. Such people, whenever they de-
bate about something, pay no attention to how things are regarding the
subject of the argument, but are instead determined that what they are
claiming seems right to the audience. And I think in my present cir-
cumstances I differ from them only a bit, for I am not determined that
my audience will think what I am saying is true—that would be a sec-
ondary concern—but rather that *I myself* will think, as much as possi-
ble, that this is how things are. I reason, my dear friend—observe how b
self-servingly!—that if what I'm saying turns out to be true, I would
benefit by believing it, while if there is nothing after dying, at least
my grief will be less unpleasant for everyone present during this time
before death. This ignorance will not last long: that would be bad; in-
stead, it will end in a little while.

"And so now, Simmias and Cebes, I am certainly prepared to take
up the argument. But you, if you obey me, should pay little attention c

1 *Euripus* The Euripus Strait is a narrow strip of water between a Greek island and the mainland, in the Aegean, where unusually strong tidal waters flow back and forth, changing four times a day and making sailing very difficult.

to Socrates and much more to the truth: agree if you think I'm saying something true, but if not, resist with every argument you have, being careful that I don't simultaneously beguile both you and myself with my eagerness, like a bee that leaves its stinger in you as it departs.

But we must proceed," he said. "And first, remind me what you
said, if I seem not to remember. Simmias, I think, was doubtful and
d afraid that the soul, although more divine and more beautiful than the
body, is destroyed first as a kind of harmony, while Cebes, I thought, agreed with me that the soul is longer-lasting than the body but said it was obscure to everyone that if the soul repeatedly wore out multiple bodies, it would leave behind the final body when it was destroyed, and that death might be just this, the destruction of the soul, as body is constantly being destroyed. Are these, Simmias and Cebes, the matters we have to look into?"

e They both agreed that they were.

"Then do you reject all of the previous arguments, or some and not others?"

"Some and not others," they said.

"Well, then," said he, "what do you say about the discussion in
which we said that learning is recollection and, based on this, that it is
92a necessary for our soul to exist previously, somewhere else, before it is
imprisoned in the body?"

"For my part," said Cebes, "it was marvelous how convinced I was by you at the time and I remain convinced now, as by no other argument."

"And certainly," said Simmias, "I too am the same way, and I would be completely amazed if anything else ever seemed so sure, on this subject at least."

And Socrates said, "But, my Theban guest, you must believe oth-
erwise, if you stick to the current opinion, that harmony is something
composite and the soul is some kind of harmony made out of parts
b stretched by the body, for you don't somehow believe, at any rate, that
prior to the harmony being composed, the things it would have to be composed of already existed. Or do you believe this?"

"Not at all, Socrates," he said.

"But are you aware," said he, "that this is what you are saying when
you say that the soul exists before it comes into a human form and body
but that it is composed out of things that don't yet exist? Harmony is
not the kind of thing as what you're comparing it to: the lyre and the
c strings and the sounds come to exist earlier, while it is still out of tune,
whereas the harmony is the last to be constituted and the first to be destroyed. So how will you attune this argument with the former one?"

"There's no way," said Simmias.

"But certainly," said he, "it is fitting that if any other argument should be in tune, it is the one about harmony?"

"That is fitting," said Simmias.

"But for you it is not in tune," he said. "And so, see which of the arguments you will choose—that learning is recollection or that soul is a harmony?"

"The former, Socrates" he said, "by a long way. For this other one d
came to me without proof but with a certain likelihood and plausibility, which makes it seem good to many other men. But I am aware of these arguments that take likelihoods as proofs are imposters, and if you aren't on guard against them, they can deceive you very effectively, in geometry and in all the other subjects. But the argument about recollection and learning was established from a hypothesis worthy of acceptance, for we said somewhere that the soul exists before entering a body, in the same way that its essence, which goes by the descriptor 'what it is', exists. e
And, I believe, I had accepted this on adequate proof and correctly. Based on this, I cannot, it seems, accept myself or others saying that soul is a harmony."

"And what about *this*, Simmias?" said he. "Do you think that harmony or any other composite can be in any other condition than what- 93a
ever condition the things it is composed of have?"

"Not at all."

"Certainly, I take it, it doesn't do or undergo anything contrary to what those things do or undergo?"

He agreed.

"And so it is not proper for a harmony to be the leader of the things from which it is put together, but to follow."

He concurred.

"And a harmony wouldn't at all move in opposition, or make an opposite sound, or do anything else that is in opposition to its parts."

"Not at all," he said.

"What next? Isn't harmony by nature however each harmony is harmonized?

"I don't understand," he said.

"Wouldn't it be a greater harmony and more full," said he, "if more elements were harmonized and to a greater extent—if such a b
thing is possible—but a lesser harmony and less full if there were fewer elements and the elements were harmonized to a lesser extent?"

"Indeed."

"So, is this the case concerning the soul, such that in some tiny way one soul, compared to another, is more full and to a greater extent a soul, or less full and to a lesser degree this very thing, a soul?"

"In no way at all," he said.

"Come, then, by Zeus," he said. "Is one soul said to have sense and
c virtue and to be good, while another is stupid and wicked and to be bad? Is it correct to say this?"

"Yes, that's correct."

"Among those who claim that soul is a harmony, what will any of them say these things are in the soul: virtue and wickedness? That they are some additional harmony and lack of harmony? That the harmonized one, the good one, has within itself—which is itself a harmony—another harmony, while the unharmonized one is just itself and does not have another within it?"

"*I* don't have anything to say," said Simmias. "But it's clear that the person working from this hypothesis would say something like this."

d "But it was agreed," he said, "that one soul is no more or no less a soul than another, which is to agree that one harmony is not a greater or more full harmony, or a lesser or less full harmony, than another. Right?"

"Certainly."

"But what is not more or less a harmony is not more or less harmonized. Isn't that so?"

"It is."

"And does what is no more or less harmonized share more or less in harmony, or equally?"

"Equally."

e "So, a soul, since it is not more or less itself this, a soul, than another, it is not more or less harmonized?"

"So it is."

"And since this is its state, it wouldn't lack or possess harmony more?"

"Not at all."

"And again, since that is its state, would one soul share more in wickedness or virtue than another, if wickedness were lack of harmony and virtue were harmony?"

"Not at all more."

94a "It's rather, I suppose, that, correctly reasoned, a soul will not have any wickedness, if it is indeed a harmony, since a harmony is absolutely just this, harmony, and would not at all be lack of harmony."

"No, indeed."

"And so, of course, neither will soul, since it is absolutely soul."

"How could it, based on what we have already said?"

"Based on this account, for us every soul of every animal will be similarly good, if souls by nature are just this: souls."

"I think so, Socrates," he said.

"Does the account seem right," said he, "to speak like this and produce these results, if the hypothesis had been correct, that soul is harmony?" b

"In no way whatsoever."

"What next?" said he. "Out of everything that a man is, is there anything else you can say is the ruler apart from the soul, especially a sensible one?"

"I cannot."

"Does it yield to the passions from the body or does it oppose them? I mean this sort of thing, such as when it is experiencing heat and thirst, it drags it towards the opposite, towards not drinking, and when experiencing hunger towards not eating, and we see in a thousand other c
ways the soul opposing the passions of the body. Or not?"

"Absolutely."

"And so, next, didn't we agree previously that it could never, as a harmony, 'make a sound' opposite to the tensings and relaxings and vibrations and whatever else of the things from which it happens to come, but follows them and is never the leader?"

"We did agree to that," he said. "How could it not?"

"And what then? Does it not now seem to us to operate in completely the opposite way, that it is the leader of all the things from which someone says it comes, opposing them throughout life in al- d
most all things and ruling over them in every way, punishing some of them most severely with pains both gymnastic and medical, and some of them more gently, threatening some and warning others, speaking to the desires and hungers and fears as one thing separate from another? Rather like Homer wrote in *Odyssey*, where he says of Odysseus that, 'he struck his chest and berated his heart with the words e
"Just bear it, heart; you have endured greater arrogance before."'[1] Do you think when he wrote these words he had in mind that it was a harmony and the kind of thing to be led by the passions of the body, or rather the kind of thing to lead and rule them since it is a thing far more god-like than harmony?"

"By Zeus, Socrates, I think so."

"Not for us, then, best of men, is it in any way good to say that soul 95a
is a harmony, for we would not be agreeing with the divine poet Homer, it seems, nor with ourselves."

"So it is," he said.

"Well, well, then," said Socrates, "the concerns of Harmonia of Thebes have somehow turned out moderately favorably for us, it

1 Homer, *Odyssey* 20.17–18.

seems. But what of the concerns of Cadmus,[1] Cebes," he said. "How will we propitiate them and with what argument?"

"I think you will find a way out," said Cebes, "This argument against the harmony account, I was amazed at how you spoke, how unexpected it was, for when Simmias was telling us what was trou-
b bling him, I wondered greatly if anyone would be able to meet his argument, and so I thought it extraordinary that right away it was unable to withstand the first attack of your argument. So, I wouldn't be surprised if the argument of Cadmus also met the very same fate."

"Don't get cocky, my good man, for fear some evil eye reverses the argument that is to come. The god will take care of these things, in any case; as for us, let us come to close quarters, as Homer's heroes do, and test if you're saying anything. The main thing you're looking
c for is this: you think it's a good thing that we are shown that the soul is indestructible and immortal, and thus, when a philosophical man is about to die, but is brave and thinks that upon death he will fare well in that other place and better than if he were ending a different life, his bravery will not be unreasonable and foolish. But with respect to the demonstration that the soul is strong and god-like, and that it also existed previously, before we came to be humans, you say that all of this shows *not* immortality but only that soul is long-lasting and previously existed somewhere for an inconceivably long time and knew and did
d many things, but for all that is not immortal, and in fact entering a human body was the beginning of its destruction, like a disease, and suffering hardship it lives out this life and meets its end and is destroyed in a so-called 'death'. Indeed, it makes no difference, you say, if it entered a body once or many times, at least with regard to what each of us fears, since it is appropriate for a person to be afraid if he
e does not know, and cannot prove, that it is immortal, unless he is a fool. Such things, I think, Cebes, are what you are saying. And I am restating it in various ways on purpose, in case something escapes us, and if you want you can add or take away something."

"For the moment," Cebes said, "there's nothing I need to take away or add. That is what I am saying."

After Socrates paused for quite a while and considered something by himself, he said, "It's no mean thing, Cebes, that you are looking for, since it requires a complete and thorough examination of the
96a cause of generation and destruction. If you want, I will go over my

---

1 *Cadmus* Husband of Harmonia and mythical founder of Thebes. Socrates is playfully comparing the two arguments to the couple who founded Cebes and Simmias' home city of Thebes, perhaps inspired by the resonance of 'Harmonia' and 'harmony.'

own experiences regarding these matters and then if anything that I say seems useful to you, you can put it towards the appeasement of your objection."

"I certainly do want that," said Cebes.

"Then listen while I speak. When I was a young man, Cebes," he
said, "I had an extraordinary desire for the particular kind of wisdom
they call 'natural inquiry'. It seemed magnificent to me to know the
causes of each thing, why each thing comes to be and why it is de-
stroyed, and why it exists. And at first, I often went up and down ex- b
amining things such as these: When heat and cold initiate
decomposition, are living things composed at that very moment, as
some[1] used to say? And is it blood with which we think, or air, or
fire,[2] or none of these, but rather the brain that allows for the senses
to hear and to see and to smell, from which come memory and
thought, while from the stabilizing of memories and thoughts knowl-
edge is produced? And as I next investigated the destruction of these
things, and what happens in the sky and the earth, I wound up think- c
ing to myself that I was unsuited to this investigation as no other crea-
ture could be. I will give you a convincing proof of this: there were
things I previously knew clearly and that in fact seemed true both to
me and to others, but as a result of this investigation I was so severely
blinded that I lost knowledge even of what I thought I knew before
this, about many various things, even including why a human grows.
For I had previously thought that this was obvious to everyone: by
eating and drinking, and then from the food, flesh is added to flesh, d
and bone to bones, and so on by the same account, the things that are
appropriate are added to each of them, and what was at the time the
lesser bulk later becomes much greater, and in this way a small man
becomes large. This is what I thought then; don't you think I was
reasonable?"

"I do," said Cebes.

"But next observe the following: I used to think it was enough to
think a large man, whenever he was standing next to a small one, ap-
peared taller by a head. Or one horse to another. And, even more ob- e
viously than that, ten things seemed to be more than eight because two
were added to it, and the two-cubit length to be greater than the one-
cubit by exceeding it by half."

"And now," said Cebes, "what do you think about them?"

---

1 *as some* Perhaps Archelaus (who may have held that everything in nature originates in the separation between hot and cold) or Anaxagoras (who saw nature as a constant disruption and composition of fundamental elements).

2 *blood ... or fire* Views held, respectively, by the philosophers Empedocles, Diogenes of Apollonia, and Heraclitus.

"That I am a long way away, by Zeus," he said, "from thinking that
I know the cause of any of them, I who cannot accept from himself,
when a particular thing is added to another, whether it is the one to
which it was is added that became two, or both the one that was added
97a and the one to which it was added that became two by the addition of
one of them to the other. I am amazed how, when either of them was
separate from the other, they were each one and not at that time two,
but when they were close to one another, this, it turns out, became a
cause of them becoming two, the *juxtaposition* that put them close to
one another. Nor again when one is divided, I cannot still believe that
this—the *division*—has in turn become a cause of their being two,
b since this is the opposite of the previous cause of their becoming two.
Previously, it was because they were gathered close to one another
and either of them added itself to the other, whereas now it's because
they were moved apart and each one separated itself from the other. I
can no longer convince myself that I know why one comes to be, or
why anything else, in brief, comes to be or is destroyed or exists, ac-
cording to this way of investigation, but I muddle along randomly in
another way and don't use this one at all.

"But then I heard someone reading from some book or other, by
c Anaxagoras he said, saying that mind was what ordered and caused
everything. I was pleased by this cause and it seemed to me that it was
good, in a certain way, that mind is the cause of everything. And I
thought, if this is how it is—by the ordering of mind everything is or-
dered and each thing arranged in the way that is best—if someone
wished to discover the cause of each thing—how it comes to be and is
destroyed and exists—that *this* is what he would have to discover
d about it: in what way it is for the best that it exists or whatever else it
undergoes or does, and that, based on this account, it is entirely ap-
propriate for a man to look at nothing else, concerning himself and
anything else, besides what is most excellent and best—and the same
man will necessarily know what is inferior, since the knowledge of
that is the same.

"Reasoning happily in this way I thought I had found a teacher of the
cause of the beings in accordance with my own mind, Anaxagoras, who
e would tell me, first, whether the earth is flat or spherical, and after
telling me that, he would go on to explain the cause and the necessity,
speaking in terms of 'the better' and how it was 'better' to be such as
it is. If he should say that it is in the center, he would go on to explain
98a why it is better for it to be in the center. And were he to show me these
things, I was ready not to pursue any other kind of cause. And I was
ready, in particular, to learn in the same way about the sun and the
moon and the other stars, both about their speed relative to one another

and their rotations and their other aspects, and how in the world it is better for each of these to do what they do and to undergo what they undergo. I did not think at the time that by saying that they were ordered 'by mind' he was introducing some other cause for these things besides that it is best for them to be as they are. And so I thought the person as- b
signing a cause to each of them and to all of them in common would go on to explain what is best for each of them, and the good common to all of them. I would not have given up my hopes even for a great price, but taking up the books with great enthusiasm, I read them as quickly as I could, so that I would learn about the best and the inferior as quickly as possible.

"From my marvelous hope, my friend, I was dragged away, when, as I continue to read, I see a man making no use of mind *at all*, nor assigning any particular causes for the ordering of things, and instead c
using air and aether and water and many other strange things. I thought it was exactly like someone who says that *all* the things Socrates does, he does by mind, but who then, when he tried to say the causes of *each* thing that I do, would say that I am now seated here, to begin with, for the following reasons: that my body is composed of bones and muscles and that bones are solid and have joints separating them from one another, while muscles are the kind of thing that tightens and relaxes, d
and they encase the bones, along with the flesh and skin that contains them. Lifting up the bones in their ligaments, by the slackening and tightening of the muscles, somehow makes me able to bend my limbs now, and hence I am sitting here bent over. Or again, concerning our talking, he should mention other similar causes, voice and air and hearing and other such parts as causes, neglecting to say the real causes, e
that since the Athenians deemed it best to vote against me, because of *that* I subsequently thought I should sit here and that it is most just for me to stay and suffer whatever penalty they order. Since, by the dog,[1]
I think that these muscles and bones would be somewhere far away 99a
like Megara or Boeotia long ago, carried by an opinion of what is best, if *I* did not think that, rather than escaping and running away, it was more just and more noble to suffer for the city whatever penalty it might prescribe. But to call these 'causes' is exceedingly strange. If someone were to say that without having such things as bones and muscles and so on I would not be able to do the things I think good, he would speak the truth, but to say I do what I do because of these,

1 *by the dog* This is a "minced oath": an exclamation changed somewhat to eliminate its original objectionable reference, in this case, to the gods. 'The dog' is presumably the dog star Sirius. (Compare 'by gosh!' as a substitute for 'by God!')

b and also that I act because of mind, but not by choosing what is best, this would be a great and large carelessness of speech. Imagine not being able to distinguish that a cause is actually one thing while that without which the cause would never be a cause is another! I think most people handle this blindly, as if in the dark, calling something by a name that does not belong to it when they categorize it as a cause. Because of this, one man puts a vortex around the Earth to make the Earth stay below the sky, while another rests it on a pedestal of air, as
c though it were [the lid of] a flat kneading trough.[1] But the power that causes these things to be currently situated as it is best for them to be placed, this they neither seek nor believe to have any divine strength, but they believe that they might somewhere discover an Atlas[2] stronger and more divine than this and more all-encompassing than this, and would not at all think that what is truly good and binding binds and holds them together. With respect to *these* causes, what in the world they are, I would have very gladly become anyone's student. But as I was deprived of this and was unable to discover it for myself or by
d learning from another, would you like me to give you a demonstration, Cebes," he said, "of the 'second sailing' that I made in the search for this cause?"

"I would like that enormously," he said.

"Well, after that I then thought," said he, "that, since I had given up investigating the things that are, it was necessary to be cautious in case I experienced what happens to those who observe the sun and look at
e it during an eclipse: some of them quite destroy their eyes, unless they look at an image of it in water or something similar. I had something like this in mind and I was afraid my soul would be completely blinded by looking for the 'things' with my eyes and trying to latch onto them with each of the senses. So, I thought I needed to seek refuge in defi-

---

1 *one man ... another ... a flat kneading trough* Empedocles ("one man") and Anaximenes ("another"). Both theories are discussed in Aristotle's *On the Heavens*: "Anaximenes and Anaxagoras and Democritus give the flatness of the Earth as the cause of its staying still. Thus, they say, it does not cut, but covers like a lid, the air beneath it.... [Various theorists] then seek a reason for its staying there [at the center]; and some say, in the manner explained, that the reason is its size and flatness; others, with Empedocles, that the motion of the heavens, moving about it at a higher speed, prevents movement of the Earth" (294b14–295a19, trans. J. L. Stocks).

2 *Atlas* One of the Titans (elder gods in Greek mythology) punished by Zeus for the Titan war against him by condemning Atlas to eternally support the pillars which separated the Earth and the heavens. The idea is that these mechanical accounts are incomplete and still require an 'Atlas' to complete the explanation, while Socrates' preferred kind of explanation—using the forms or essences—'holds everything together' in itself.

nitions and look in them for the truth of the things that are. Well, per-
haps in a way this is not a fitting analogy for what I am comparing it 100a
to, for I do not much agree that a person who examines definitions is
examining real things in images, any more than the person who ex-
amines them in action. In any case, that is how I set out, taking as a hy-
pothesis in each case the definition that I judge to be strongest and I
set as true whatever things seem to me to harmonize with it—con-
cerning both causes and all the rest—and as not true whatever things
do not. I wish to tell you more clearly what I mean, as I don't think you
understand at present."

"No, by Zeus," said Cebes, "not completely."

"Well, it's nothing unusual," said he, "just what I never stop say- b
ing, both on other occasions and in our preceding argument. I am going
to try to demonstrate to you the form of the cause that I have been
busying myself with, and I return again to those much-discussed things
and begin from them, hypothesizing that there is such a thing as beauty
itself, and goodness, and largeness, and all the others, and if you grant
me these and agree that they exist, I hope from them to demonstrate to
you the cause and to discover that soul is immortal."

"But of course," said Cebes, "consider them granted and proceed at c
once!"

"Well, consider," he said, "what follows them, and whether you
think as I do. It appears to me if something is beautiful (besides beauty
itself), it is beautiful on account of nothing other than by sharing in that
beauty, and the same for everything. Do you agree to a cause of that
sort?"

"I agree," he said.

"I can no longer understand," said he, "or acknowledge those other
wise causes, and if someone should tell me that the reason why any d
thing whatsoever is beautiful is its pretty color or shape or anything
else of this sort, I ignore those reasons, since I am confused by all of
them. Instead I plainly and simply and perhaps foolishly keep close to
me that there's nothing else that makes a thing beautiful except beauty's
presence—or its association, or whatever the mode and method may
be, as I am not yet confident about this, only that it is by the beautiful
that things are beautiful. This seems to me the surest reply to myself and e
to others. And by keeping to this, I believe that I would never fall, and
that it is safe—both for myself and for whoever else—to reply that it is
by the beautiful that beautiful things are beautiful. Or don't you think
so?"

"I do."

"And by largeness large things are large, and larger things larger,
and by smallness smaller things smaller?"

"Yes."

"And you would not accept it if someone should say that one person is larger than another 'by a head', and the smaller is smaller by this
101a same thing, but you would protest that you just say that every larger thing is larger than some other by nothing other than largeness, and the reason it is larger is this: because of largeness; and smaller things are smaller by nothing other than smallness, and the reason it is smaller is this: because of smallness. You're afraid, I suppose, that if you were to say that someone is greater *and* smaller by a head, someone would accuse you of a contradictory account, that firstly, the larger is larger and the smaller is smaller by the same thing, but then, it's by a head,
b which is small, that the larger person is larger, and this is a monstrosity: that a person is large by something small. Or would you not be afraid of this?"

And Cebes burst out laughing and said, "I would."

"Well, then," said he, "wouldn't you be afraid to say that ten is more than eight 'by two' and exceeds it due to that cause, rather than 'in manyness' and 'because of its manyness'? Or that two cubits[1] is more than one cubit by a half rather than 'in lengthiness'—because of the same fear, I suppose?"

"Indeed," he said.

"What next? Wouldn't you be wary of saying that by adding one to
c one the addition is the cause of two coming to be, or in the case of dividing, it's the division? And you would shout loudly that you do not know any other way that each comes to be except by each of the respective natures participating in whatever it participates, and in these cases you have no other cause of two's coming to be except the participation of duality, and that anything that is going to be two must share in this, and singularity in the case of anything that is going to be one, and to let go of their division and addition and other such subtleties, letting them pass for use in the responses of people much wiser
d than you. You would be afraid, as the saying goes, of your own shadow, of your inexperience, and hold onto the security of that hypothesis, and would answer accordingly.

"And if anyone were to attack this hypothesis, you would dismiss him and not respond until you had examined whether the things that followed from it were, for you, in harmony or disharmony with one another. And if you should be compelled to give an account of it itself, wouldn't you give it in the same way, setting up another hypothesis in
e turn that seems best among the higher ones, until you arrived at something sufficient, but at the same time you would not confuse, as the

1 *cubit* An ancient measure of length; about 44 cm or 17 inches.

quarrelsome do, what you say about the principle and what follows from it, if indeed you wished to discover some of the things that are? For those people, perhaps, there is no single account of this nor a single care; in their wisdom they are capable of confusing everything together while still being able to be pleased with themselves, whereas you, if you are one of the philosophical people, will, I think, proceed 102a
as I describe."

"You are absolutely right," said Simmias and Cebes in unison.

Echecrates: And with good reason, by Zeus, Phaedo: it's amazing to me how clearly he put these things, even for a person of little intelligence.

Phaedo: Completely, Echecrates, and everyone present thought so, too.

Echecrates: As do we who were not there but are hearing it now. But then what was said after that?

Phaedo: As I believe, when these points had been granted to him, and b
it was agreed that each of the forms existed and that the other things receive their name from participating in them, the very next thing after that was him asking, "If, then," said he, "you describe these things in this way, isn't it the case that, whenever you say that Simmias is larger than Socrates but Phaedo is smaller, you are saying that Simmias at the time possesses both of them, both largeness and smallness?"

"I do."

"And yet," said he, "you agree, when it comes to 'Simmias exceeding Socrates', that the truth is not as stated in these words? For I c
suppose you agree that it is not Simmias' nature to exceed Socrates, by being Simmias, but by the largeness that he happens to have. Or again, concerning Socrates being exceeded, it's not because Socrates is Socrates, but because he possesses smallness in comparison to the other man's largeness?"

"True."

"Or again, being exceeded by Phaedo is not due to Phaedo being Phaedo, but because Phaedo has largeness in comparison to the smallness of Simmias?"

"That's how it is."

"In this way, Simmias gets both the names small and large, being
in the middle between them, by submitting his smallness to the d
largeness of one of them and providing a largeness that exceeds the smallness of the other." And cracking a smile at this he said, "It

seems as though I'm about to talk like a book, but in any case it's just as I say."

He agreed.

"I'm talking like this because I want it to seem to you how it seems to me: it appears to me that not only largeness *itself* is never able to be large and small simultaneously, but also that the largeness *in us* never accepts the small or is able to be exceeded by it; instead, one of two
e things happens: either it flees and withdraws whenever its opposite, the small, is at hand, or it is destroyed when the other approaches. But it is *not* able to be other than what it is by admitting and receiving the smallness. In the same way, I, who have received and admitted the smallness, while still being who I am, I, this same person, am small, but the largeness, being large, has not submitted to being small. And in the same way, too, the smallness in us is never able to become or be
103a large, nor will any other of the opposites, while still being what it is, at the same time become and be its opposite, but either it withdraws or is destroyed when this happens."

"This is exactly how it appears to me," said Cebes.

And one of the people present—I don't clearly remember who it was—said, when he heard this, "By the gods, didn't we agree in our earlier conversation to the exact opposite of what we're now saying, that the more comes from the less and the less from the more, and in short that this is the coming-to-be for opposites, from their opposites? It now seems that we're saying that this is never how it happens."

b And Socrates, who had turned his head and listened, said, "You have brought it up manfully, but you are not keeping in mind the difference between what is being said now and what was said before. Before, it was said that an opposite thing comes from the opposite thing, but now, that the opposite itself could never become opposite to itself, either in us or by nature. Previously, my friend, we were talking about the things that *possess* opposites and which are given their names, whereas now we're talking about these them-
c selves, which give their name to the things, by being in them. It's these that we are saying are never able to accept a coming-to-be from each other."

And speaking as he looked towards Cebes, he said, "Well, then, Cebes, what about you? Is there anything that this man has said that troubles you?"

"Not anymore," said Cebes. "Though I certainly can't say that many things don't bother me."

"We are agreed, then," said he, "that, simply put, an opposite will never become the opposite to itself."

"Absolutely," he said.

"Look and tell me about the next thing," he said, "whether you agree with it. Do you call something heat, and cold?"

"I do."

"And you call these snow and fire?"

"By Zeus, I do not." d

"Rather, heat is a different thing than fire and cold is a different thing than snow?"

"Yes."

"But the following, I suppose, you do believe: that snow cannot exist if it 'receives' heat, as we put it earlier, and still be what it is, snow, with heat; rather, when heat approaches, the former will either withdraw or be destroyed."

"Indeed."

"And again, fire, when cold approaches it, either backs away or is destroyed, and can never receive the coldness while still remaining what it is, fire, with cold."

"You are right." e

"Now, is it the case, concerning some of these, that it's not just the form that is thought worthy of its name for all time but also something else that is not that form but which, whenever it exists, always has the same outline as it. Perhaps what I mean will be most obvious in this way: oddness must, I suppose, always bear this name that we are now calling it? Or not?"

"Indeed."

"And *only* this among the things that are?—this is what I am ask-
ing—or is there also something else that is not the very thing that odd- 104a
ness is but nonetheless it is necessary to call it this also, using that
thing's name, since by nature it is the kind of thing that is never sep-
arated from oddness? I mean, as an example, what happens with three,
and many others. Consider three. Don't you think that it must always
be referred to by its own name *and* by oddness, even though this is
not the same thing as three? And yet three and five and entirely half
of the numbers have this same nature, such that, although they are not b
oddness, each of them is always odd. And again with two and four and
all the various others in the series of numbers: they are not evenness
but nonetheless each of them is always even. Do you agree or not?"

"Of course," he said.

"Observe," he said, "what I want to make clear, which is this: it
seems it is not only the opposites that cannot receive one another, but
also those things which possess opposites even though they are not
themselves opposites to one another. It is not fitting for these to re-
ceive the form that is opposite to the one in it, and instead when the lat-
ter is approaching the former it is either destroyed or withdraws. Or c

won't we say that threeness will be destroyed and would endure anything else at all, before becoming even while remaining three?"

"Absolutely," said Cebes.

"But two is definitely not the opposite of three."

"Not at all."

"So, it's not only the opposite forms that do not remain when they approach one another but there are also various other things that don't remain when opposites approach."

"Very true," he said.

"Do you want, if we can," said he, "to define what sort of things these are?"

"Indeed."

d "Well, then, Cebes," he said, "would they be the things which, whatever they possess, compel those things to not only have their form but also to always have the form of some opposite?"

"How do you mean?"

"Only what we were saying just now, since you know of course that things possessed by the form of three must be not just three but odd, too."

"Indeed."

"And into this could never enter the opposite form to the outline which produced this result."

"No."

"And it is oddness that produced it?"

"Yes."

"And the opposite to this is the form of the even?"

"Yes."

e "Into threeness, then, the form of the even will never enter."

"Certainly not."

"Threeness has no share in the even."

"None."

"And threeness is uneven."

"Yes."

"So, then, what I said we would define—the things that, although
they are not the opposite of some being nevertheless do not receive it,
the opposite itself, such as, in the present case, although three is not op-
posite to the even, it does not receive it at all, since it brings the op-
105a posite to it, and two in the case of odd, and fire in the case of cold and
so many others—well, see if they are defined as follows: that the opposite will not receive its opposite, but in addition there's also this, that the thing that brings along something that is opposite to whatever it approaches, this thing doing the bringing never receives whatever is opposite to the thing being brought. Go over that once more, since it

is not bad to hear it several times. Five won't receive the form of the even, nor ten, its double, that of the odd. And so, the double itself is also opposite to something else, but nevertheless it won't receive that b
of the odd. And certainly neither the one-and-a-half nor the others like it, with 'and a half,' will receive that of the whole, nor again will the thirds and all such things, if you follow me and it seems the same way to you."

"It absolutely does," he said, "and I follow."

"Well, then, tell me again," he said, "from the beginning. And don't reply to me with what I said, but by following my example: I am going beyond what I said in my first answer, the sure one, as I now see another assurance based on what is being said now. If you asked me what it is that, by coming to be in a body, will make it hot, I won't give you that sure but ignorant answer, that it's because of heat, but more cleverly based on the recent discussion, that it's by fire. And if you ask what it is that when it comes to be in a body will make it sick, I won't c
answer that it's because of sickness, but rather because of fever. Or, what it is that by coming to be in a number makes it odd, I won't answer it's because of oddness, but because of oneness. And so on for other cases. So, see if now you sufficiently understand what I want."

"More than sufficiently," he said.

"So answer, then," said he, "what is it that when it comes to be in a body will make it alive?"

"It would be by the soul," he said. d

"Isn't this always the case?"

"Of course," said he.

"And whenever it possesses a thing, soul always comes upon it bringing life?"

"It certainly does," he said.

"And is there an opposite to life, or not?"

"There is," he said.

"What?"

"Death."

"And soul absolutely never admits the opposite of what it always brings, as was agreed in the previous conversation?"

"Very much indeed," said Cebes.

"So, then, what name do we give the thing that refuses to admit the form of the even?"

"Uneven," he said.

"And the thing that does not admit the just and that which does not admit the musical?"

"The unmusical," he said, "and the unjust." e

"Well, then. What will we call the thing that does not admit death?"

"Immortal," he said.

"And soul does not admit death?"

"No."

"So, soul is immortal."

"Immortal."

"Well, then," he said, "shall we say that this has been proven? Or what do you think?"

"Most sufficiently, Socrates."

106a "What else, Cebes?" said he. "If it were necessary for the uneven to be indestructible, would three be anything other than indestructible?"

"How could it not?"

"And if it were necessary that the heat-less is indestructible, then whenever someone brings heat to snow, wouldn't it withdraw, safe and unmelted? For it could not be destroyed nor again could it receive the heat and remain."

"You're right," he said.

"And in the same way, I think, if the uncoolable too were indestructible, then whenever something cold approached fire, it would never be extinguished or destroyed but it would depart and head for safety."

b "Necessarily," he said.

"And isn't it necessary," he said, "to speak about the immortal in this way, too? If the immortal is also indestructible, it's impossible for soul, whenever death advances towards it, to be destroyed, since death, based on what was said earlier, will certainly not admit it nor will it be dead, just as the three will not, we said, be even, and neither will the odd, and the same with fire and cold, nor the heat in the fire. 'But,' someone might say, 'isn't it possible that the odd does not become
c even when the even approaches, as was agreed, but instead it is destroyed and the even comes to be in its place?' We would not be able to assert against the person saying this that it is not destroyed, since the uneven is not indestructible. If this were granted to us, we would have easily argued that when the even comes forward the odd and the three go off and leave. And we would argue the same about fire and heat and the others. Right?"

"Absolutely."

"And now concerning the immortal, if we were granted that it too is indestructible, soul would be indestructible in addition to being im-
d mortal. But if not, it would require another argument."

"There's no need," he said, "as far as that goes. It could hardly be that other things won't admit destruction but the immortal, being everlasting, will accept destruction!"

"Well, God, I think," Socrates said, "and the form of life itself, and if there is anything else immortal, everyone would agree these are never destroyed."

"By Zeus," he said, "every human would agree, and so would the gods, I believe."

"Since then the immortal is also imperishable, would soul be any- e
thing other—since it turns out to be immortal—than indestructible?"

"It absolutely must be."

"So, when death approaches a mortal human, it seems, he dies, but the immortal part goes off and leaves, safe and indestructible, withdrawing from death."

"It seems so."

"More than anything, then, Cebes," he said, "soul is undying and in- 107a
destructible, and in reality our souls will exist in the land of Hades."

"Socrates," he said, "I, at least, can't say anything to contradict this or to cast doubt on the arguments in any way. But if Simmias has anything to say, or anyone else, they would do well to break their silence, as I don't know until what better time they would put it off than the present moment, if they wish to speak or hear about these matters."

"I, certainly," said Simmias himself, "don't have any further way of casting doubt beyond what was said. But because of the magnitude
of the subject of the arguments, and having a poor opinion of human b
weakness, I must retain some disbelief in my mind concerning what was said."

"Not just that, Simmias," said Socrates, "but what you say is right and the initial *hypotheses*, even if they are credible to us, must nevertheless be examined more thoroughly. And if you analyze them sufficiently, you will, I think, follow the argument and pursue it to the highest point possible for a human. And if this itself becomes clear, you will seek nothing further."

"You are right," he said.

"But it is right to consider *this*, men," he said, "that if the soul is in- c
deed immortal, then it needs attention not only during the time that we call life, but also for the whole of it, and a terrible danger now presents itself, if a person does not pay attention to it. Because if death meant being released from everything, it would be a stroke of luck for the wicked, when they died, to be released from their body and, at the same time, from their wickedness with the soul. But now, since it appears to
be immortal, it would have no other escape or deliverance from its d
wickedness except to become as good and as moderate as possible. For the soul goes to the land of Hades possessing nothing else except its upbringing and nurturing, which are said to be either the greatest help or hindrance to a person meeting his end as he begins his journey there.

"It is described as follows: that as each person meets their end, their spirit,[1] which was allotted to them during life, tries to lead them into a certain place, where those who have been gathered together must be
e judged, and then travel to the land of Hades with a guide appointed to lead them from here to there, and once they have undergone the experience there and stayed for the requisite time another guide brings them back here over a long time and a great cycle.

108a "The journey is thus not as Aeschylus' *Telephus*[2] describes it, as he says that the road to the land of Hades is simple, but it is not simple and there is not, it appears to me, just one, since there would be no need for a guide; if there is only one road there, a person could never somehow get off track. Rather, judging from the sacrifices and customs here, I say there are likely to be many forks and crossroads. The well-ordered and wise soul follows and is not ignorant of its circumstances, whereas the one that desires to possess bodily things, as we
b said earlier, flutters around it for a long time, in the visible realm, and after greatly resisting and suffering many things, departs under duress and with difficulty, being led by the appointed guide.

"And the impure soul that has done such things as committing unjust murder, or carried out other deeds that are kindred to those and the deeds of similar souls, when it arrives at the place where the others are, they all flee and turn away from it and are unwilling to be-
c come either a fellow traveler or a guide, and the soul wanders by itself in great frustration until certain periods of time have passed, after which it is carried by necessity into a suitable dwelling, whereas the soul that spent its life purely and moderately finds it has gods as traveling companions and guides, and inhabits the place that is fitting for it in particular.

"There are many amazing regions of the earth, and it is neither the sort nor the size that it is thought to be by those who typically speak about the earth, as I was persuaded by someone."

d And Simmias said, "What do you mean by this, Socrates? I myself have certainly heard many things about the earth, but not what has persuaded you. So, I would be glad to hear of it."

"But of course, Simmias. I don't think it requires the skill of Glaucus[3] to explain what it is, though to show that it is true seems to me too

---

1 *their spirit* Their *daimon*, or personal divine guiding spirit.

2 *Telephus* This play by the great Greek tragic playwright Aeschylus has been lost.

3 *the skill of Glaucus* Plato scholar David Sedley, following Konrad Gaiser, identifies this as a reference to the Glaucus named by Herodotus (1.25) as the inventor of welding. ("Teleology and myth in the *Phaedo*," *Proceedings of the Boston Area Colloquium in Ancient Philosophy* 5, 1990.)

difficult for the skill of Glaucus, partly because I am not capable, per-
haps, and partly because even if I did know, my life appears insuffi-
cient, Simmias, for the length of the explanation. But certainly there's
nothing stopping me from describing the form of the earth and its re- e
gions that I have been convinced of."

"That would be plenty," said Simmias.

"I am convinced, then," said he, "that first, if it is in the middle of
the sky and circular, there is no need at all for air or any other such ne- 109a
cessity to prevent it from falling, but the similarity throughout sky it-
self on every side, and the equilibrium of the earth itself, is sufficient
to hold it in place. A well-balanced object sitting in the middle of
something homogeneous like this will not be able to incline in any di-
rection to any greater or lesser extent, and because of the similar con-
ditions will remain upright. This is the first thing," said he, "that I am
convinced of."

"And quite rightly so," said Simmias.

"And further," he said, "that it is something very large, and that we
who live between the pillars of Heracles and the river Phasis[1] dwell in a b
small portion of it, living around the sea like ants or frogs around a pond,
and many other people live in many other similar places. For everywhere
around the earth there are many chasms of every kind of shape and size,
in which water and mist and air have flowed together,[2] though the earth
itself is pure and lies in a pure atmosphere, which is where the stars re-
side, and which is called 'aether'[3] by the many who are accustomed to c
talking about such things, and those three—water, mist, and air—are the
sediment of aether and they are constantly flowing together in the chasms
of the earth. We are unaware that we live in its chasms and we think we
live up above on the surface of the earth, just as if someone living down
in the sea floor thought that he lived upon the water, and when he looks
through the water at the sun and the other stars thinks that the sea was
sky, but because of slowness and weakness, he never ever reached or d
saw the top of the sea or emerged out of the sea and lifted up his head
into this region, and seen how much more pure and beautiful it was com-
pared to their own, nor had heard about it from another person who had
seen it. This is exactly what we are also convinced of, since even

1 *the pillars of Heracles and the river Phasis* The pillars of Heracles are the two sides of the Strait of Gibraltar; the river Phasis flows into the eastern end of the Black Sea, in Georgia.

2 *in which water... flowed together* That is, they are present together locally (rather than being in their proper universal striations) creating a sea (with mist) and a pocket of air.

3 *aether* According to ancient science, this is the substance that fills the universe, the only substance in the extra-terrestrial "space."

though we live in some chasm of the earth we think we live on top of
it, and we call the air 'sky' on the grounds that what has room for the
e stars is sky. But it's the same: by weakness and slowness *we* are un-
able to break through to the upper air. For, if someone got to its high-
est point or became winged and flew up and lifted up his head to look
back—just as if, in the analogy, the fish stuck their heads out of the sea
and saw what was here—in this way someone might see what is up
there, too, and—if its nature were sufficient to sustain seeing—to
110a know that that is the true sky and the actual light and the real earth. For
this earth and its stones and the entire place here has been corrupted
and corroded, just like brine does to the things in the sea, and nothing
in the sea has a nature worth mentioning, nor is anything complete, so
to speak, and anywhere there is earth, there are sea caves, sand, un-
manageable mud and filth, and compared to the things around us they
are in no way worthy of being judged beautiful. But those upper things,
in turn, would seem to be superior to those where we live by an even
b greater extent. Indeed, if it is appropriate to tell a story, it is worth
hearing, Simmias, about what kinds of things there are upon the earth
and beneath the sky."

"But of course, Socrates," said Simmias, "we would be glad to hear
this story."

"Well, then, my friend" he said, "first of all they say that the
earth itself is something like this to look at, if someone should see
it from above: like a sphere of twelve leather panels, variously col-
ored, but divided by color, of which the colors here are like samples,
c such as painters use. There, the whole earth is of such colors, more
brilliant and pure even than our colors: one is a purple of amazing
beauty, another is golden, and whatever is white is whiter than chalk
or snow. And it is made in the same way from other colors still
greater in number and in beauty than those that we have seen. For
d even these chasms, full of water and air as they are, give the ap-
pearance of color, gleaming in the variety of other colors, so that it
gives the impression of a single, continuous, multi-colored form.
And on this upper earth, given that it is like this, the growing things
have a corresponding nature, the trees and flowers and crops, and
the mountains similarly and the rocks are similarly more beautiful
in smoothness and transparency and color. And the pieces
that people here hold precious—of sard,[1] jasper, emerald and all
e the rest—are fragments of these. But in that place, everything is
of this sort and even more beautiful than these: the reason for
this is that those stones are pure and have not been corroded or

1 *sard* A dark reddish-brown semi-precious stone (chalcedony).

corrupted like the ones here by decay and brine caused by the conflu-
ence in this location which brings ugliness and illness both to stones
and earth and to plants and other living things. But the earth itself is
adorned with all of these and also with gold and silver and the others 111a
that are like these. They are naturally noticeable, since they are great
in number and size and exist everywhere on the earth, so that to behold
it is to gaze at a blessed spectacle. There are living things upon it, both
humans and many others, some inhabiting the interior and others near
the air, just as we live near the sea, and others in the islands that the
air flows around, next to the mainland. And in a word, what the water
and the sea are for our needs, so the air is there, and where we have air, b
they have aether. Their seasons are mixed together in such a way that
they are without illness and they live for a much greater time than peo-
ple here, and in sight and hearing and intelligence and everything like
that they are as far removed from us as air is removed from water, in
purity, and air from aether. And in particular they have groves for the
gods and temples for them, of which gods really are inhabitants, and
they interact with them, through utterances and prophecies and visions c
of the gods, and the sun and the moon and the stars are seen by them
as they really are, and their happiness in other respects is a conse-
quence of this.

"This is indeed the nature of the entire earth and of the things around
the earth. But it has places, many of them, in its chasms in a circle
around the whole, some deeper and more spread out than the one in
which we live, some deeper but with a smaller opening than ours has, d
and some that are shorter in depth than here but wider. All of these are
connected to one another by underground channels that are everywhere,
some narrower, some broader, and they have outlets by which a lot of
water flows out of one and into another, as if into mixing bowls, and
ever-flowing underground rivers of inconceivable size, of both hot and
cold water, and a lot of fire and great rivers of fire, and many of moist
clay both cleaner and muddier, just as in Sicily rivers of mud precede e
the lava flow, and then the lava itself. And each region is filled with
these things, each time the stream comes around to each of them. All
of these move up and down as if there were some oscillation in the
earth, and this oscillation is because of a natural process such as the
following: one of the openings in the earth happens to be very large in 112a
various ways including being bored right through the earth—this is
what Homer was speaking of, describing it as 'A great distance hence,
where is the deepest pit under the ground'[1] and which, in another place,
he in fact calls 'Tartarus', along with many other poets—into this open-

1 Homer, *Iliad* 8.14.

ing flow all the rivers and out of it again they flow, and each of them
b becomes like the earth through which it flows. All the streams flow in
and out of there because this liquid matter has no base or foundation,
and so it oscillates and swells up and down, and makes the air and the
wind around it do the same, since it follows it whenever it pulses to-
ward the earth up here and then into the part down there, and just as
with people breathing the flowing breath is always breathed out and in
again, so also there the wind, oscillated by the liquid, produces terri-
c ble and uncontrollable gusts, as it goes in and out. Whenever, there-
fore, the water is returning to the so-called 'lower' region, it flows
through the earth to those places by filling the streams there, just as in
irrigation, and whenever in turn it leaves them and starts for here, it
fills the streams here again, and when full it flows through the chan-
nels and through the earth, and having arrived in each place, into which
it has made its way by each stream, it makes seas and marshes and
d rivers and springs. From here, it sinks back again under the earth, some
streams going through longer places and more of them, some through
the shorter ones and fewer, and they rush once again into Tartarus,
some much lower than where they were pumped up, some only a lit-
tle, but all flowing in below their exits, and some pour out directly op-
posite to where they come in and some on the same side. There are
those that make a complete circle, winding around the earth once or
even more times, like snakes, going down as far as possible before
e rushing back again. It is possible to descend on each side as far as the
middle, but no further, since for both streams there is a steep section
on each side.

"Now there are certainly many other large streams all over, but
among all of these are four particular streams, of which the largest and
outermost, flowing around in a circle, is called 'Okeanus,' and oppo-
site this and flowing the opposite way is 'Acheron,' which flows
113a through various desolate places and in particular, when flowing be-
neath earth, arrives at the Acherusian lake, where the souls of most
people who have died arrive, and when they have remained for some
allotted time, some for longer, some for shorter, they are sent away to
be born as animals. The third of these rivers comes out in the middle
of these and falls, near the outlet, into a large area with a lot of burn-
ing fire, and it makes a lake greater than our sea, boiling up with water
b and mud. From there it goes in a circle, cloudy and muddy, and wind-
ing around the earth it arrives at another place at the farthest end of the
Acherusian lake, not mixing with the water. Having been cycled
around many times under the earth, it rushes out further down in Tar-
tarus. This is what is called Pyriphlegethon, fragments of which, in
fact, are sprayed up by the rushing streams in the various places where

they occur on the earth. And opposite this, the fourth comes out first
into a wild and terrible place, they say, colored all over like lapis lazuli,[1] c
to which they give the name 'Styx,' and 'Stygian' to the lake that the
gushing river makes. And by rushing into it the water has gained terri-
ble powers, it sinks below the earth, and it winds around and travels
opposite to Pyriphlegethon and meets it in the Acherusian lake from
the opposite direction. And its water never mixes with any other's but
it too, after circling around, rushes into Tartarus, opposite Py-
riphlegethon. And its name, the poets say, is Cocytus.

"Such is the nature of these four. When those who have died arrive d
in the place to which the spirit has brought each of them, first they are
judged, both those who lived nobly and piously and those who did not.
And those who seem to have lived in a neutral fashion, they are
brought to Acheron, climbing onto the rafts for them, they arrive on
them into the lake, and there they reside and are purified, and if any-
one has done some injustice, when they have paid the penalty for their
injustices, they are released, and for their good deeds they receive an e
honor proportional to the value of each one. Those, on the other hand,
who seem to be incurable on account of the magnitude of their wrong-
doings—having committed frequent and substantial theft from tem-
ples, or unjust and illegal murders, or various other such things—these
the appropriate fate casts into Tartarus, from where they never re-
emerge. But those who are curable but appear to have committed se-
rious errors, such as in anger doing something violent against their 114a
father or mother but then repenting and leading a different life, or com-
mitting homicides for some other similar reason, these must fall into
Tartarus, and having fallen and having spent a long time there, the
swell casts them out, the murderers along Cocytus and the patricides
and matricides along Pyriphlegethon, and as they are being carried
along towards the Acherusian lake, they shout and call out, some to
those they have killed, others to those they have dishonored, they call
out, begging and asking them that they be allowed to go out into the b
lake and be received, and if these people are convinced they proceed
out and give up their wrongdoings, but if not, they are carried again
into Tartarus and from there back into the rivers, and they suffer in
this way without ceasing until those they have wronged are convinced,
since this is the penalty set for them by the judges.

"But when it comes to those who are thought to have excelled in
living piously, they are the ones who are set free from these places in
the earth and are released, as though from prisons, and they arrive up c
in the pure territory and settle there on the earth. And of these, those

---

1 *colored all over like lapis lazuli* That is, deep blue.

who have been sufficiently purified by philosophy live without bodies for absolutely all of the rest of time and come to yet more beautiful territories which cannot be described with ease or in the insufficient time available at present. But for these reasons that we have gone over, Simmias, we must do everything to share in virtue and prudence, since beautiful is the prize and the hope great.

d "To affirm with confidence that these things are just as I have de-
scribed them would be unreasonable for a man of sense. However, since the soul indeed appears to be undying, that either this or something like this is the case—concerning our souls and where they reside—seems reasonable to me and a risk worth taking for the person who believes that this is how things are—for the risk is a fine one—and he must chant these things to himself, which is why I have drawn out the story so long. These are the reasons why a man ought to be
e confident about his soul if, during his life, he has shunned glamorous things and the other pleasures of the body, considering them foreign to him and causing more harm than good, but instead has devoted himself to the pleasures of learning. And having beautified his soul with
115a nothing but its own adornments—namely self-control and justice and courage and freedom and truth—in this state he awaits his journey to Hades, prepared to go whenever fate calls. So while you," he said, "Simmias and Cebes and you others, will each make this journey later when his time comes, fate is now, as a tragedian would say, already calling me, and it is nearly time that I go to the bath, because I think it is clearly better to bathe myself before drinking the poison and save the women the trouble of bathing a corpse."

b When he said this, Crito asked, "Well then, Socrates, do you have any final requests for these men or myself, concerning your children or anything else, which we could do for you and so be of some particular service to you?"

"The things I always say, Crito," he replied. "Nothing very new. By taking good care of yourselves you are of service to me and my family as well as yourselves, no matter what you do, even if you don't think so at present. But if you neglect yourselves and are unwilling to live, as though following tracks, in accordance with what we now say and have said in the past too, then you will accomplish next to noth-
c ing, no matter how much or how earnestly you agree with me at present."

"We will certainly be eager to act in this way," he replied. "But how should we bury you?"

"However you want to," he responded, "if you can actually catch me and I don't escape you." And laughing quietly he turned to face us and said, "Men, I can't convince Crito that I am this man Socrates who

is speaking right now and arranging each of his sentences. Instead, he
thinks I am what he will shortly see as a corpse, and so he asks how d
he should bury me. And what I have been going on about at length—
about how, after I drink the poison, I will no longer be with you but
will have departed, on my way to the particular joys of the blessed—
it seems I was saying these things to him for some other reason, to en-
courage you and myself at the same time.

"So give Crito a guarantee for me," he said, "the opposite guaran-
tee to the one he gave the judges; for his was that I would stay, but
you must guarantee him that I won't stay when I die, but will go away e
and leave, so that Crito will more easily bear it and won't be angry on
my behalf, as if I am suffering something terrible, when he sees my
body being burned or buried, nor say at my funeral that *Socrates* is
being laid out, or carried out, or buried. For rest assured, great Crito,"
said he, "speaking poorly is not only discordant in itself, but also
causes some harm to souls. But you must be brave and say that you
will bury my body, and bury it in whatever manner you like and as 116a
you think is customary."

Having said this, he set off to bathe in another room, and Crito fol-
lowed him, but he ordered us to stay behind. So we stayed, talking
among ourselves about what had been said and re-examining it, and
then returned to dwell on how great a misfortune had befallen us,
thinking that since we were being deprived of a father, we would lit-
erally be spending life hereafter as orphans.

When he had bathed and his children had been brought in—he had b
two small sons and one older one—and the women of the family had
come and he had spoken to them in Crito's presence and instructed
them as he wanted, he ordered the women and children to leave and
joined us. It was already close to sunset, for he had spent a long time
inside. He came from his bath and sat down and didn't say much more
after that. The servant of the Eleven came and, standing next to him, c
said, "Socrates, I won't observe from you the behavior I see from oth-
ers, who are angry with me and curse me when, on the orders of the
magistrates, I tell them to drink the poison. This whole time I have
found you in other ways to be the most noble and kind and best man
of those who have ever come here. And so I am sure that now too you
will be angry not with me but with those others, since you know who
is responsible. So now, since you know what I have come to tell you, d
farewell, and try to bear what must be as easily as possible." And he
cried as he turned and left.

And Socrates looked in his direction and said, "Farewell to you too.
We will do it." And then to us he said, "How polite the man is.
Throughout this whole time, he has come to check on me and some-

times talked with me and was as kind as could be, and how genuinely
he weeps for me now.

"But come on, Crito, let's obey him. Have someone bring in the
poison, if it has been ground. If not, have the man grind it."

e And Crito said, "But I think there is still sun on the mountains,
Socrates, and it is not quite sunset. And I know that others have taken
the poison very late, after the order has been given to them, eating and
drinking exceedingly well and having sex, some of them, with people
they love. So don't hurry. There is still time."

And Socrates said, "The people who act in this way, the ones you
mention, Crito, act reasonably because they think it will benefit them
117a to do such things. But I will be reasonable by not doing them. For I
think that drinking a little later will bring me nothing except to make
me ridiculous in my own eyes, clinging to life and being thrifty with
it when there's nothing left in it. So come, obey me and don't do
otherwise."

And Crito heeded him and nodded to the boy who had been standing
nearby, and the boy went out. After a long time had passed he
came back leading the man who was to present the poison, which was
ground up in a cup he was carrying. Seeing him, Socrates said, "Well
then, best of men, since you are the expert in these matters, what
should I do?"

b "You only have to drink it," he said, "and walk around until you
feel your legs become heavy. Then lie down, and from there it will
work on its own." And at the same time he handed the cup to Socrates.

And taking it very good-naturedly, Echecrates, without fear and
without changing color or expression, he looked at the man as would
a bull and said, "What do you say about pouring out an offering to a
god from the drink? Is it allowed, or not?"

"We only prepare as much as we think is needed, Socrates," he said.

c "I understand," said he. "But surely it is permissible, and necessary,
to pray to the gods, that my migration from here to there will
be blessed. So I pray for this, that it will happen in this way." And
as he said this he raised the cup and drank it down, very gently and
calmly.

Until then the majority of us had been able to keep ourselves from
crying reasonably well, but when we saw him drinking, and then that
he had finished it ... no longer. And my own tears poured out of me
with the force of a flood, and I hid myself in shame and cried for myself—for
truly I was crying not for him but for my own misfortune,
d that I was being deprived of such a comrade. Crito had turned away
even before I did, when he was unable to restrain his tears. Apollodorus
had been crying the entire time, and when he howled with

grief and anger at this particular moment, nobody who was present could help breaking down, except Socrates himself.

And he said, "What a way to behave, you remarkable men! I sent the women away mainly for this reason, so that they would not make e
such an offensive sound, because I have heard that one must meet one's end in calmed silence. So be quiet and collect yourselves." And when we heard this we were ashamed and ceased crying.

He was walking around, and when he said his legs had become heavy, he lay down on his back—since this was what the man had instructed—and the man who had given him the poison took hold of him, and after a while examined his feet and legs and then squeezed his foot hard and asked if he felt it. He said that he didn't. After this, the man squeezed his calves, and going higher in this way he showed us that he was cold and congealed. Socrates grasped himself and said that when it reached his heart, he would be gone.

And then when nearly all of the area around his belly was growing cold, he uncovered his head, for he had covered it, and said—he uttered his final words—"Crito," he said, "we owe a cock to Asclepius.[1] Make the offering and don't forget."

"It will be done," Crito said. "But see if you have anything else to say."

He said nothing further in response to the question, but after a short time he shuddered. The man uncovered him. His eyes were fixed. And Crito, seeing this, closed his mouth and eyes.

This, Echecrates, is how our friend passed away, a man who, we would say, was the best of those we have ever known, and the wisest and most just.

Suggestions for Critical Reflection

1. Socrates' last words are said to have been a reminder to Crito to make a sacrifice to Asclepius, the god of healing (118a). What do you think might be the significance of this request?

2. Socrates bases one of his arguments on the principle that opposites come from opposites. Is this principle valid? Are his examples evidence of the present question?

3. Socrates gives several arguments other than the "opposites come from opposites" argument for the life of the soul before and/or after bodily death. Outline these arguments, and consider whether or not they give genuine reasons for believing their conclusions.

1 *a cock to Asclepius* A sacrifice of a cockerel to the god of medicine and healing.

4. Socrates says, "those who truly undertake philosophy practice nothing other than dying and being dead" (64a). What does he mean, and how well does he manage to make a case for this?

5. What do you make of the long section at the end in which Socrates gives his vision of the geography of the universe and the place of souls after death in it? He says earlier that he has been writing poetry (61b); should this be interpreted literally or poetically? Could a "poetic" vision have any real effect on how one faces death?

6. Critics sometimes claim that, in various parts of this dialogue, Socrates is presupposing different notions of what a "soul" is: sometimes, for example, it's the animating principle of bodies, and sometimes it's the mind: the thinking/knowing part of a person. See if you can distinguish various notions of "soul" operating in different parts of this work.

7. Socrates throughout urges on his hearers the view that real philosophy concentrates on the "soul," not the body, and on the invisible, not the visible. What is his picture of the invisible things, having to do with the soul, that he thinks real philosophers concentrate on? Do you think that there is any reality to these things? Or, if there is, is it the proper business of philosophy to deal with them?

8. Socrates, with his "philosophical" vision, appears to be the only one not greatly upset by his impending death. Can a "philosophical" vision really bring about that sort of state of mind? Might he really (excusably?) be desperately trying to fool himself into accepting his fate?

Index

About the Publisher

The word "broadview" expresses a good deal of the philosophy behind our company. Our focus is very much on the humanities and social sciences—especially literature, writing, and philosophy—but within these fields we are open to a broad range of academic approaches and political viewpoints. We strive in particular to produce high-quality, pedagogically useful books for higher education classrooms—anthologies, editions, sourcebooks, surveys of particular academic fields and sub-fields, and also course texts for subjects such as composition, business communication, and critical thinking. We welcome the perspectives of authors from marginalized and underrepresented groups, and we have a strong commitment to the environment. We publish English-language works and translations from many parts of the world, and our books are available world-wide; we also publish a select list of titles with a specifically Canadian emphasis.

broadview press

MIX
Paper | Supporting responsible forestry
FSC® C013916
www.fsc.org

The interior of this book is printed on 100% recycled paper.